To my mother and father,
whose care, example, creativity,
articulation, and prayers
inspired the contents of this volume.

Robert J. Spitzer

The Spirit of Leadership

Optimizing Creativity and Change in Organizations

For permission requests, contact the publisher at:
Executive Excellence Publishing
1344 East 1120 South
Provo, UT 84606
phone: 1-801-377-4060
toll free: 1-800-304-9782
fax: 1-801-377-5960
www.eep.com

For Executive Excellence books, magazines, and other products, contact Executive Excellence directly. Call 1-800-304-9782, fax 1-801-377-5960, or visit our Web site at www.eep.com.

Printed in the United States

10 9 8 7 6 5 4 3 2 100

Cover design by Nichole Klein

Printed by Publishers Press

Library of Congress Cataloging-in-Publication Data

Spitzer, Robert J., 1952-
The spirit of leadership : optimizing creativity and change in organizations / by Robert J. Spitzer.
p. cm.
Includes bibliographical references and index.
ISBN 1-890009-89-X (hard : alk. paper)
1. Leadership. 2. Industrial management. 3. Creative ability in business.
4. Organizational effectiveness. I. Title.
HD57.7.S697 2001
658.4'092--dc21

00-008728

Table of Contents

Acknowledgements

My deep and sincere gratitude to Camille E. De Blasi, M.A. who typed and critiqued two full drafts of this text from dictation. The many more hours she spent on proofreading, diagramming, and researching footnotes complemented the many weekends she spent with the text itself. Her skill, creativity, patience, and attentiveness to detail were invaluable in making this book a reality.

My special thanks to Lou and Diane Tice of the Pacific Institute, whose friendship and generosity made the video series, which inspired this book, a reality. Lou's mentorship and know-how allowed me to dream of a bigger reality for this curriculum than I ever thought possible.

My thanks also to Steve Gandara and Jack Fitterer of The Pacific Institute, whose encouragement, friendship, and expertise ushered this project along the way; and to so many other friends at The Pacific Institute whose support made this project possible.

My thanks also to Gill Tumey and Jed Selter of the Boeing Corporation, whose advice and encouragement led to the development of many aspects of the teaching curriculum. My thanks also to Peter Morton, Alan Mullaly, and the many members of the Boeing Corporation who provided many occasions to develop the teaching curriculum, as well as encouragement and feedback.

Finally, and by no means least, I would like to thank the administrators, Jesuits, faculty, staff, and students of Gonzaga University, who have not only labored under these leadership principles, but given me so much generous feedback in our co-participative program to make Gonzaga University the finest possible experience of spirit and education.

Introduction

Once there was a CEO of Widgets International named Joe Driver,[1] a leader of great vision and energy. Joe was a rather remarkable "opportunity seizer." He had a capacity for making 30 important decisions per day, each of which could effect the lives of hundreds of people. Joe had an intense desire to create. He wanted to see Widgets not only grow in market share and quality, but also serve the public's need for widgets in more useful ways. People were continually amazed at how much he could hold together in his mind, how much he could accomplish, and how far into the future he could see. Without question, Joe was destined for greatness.

The Board of Directors knew that Joe was the right man for Widgets. He could bring an already successful, "opportunity-seizing," innovative organization to the next level. After obtaining a lucrative salary and restricted stock option agreement, Joe embarked on his plan with great zeal. He constructed a four-fold plan: 1) To increase market share by designing new widget products and to invade competitors' market share; 2) To implement a new computer system to promote "just-in-time inventory"; 3) To initiate a total quality improvement system to show improvement in a) customer satisfaction, b) product quality, c) waste reduction, and d) processes; and 4) To corner the market on widget designers, to create a veritable think-tank of widget geniuses to assure competitive edge.

Within seven months, Joe had implemented these plans with incredible drive. He had designed most of the processes, worked with quality consultants to set up a Deming system, hired the best and the brightest in widget design, and purchased the best system to promote "just-in-time inventory."

Joe then stepped back to take a look at his new creation ...but something was terribly wrong.

The goals he had set for new market share were not being reached. Indeed, in several areas he was losing market share. His two primary competitors had moved into new market areas more quickly, and customer satisfaction seemed more tenuous. The "just-in-time inventory" system had fallen on equally bad times. Many divisions were simply not using the new technology and had reverted back to the "old system." Other divisions were so angered by the imposition of this "colossal monster" on them, that they intentionally misused the system, thereby disrupting delivery schedules. Joe was furious and retaliated by threatening to make the "foot draggers" comply. The more he pushed, the more his people pushed back. The new computer system began to look like a $100 million mistake. It even seemed to be less efficient than the old one—a perception which Joe's people wanted to promote.

After making some initial gains, the quality system seemed to hit a wall. Joe attempted to get additional improvements by adding feedback loops and paper trails to more parts of the manufacturing and delivery process. For all the time and effort that went into it, not a single improvement could be detected. Instead, his people became disillusioned, angry, and cynical. They were literally "burning out" trying to accommodate mounds of additional data. They knew that the data had limited usefulness, but they had to collect it, because Joe was going to break the previous quality parameters come "hell or high water." An atmosphere of passive-aggression and compulsive cynicism seemed to pervade the organization. Ironically, a new sense of unity began to emerge among the disaffected.

Finally, Joe found that his attempt to stockpile widget geniuses was being interrupted by the fact that his old widget geniuses were leaving the firm. People with years of experience, and customer and vendor contacts, were hiring themselves out to the competition. Joe did not bother to ask for exit interviews because he knew that they were either slothful or scared of the new pace and could not accommodate themselves. At the end of one year, Joe had lost market share, spent $100 million on an inefficient inventory system, purchased small quality improvements at the cost of tremendous collective resentment and cynicism, and accelerated the turnover of his top critical skills people. His competition had hired away several of his key design engineers, and many of his top salespeople. The effects on the bottom line were quite negative, and long-term prospects seemed bleak at best.

How could this all-too-typical scenario happen? Joe had high goals, energy, charisma, intelligence, and a remarkable ability for process design and improvement. Notice also that the failure of Joe's four-fold plan did not arise out of daunting market exigencies. Neither did it arise out of a need for greater self-accountability on the part of his people. Rather, in excellent market conditions with a group of people who had already proven themselves, Joe had driven the synergy, common cause, excitement, and *esprit de corps* out of them.

What happened? I submit that Joe had one "easy to overlook" Achilles Heel in his leadership style. He did not try to achieve partnership with his people around his plans. Instead of allowing his people to get enthusiastic about their part of the plan, he enthusiastically gave them the plan. Instead of showing them the goal, the challenge, and his need for their responsiveness, he told them that his goals "should be no problem for them to achieve." Instead of letting his people develop the "how" to the goal, he tried to develop the "how" for them. Instead of anticipating the suspicion with which a new computer inventory system might be greeted, he expected people not to show typical human responses to radical change. Indeed, he was outraged. Instead of finding out why his best critical skills people were leaving, he attributed the whole matter to sloth and fear. He admitted later that he didn't even know that people were angry about the new quality improvement system. When he heard complaints about "burnout," he thought it was just typical complaints of whiners who didn't like being pushed to new levels.

Joe had blinded himself consistently to one of the three Ps of leadership. By concentrating on *product* and *process*, he had altogether ignored *people*.

How does a leader get to the point where he is almost blind to one of the main components of leadership? How can he not only ignore data, but assiduously avoid it when the welfare and future of the organization is at stake? How can a genius at process development miss the most obvious aspects of process implementation by people? How can he destroy a people system while trying to improve processes and products?

The answer lies in a leader's awareness, openness, and sensitivity to "people data." The problem is not one of knowledge or skill, but of identity, purpose, and heart. This problem, therefore, cannot be resolved by learning something new, but only by choosing and even embracing something new.

In writing this book, my intent is to educate you toward the most important choice of your life: the choice about identity, that is, what gives meaning and purpose in life. This choice, in turn, opens or closes your awareness of the people component of leadership, which, in turn, determines whether you will produce common cause or blame, whether you will energize or enervate, whether you will achieve partnership or resentment, and whether you will induce trust and creativity or fear, anger, blame, suspicion, passive aggression, and compulsive ego. Oddly enough, your choices about identity and purpose in life control your capacity to let people share the excitement of vision. If you are the only one excited by the vision, you will be moving rapidly toward the goal, while your people are digging their heels into the floor.

The Board of Directors might have detected early whether Joe's genius could be translated into an organization-wide enthusiasm for the common good. But they would have had to attend to little things in his answers to interview questions. Did he need to have all the control, or could he share control with people who needed it more than he for organizational efficacy? Did he have to know more than everyone, or could he listen to people who had to know more than he? Did he have to decisively win every showdown, or could he negotiate, or even seek a "win-win?" Did he care about his people burning out, having adequate resources, getting credit? Did his presence manifest direction and respect? Greatness and humility? When the Board hired Joe, it might have anticipated what would happen to its culture and people.

A leader does not have to ruin a culture, a company, or even a team before the Board has a clue about his "people choices." They simply must know what to look for. I call it "contributory vs. comparative identity."

Inspired Leadership Reconsidered

Leaders determine whether the organization is capable of rapid change, innovation, reasonable risk-taking, self-motivated quality improvement, and the actualization of opportunity. Leaders who concentrate on the product and process components of quality, but virtually ignore the people component will drive not only work, but people into the ground. They will stifle spirit, common cause, co-participation, individual efficacy, team efficacy, and the actualization of opportunity.

Leaders who give equal billing to the people component of quality encourage the development of trust, vision, and spirit. These qualities, in turn, cultivate optimal change, creativity, common cause, and optimal actualization of opportunity.

Every leader is aware that many people must know more about specific areas than she, if the organization is to progress. Similarly, many people will need to have more "hands-on control" over specific areas than executive leadership, if the organization is to prosper. The cultivation of trust, vision, and spirit, therefore, requires that a leader not suppress the knowledge and appropriate control of people. This requires humility.

This humility, however, cannot interfere with the leader's vital energy, enthusiasm, and vision toward the goal. Every successful leader has an inner dynamism, a desire to create, a desire to see an organization bigger and better. This inner drive and enthusiasm to create can either foster common cause (teamwork toward a common good), or debilitate common cause ("every man for himself—be prepared to foist blame, make excuses, defend yourself, and appear better than all other team members"). If a leader does not foster common cause, there is no "us." Thus, each employee is left to fend for the only remaining residual: "me." Humility, then, is critical for bringing common cause into the drive toward goal. Rather than stifle drive, humility allows this drive to be filled with co-participation, open communication, common cause, and teamwork. It converts the drive toward goal into "inspiration of the 'us' toward goal." It invites people into the excitement, into the growth, the quality improvement, the opportunity seizing; it gives people a sense of importance and meaning.

"Excitement toward goal" plus "humility" equals "inspired leadership toward common cause."

To enter into a bond of common cause, people must not only trust in their leaders and one another, but also have confidence in the vision and the team. Humility cannot interfere with this sense of confidence in the vision and people. Rather, it must invite all stakeholders into this confidence by showing that the leader's vision is not "ego-driven," but rather, an invitation to all stakeholders to reach greatness (optimal potential) together. Humility shares greatness generously by allowing others to bask in the achievement of great vision, to recognize and appreciate people for their contribution to this collective enterprise, and to allow people to feel their true importance and dignity in light of their invaluable contribution.

Effective leaders must possess three virtues: prudence to promote balanced judgment, courage to avoid shrinking before challenge, and self-discipline to avoid being dominated by base emotion. Humility assures that these virtues will promote common cause rather than destroy it. If prudence lacks humility (i.e., is done for the sake of ego-gratification rather than common cause), it becomes arrogance, which undermines spirit, vision, and trust.

Similarly, if courage is motivated by ego-gratification, it becomes mere bravado. Bravado never moves a group beyond daunting challenges. It belittles the "lesser" members of the group. Instead of calling the group to greatness, it says, "You are unworthy of *my* greatness."

Finally, if self-discipline is motivated by ego-gratification, it becomes sheer disdain for the undisciplined. Again, it does not call the group to make sacrifice; it states only that "My strengths will always be better than yours."

Without humility, such virtues as prudence, courage, and self-discipline become mere tools of self-aggrandizement, and therefore the vices of leadership.

What kind of "humility," common cause, trust, and spirit inspires confidence toward participation in greatness; invites people into a leader's vital excitement toward goal; and transforms prudence, courage, and self-discipline into a catalyst for group spirit instead of arrogance, bravado, and disdain? It cannot be an obsequious humility, a false modesty, or an understatement of gifts or vision. Humility is not an encouragement of passivity or weakness. It does not run away from calling people to self-accountability, or excuse unaccountable behavior.

Rather, humility is grounded in a true assessment of our abilities and vision. It promotes strength based on truth and makes us more active rather than passive. It lets us share the truth that leads to the common good through common strength and common cause. I describe this humility as the ability to allow our contributory identity to take precedence over our comparative identity.

I devote the rest of this book to explaining this identity decision, and how to cultivate it. I will show how this identity decision can heighten happiness, creativity, and accomplishment in personal, organizational, and community life. I will show how to foster a common cause outlook, and how to direct this toward the development of trust, vision, and inspiration. I will show how the mind and heart of inspired leaders can liberate *esprit de corps*.

Before considering this most important identity decision, I will review the trends that have brought us to a people orientation in leadership. This will be the objective of the first chapter.

1 Spirit, Trust, and People

Effective people, teams, and organizations require not only skills and structures, but also spirit, trust, and vision, because these qualities are necessary for open communication, common cause, and synergy. Skills and structures support and complement effective teaming, but cannot produce it without spirit, trust, and vision.

When leaders fail to inspire to common cause, to set clear performance objectives, goals, and accountability, when individual pride in work is glossed over by forced equivalence, then people seem to play to the lowest common denominator, superstars seem to lose enthusiasm, and team efficacy decreases. But teams need not play to the lowest common denominator of individual performance. If leadership accentuates both individual efficacy skills and team skills in a complementary way, then the organization will actualize self-motivation, self-accountability, empowerment, adaptability, creativity, specialization, and cross-functionality.

When we experience spirit, trust, and vision in a team, our creativity and energy increase substantially. Indeed, in these circumstances, our work can give us energy rather than take it away.

Why is so little time spent on spirit, trust, and vision in the leadership literature? First, these are intangible, and therefore easy to ignore in a world filled with concrete problems, quantitative parameters, and growth expectations. Second, they seem to be "soft" disciplines that do not enjoy as much prestige as the "hard" quantitative and analytical disciplines. Third, their involvement with the inner disposition of people makes them seem more ambiguous and difficult to control than processes, technology, and product innovation. It's easier to hold a conflict resolution workshop than deal with the "vague" notions of spirit and trust, and easier to study personality inventories[1] (which do not involve human choices and values) than assess character inventories[2] (which do involve human choices and values).

Nevertheless, leaders need to give serious consideration to these intangibles, for they show up poignantly on the bottom line as an increase in opportunity costs.[3] "Opportunity costs" reflect the revenue lost from missed opportunities. For example, if employees lack spirit, trust, and vision, they may engage in shoddy customer relations; may not pursue new, viable opportunities; may not contribute to the elimination of waste and product defects; or may lack the desire to improve processes. Opportunity costs are probably more responsible for the stagnation and demise of organizations than any other single factor. Yet, they are the most invisible of costs because they are not reflected in the income statement as a "tangible expense." It is, for example, much easier to see an increase in one's utility expenses than to see the lost revenue resulting from unexploited opportunities in developing market share. Also, opportunity costs generally take a year or two to manifest themselves. For example, a lack of spirit, trust, and vision could take one or two years to become evident as missed opportunities for new customers, new processes, and new product lines. But when this slow process manifests itself, it will reap a terrible harvest, for it will take a long time, and much inspiration to reinvigorate the unhealthy organization. Sometimes it is too late, and an organization simply becomes spoils for the victor.

If, however, leaders foster a community of spirit, trust, and vision, the five organizational debilitators (fear, compulsive ego, passive aggression, resentment/anger, and suspicion) will decrease. Performance objectives, empowerment, and self-accountability need no longer be threatening to anyone who has the skills and intentions to contribute to the team's common cause. Good team leaders can frequently identify and assist those who have problems with skills and intentions. After doing this, leaders can help team members with connecting, communicating, and moving toward a common cause by listening to and acting on feedback, and showing appreciation for self-motivated, self-accountable, openly communicative, creative, and synergistic behaviors. As a result, opportunity costs are significantly reduced, giving the organization a future of quality, adaptability, and growth.

How can we infuse these qualities of spirit, trust, and vision in our organizations? I suggest two steps:

1) developing the mind and vision of the inspired leader, (Chapters 2-5) and
2) developing the heart of the inspired leader through personal commitments (Chapters 6-11), people commitments (Chapter 12), ethical commitments (Chapter 13) and leadership commitments (Chapters 14-18).

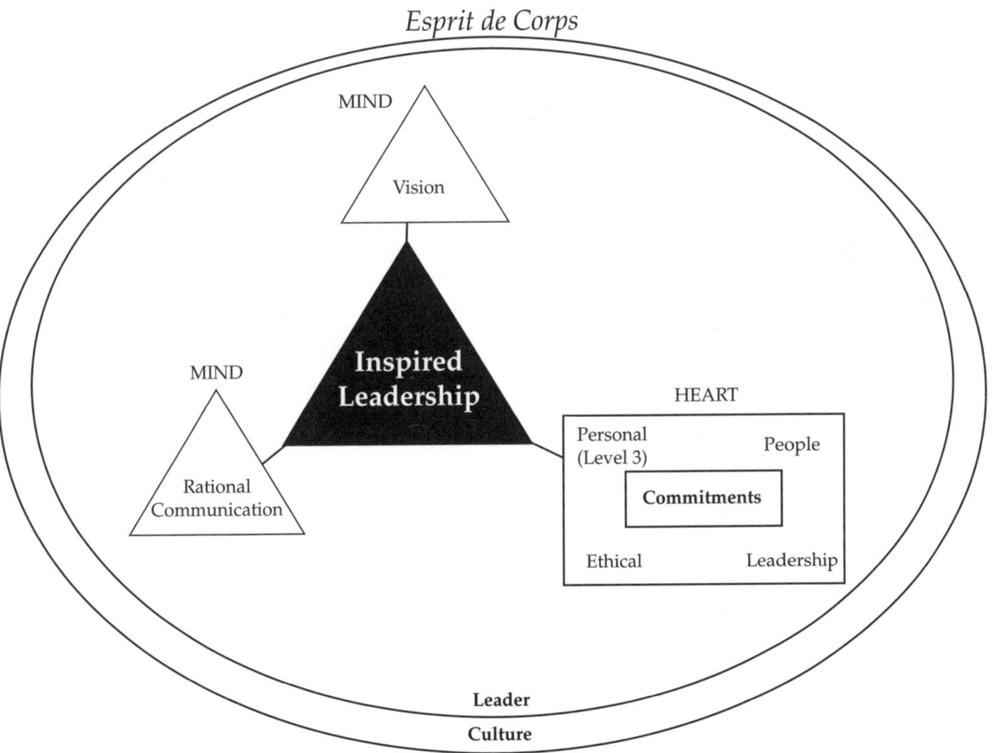

These steps will not only significantly improve quality and reduce opportunity costs, they will also invite stakeholders to a better quality of life.

My intent is to help you develop the mind and heart of inspired leadership and to apply these mental, emotional, and spiritual habits to the benefit of your family, team, and organization.

"The heart" refers to a set of interior attitudes that place a contributory identity over a comparative one. These attitudes are essential for the development of spirit, vision, and trust not only in a leader, but in a family member, a community participant, and a citizen. A "good heart" leads to happiness, purpose, drive, depth, ideal, and hence the capacity to inspire. So, the contents of this book are applicable to every dimension of your life.

By the end the book, I hope you will begin using the habits and attitudes essential to inspired leadership. These attitudes will reduce opportunity costs, increase willingness to change and grow, break the parameters of quality improvement, and create a culture that stakeholders enjoy. These attitudes will also positively affect your personal life and your stakeholders by helping to integrate work life with home and community life. By integrating heart and mind, leaders will not only produce better organizations, but also a better world.

Our Changing World

The environment of the contemporary organization has experienced a radical change over the last 20 years. This change has benefited both organizations and the world population. Organizations have become more adaptable, more efficient, and are achieving better quality. And, as population has increased, the per capita wealth and welfare has also increased dramatically. As the world becomes more densely populated, its citizens, as a whole, are much better off.[4]

Many books have been written about this phenomenon,[5] and most experts attribute growth and broad distribution of wealth to improvements in 1) education, 2) technology, 3) communication and information systems, and 4) workplace environment.

Paul Pilzer goes so far as to suggest that resources will not become scarce so long as these human factors continue to grow, for resourceful people find abundant substitutes for what was formerly thought to be scarce.[6] For example, hydroponic farming (which is water-based) may one day take the place of soil-based farming because it does not require large tracks of arable land, is far more efficient, and can be used in multiple levels. Solar power and other more plentiful energy sources like hydrogen may one day take the place of all fossil fuels for similar reasons. This upward shift in the global economy has, in large part, been produced by innovative people and adaptable organizations that have brought breakthroughs in information, technology, and education to the marketplace.

The continuance of the increase in world per capita wealth depends on people and organizations adapting to this increased complexity and change. From the outset, the organization was designed to respond quickly to shifts in supply, demand, and technology. If organizations fail to adapt, the increase in world wealth will discontinue. If organizations do adapt, world wealth will continue to increase.

I see no intrinsic reason why organizations cannot continue to adapt to this increased rate of change and complexity. Any organization that does not adapt to it will fade away.[7]

The key to adaptation and change is to shift from hard, mechanistic, inflexible structures to malleable and adaptable structures (based on the creativity and interconnectedness of people).[8] Surprisingly, the vast literature on organizational change concentrates on strategic planning,[9] process building, and re-engineering,[10] but pays little attention to the most important factor in change: people. People alone ask questions, see problems, form goals and ideals, transcend their present state, surmount obstacles, shift thinking, create environments, form unities, and pursue common causes. People alone have the most essential principle of adaptation: spirit that engenders resilience, hope, community, and creativity.

The art of organizational change in the last 30 years has concentrated more on product and process than people. This is not to say that the role of people in organizations has not changed. Government mandates and the need for increased critical skills have compelled organizations to treat people with greater dignity and respect. This practice is extraordinarily beneficial for business because it enhances creativity, co-participation (teamwork), and adaptability to change.

Moreover, it fits our increased awareness of the intrinsic dignity of people and work.

Despite these obvious benefits of fostering a "people-friendly" culture, some experts in the art of leadership tend to de-emphasize it. They argue that product and process development are "hard" disciplines, but people development is a "soft" discipline. They suggest that when a business gets in trouble, leaders should naturally look to product and process improvement, and then, take a quick glance at people. This prioritization tends to de-emphasize one of the most important characteristics of leadership for creatively changing organizations: *the capacity to build a community of spirit, vision, and trust.*

Leadership courses tend to stress analytical and quantitative abilities (for problem-solving), and entrepreneurial abilities (for growth). Obviously, these skills are important; however, they cannot take the place of the ability to foster spirit, vision, and trust, for these characteristics inspire people to embrace change together—to see change as exciting, challenging, and beneficial.

Anyone who has led an organization for more than a week will know that people dread change. People fear it, resent it, and, consequently, resist it, unless they are inspired by vision and trust opening upon common cause. When they share a common cause, change engenders exhilaration, resilience, and creativity.

If we know this to be true, then why do we continue to classify spirit, vision, and trust, indeed, the "people" part of leadership, as "soft" and secondary?

Eight Steps to People-Orientation

We can no longer afford to restrict our vision to product and process analysis. Failure to adapt to people-oriented leadership will be a failure to adapt to increased complexity and rate of change.

We might begin our analysis of people-oriented leadership by building on eight developments of the recent past.

1. Education. The remarkable increase in per capita education resulting from the proliferation of schools, the availability of higher education, the increase in on-site and workplace training, the development of the community college system, the advent of educational television, the increased availability of publications, and the Internet has led not only to developments in production and communication technology, but also to a heightened capacity for interpersonal communication. These changes have increased resources, production, and per capita wealth. In so doing, they have benefited organizations tremendously. They also brought with them changed workers, customers, suppliers, and communities. To benefit from the information revolution, organizations had to adapt to these changed stakeholders.

Education allows stakeholders to become far more flexible and open to change. Increased self-understanding, higher viewpoints on various facets of production, and awareness of company vision and goals allows them to progressively release their grip on fixed beliefs and hard structures. As long as workers are communicating, sharing information, and acting for common cause, greater specialization produces tremendous efficiencies and creativity. However, if trust is replaced with suspicion, communications break down and internal competition takes over.

Education also brings with it higher expectations. People have a greater sense of independence; they are more aware of their rights, legal recourses, and autonomous dignity; they have a higher sensitivity to psychological health.

To adapt to these changes in the environment, managers and leaders have started to view workers as thinking implementers.

Thinking implementers can listen and adapt to customer needs, to vendors' innovations and specifications, to the requirements of manufacturing, and to the refinements of administration within the changing environment. Thinking implementers provide four major benefits: 1) they allow for increased specialization in product, design, manufacture, and customer and vendor relationships; 2) they adapt far more rapidly than just top-tiered thinkers; 3) they are far more creative in their area of specialization; and 4) they can mentor the newly initiated. These benefits provide the framework for long-term growth and viability of organizations, and even world wealth and resources.

Today, we can clearly see that specialization of labor and increased adaptability to change require thinking implementers who enjoy increased empowerment, self-efficacy, and self-motivation, and increased team performance and team spirit. An increase in these qualities requires replacing the five debilitators of team spirit (fear, compulsive ego, passive aggression, resentment/anger, and suspicion) with trust, cooperation, common cause, friendship, open communication, and synergy. An increase in cooperation requires a change in people's identity focus from a comparitive one to a contributive one. Indeed, the environment has irrevocably changed in response to the need to adapt and specialize.

2. Theory Y. Theory Y was one of the first major responses to the need for thinking implementers. During the 1960s, organizations began to move from Theory X (fear, force, bribe, oversight, and supervision) to Theory Y (self-motivation, inspiration, recognition of dignity, and open communication). It did not take long for managers to recognize empirically that Theory Y worked much better than Theory X. Turnover rates were lower, specialization continued to increase, and workplace satisfaction increased efficiency and synergy. Theory Y simultaneously changed organizational environment, leadership style, and workers' expectations. Hence, changing back to Theory X would mean dashed expectations, a feeling of being used, a return to non-thinking implementers, and an increase in the five debilitators. This, in turn, would lead to a decrease in openness to change (indeed, defensiveness and intransigence) and a decrease in the efficacy of specialized labor. Both consequences would seriously jeopardize long-term competitiveness.

3. Total Quality Management. Dr. W. Edwards Deming outlined the requirements for setting up continuous feedback and evaluation through careful attentiveness to all facets of product and process.[11] Deming's quality improvement model depended considerably on both specialization of labor and thinking implementers, for the more self-motivated and specialized workers are the more conscious of quality they can be. Deming's methods were so successful in Japan that the United States could not fail to incorporate them into its own complex processes. This worked for a while until natural limits were reached. No matter how much organizations increased their paperwork or adjusted their feedback loops, quality seemed to be reaching a plateau.

4. Systems theory. Systems theory came into the work environment closely behind TQM.[12] By looking at an organization as a dynamic, complex organism with a fundamental momentum, systems theorists gave a more comprehensive and long-term picture of organizational life. It was much easier to see long-term interdependence and interrelationship. As a consequence, "stakeholders" (the integral, interdependent constituents—customers, employees, stockholders, management, suppliers, community, etc.) replaced "stockholders" in the parlance of business theorists.[13] This allowed the principle of optimal benefit to be recognized: in the long term, a benefit to one stakeholder (e.g., employees), which does not undermine the common good or cause unfairness to another stakeholder group, will become a benefit to all stakeholders (e.g., customers, suppliers, stockholders) and therefore to the organization.[14]

5. Win-win thinking. This ushered in the notion of the "win-win."[15] If all stakeholders with diverse interests could maximize one another's benefit, then quality and long-term viability would result. If one stakeholder won at another stakeholder's expense, it would give rise to resentment, passive aggression, and even vengeance. To the extent that organizations could optimize the "win-win," they could also optimize stakeholder interrelationship. This cleared channels of communication and allowed for interaction without endless rungs of bureaucracy, supervision, and bargaining.

6. Industrial psychology. Industrial psychologists could now make an even greater impact on organizations. To pursue Theory Y, continuous quality improvement, and the "win-win," it became essential for people to recognize and respect different personalities. Human resource persons gave workshops on personality inventories, while industrial psychologists fine-tuned these theories within teams and organizations. In addition, other experts provided assistance in conflict resolution skills, communication skills, group dynamics, and team-building skills.

7. Empowerment theory. These contributions of industrial psychology paved the way for the first approach to empowerment theory.[16] The initial hopes for empowerment theory far exceeded the reality. Leaders believed that if they simply reduced oversight and supervision, and gave stakeholders free reign to take responsibility for their area of specialization, productivity and efficiency would increase. Unfortunately, this did not happen because the workforce was not prepared for the change. Workers did not yet see themselves as thinking implementers. Fear of accountability, blame, risk, and change froze the workforce in its place. The rewards of self-accountability were not as great as the risks. Finally, people were not educated or prepared to become self-accountable or operate within teams. The failure of empowerment made leadership cautious about even using the word. Unfortunately, the need for thinking implementers still existed. So, the empowerment approach would have to be reconfigured to avoid some of its earlier drawbacks. This reconfiguration came in various forms such as open-book management,[17] values-based leadership,[18] servant leadership,[19] and new approaches to team theory (e.g., the organization as cross-functional team[20]).

8. Team theory. Team theory has emerged as the most well developed encapsulation of people-oriented leadership because it helps people to become empowered and take reasonable risks. As the cliché goes, "there's safety in numbers." If people can be convinced to change together, to be open to risk together, and to create together, there should be less resistance to self-motivation and risk-taking. Furthermore, a good team would optimize the specialization of labor, for when groups of specialized individuals operate with open communication, trust, friendship, and common cause, greater efficiency and performance are inevitable.

Two groups of theorists seized the initiative: 1) the team skills (coaching) advocates,[21] and 2) the team structure advocates.[22] Team skills advocates emphasized conflict resolution, communications, and team building skills. They assisted in opening channels of communication, but had difficulty improving actual communication. Something was still missing.

The team structure advocates concentrated on moving organizations from hierarchical structures to horizontal or circular ones. They asserted that hierarchical structures made one group of people not only more responsible and empowered, but seemingly more dignified as people. This hierarchical structure also tended to emphasize the "oversight and supervision" view of management. The one on top is supposed to oversee and supervise the ones below.

Team champions began to replace hierarchical structure with horizontal or circular team structures.

Their intent was to show that each individual could be empowered to move toward a common task through interdependence with others. The primary function of team leaders was not oversight or supervision, but rather, inspiration, facilitation, and empowerment toward a common objective. The team leader is also recognized as the conduit to other teams. If reality could correspond to this structure, it would give rise to a highly adaptable and synergistic integration of specialized labor.

But even the best plans of team structure advocates seemed to fall on hard times. Rather than moving to maximal empowerment and adaptability, many teams moved toward mediocrity. "Superstars" felt they were not being properly recognized, and protection of people's feelings often outweighed high performance.[23] In short, people on the team were playing to the lowest common denominator. Some began to be overtly critical of teams, even though they recognized their necessity for meeting the demands of faster change and greater complexity.[24]

If teams are to be effective, indeed, if teams are to result in a genuine feeling of partnership and co-participation, if they are to reach the epitome of high performance, rapid change, synergy, and creativity, then they will have to be infused with spirit. The rest of this book will be devoted to explaining this most important enterprise.

Section 1

The Mind of the Inspired Leader

My objective is to help leaders not only to create high-performance teams, but also to use their talents, strengths, and strategies effectively. In the *Introduction*, I noted that this task requires both a passionate vision of greatness and a humility that allows all stakeholders to participate in the excitement of vision. When these two characteristics are combined, spirit abounds. And when spirit abounds, the organization functions as a creative, passionate community toward its common cause. This spirit will not only lower opportunity costs significantly, but also elevate organizations to their optimal level of creativity, change, performance, and quality.

How do leaders create this spirit? It requires vision, rational communication, and four sets of commitments toward spirit and trust (personal, people, ethical, and leadership commitments). Leaders also need to model these things, make them part of a noble purpose, and invite stakeholders into the excitement and nobility of the "great enterprise."

How can leaders prepare to do this? They must deepen their sense of purpose and their commitments to other people. This involves both habits of the mind and habits of the heart. The mind seeks clarity of purpose while the heart seeks passion of purpose. The mind seeks the reason and evidence for goals while the heart strives for the nobility and challenge of goals. The mind measures while the heart endeavors. Clearly, the heart liberates the mind while the mind liberates the heart, and spirit emerges through their interaction.

This section concerns habits of the mind, while Sections 2, 3, and 4 concern habits of the heart. Obviously, habits can be either good or bad. Both must be examined so that bad habits can be replaced by good ones. The only way to do this is to understand clearly why the good ones are better. Without clear understanding, we will never muster the internal strength to move beyond the comfort and inertia of even our most negative habits of mind.

Chapter 2 contrasts driven leadership (a negative habit) with inspired leadership (a positive habit). Chapter 3 then discusses three indispensable qualities for producing spirit, trust, and enthusiastic co-participation—vision, rational communication, and the four sets of commitments that condition the activities of the heart. The discussion of vision and rational communication reflect the positive habits of the mind required for inspirational leadership. Chapter 4 then looks at negative habits of the mind that undermine not only inspirational leadership but also every form of noble purpose and common cause. I call this set of negative mental habits "the seven myths of mediocre leadership." Chapter 5 then looks at the measurement of spirit. The mind needs to measure, evaluate, assess, correct, nuance, and move ahead. But if the mind is oriented in a skewed direction, it may overlook crucial data. In organizations, the most overlooked data, the most serious errors of omission, are concerned with opportunity costs (the cost of lost opportunity). Chapter 5 alerts you to the 10 major categories of opportunity costs, and then summarizes the steps and consequences of inspired leadership.

When set within the three-step process given at the end of Chapter 5, the habits of inspired leadership will open the door to the heart and provide the passion, hope, resilience, strength, noble purpose, and common cause that incite and excite individuals and communities towards extraordinary endeavor.

2 Inspired Leadership vs. Driven Leadership

Inspired leadership and driven leadership have one thing in common: they get to the goal. As most leaders know, the capacity to formulate and achieve goals is, perhaps, the most important determinant of success. Goals give a concreteness to dreams. They provide a conduit between the world of dreams and the steps taken to actualize them. Therefore, they engender a desire that lends itself to creativity, energy, and above all, spirit. When leaders are both dreamers and aggressive pursuers of the dream, they are likely not only to achieve, but also to achieve creatively. Their desire to reach the goal inspires them to adapt, to find ways around obstacles, to transcend inadequate patterns of thought, and to push beyond tepidity. Goals give courage, ardor, and strength.

If inspired and driven leaders are essentially the same in their ability to formulate and pursue goals, how are they different? In the way they pursue these goals. As I note throughout this book, there are far more errors of omission than commission. When we make errors, particularly fatal errors, they generally do not arise out of being illogical, possessing false information, believing in lies, or being irrational. Often, they arise out of oversights. We miss, ignore, or blind ourselves to data that is vital to our decisions.

Such is the case with the driven leader who commonly forgets about "collateral issues." These include enthusiasm, goodwill, morale, serendipity, open communication, and trust. They are, of course, issues that concern at once the culture of organizations and the minds and hearts of individuals. They control whether energy, creativity, and adaptability are increased or substantially decreased. They determine whether self-accountability and self-motivation are present. They can debilitate in five ways: fear, resentment, suspicion, compulsive ego, and passive aggression. They can also produce the opposite: trust, goodwill, self-accountability, *esprit de corps*, and creative collegiality.

If leaders attend to these collateral issues, they will leave a longstanding legacy. If they do not, they will engender anger, resentment, negativity, "push back," aggression, and eventually a swing of the pendulum in a direction opposite of where they intend to go.

An inspired (spirit-imparting) leader leaves a longstanding legacy because she cultivates open communication, an atmosphere in which risk can be taken, a desire to imitate her spirit, a sense of collegiality, trustworthiness, and a confidence about the imminence of success. She gets to the goal not by creating dysfunction (e.g., fear and resentment) but by reducing it. She does not get to the goal by ignoring the needs of her colleagues and co-workers, but rather welcomes all stakeholders through her attentiveness, confidence, and ability to listen. She has a depth and breadth of vision that moves beyond the errors of omission to a horizon surpassing present expectation.

How does the inspired leader come to this deep and encompassing vision of the goal amidst collateral issues? She is at peace—a peace arising out of a deep awareness of self, others, and the world—a peace grounded in a firm sense of purpose—not merely purpose for oneself, but beyond oneself, toward the common good. This peace may not be directly felt. It could manifest itself in the lucidity and clarity of thought, in the profundity of good judgment, and in the effectiveness of well-conceived action. When this peace is absent, thoughts tend to be confused, judgments poor, and actions beleaguered by the endless spinning of wheels.

The most obvious difference between an inspired leader and a driven leader is the inspired leader's possession and communication of spirit. Inspired leaders impart common cause, hope, resilience, creativity, energy, synergy, and optimal fulfillment of optimal goals. They give rise to "*esprit de corps.*" In so doing, they not only reduce opportunity costs, they transform environments into highly productive, exhilarating, and even fun places to be. Perhaps the best way of describing the inspired leader's most fundamental quality is to describe the spirit he puts into the community.

We hear the word "spirit" used in a variety of contexts: "the spirit of leadership," "*esprit de corps,*" "he is a spirited person," "she is inspired." It connotes energy, enthusiasm, a psychic surge that goes beyond the laws of physics.

Seven Effects of Spirit

How does spirit affect individuals? I assume that spirit is present in every human being, so what does it do when it's "switched on?" It seems to have seven major effects:

1. Spirit imparts heightened energy. When the human psyche is fascinated, absorbed in, or taken by something life-enhancing, meaningful, noble, worthy, or even heroic, it seems to gain energy with each expenditure of energy. Have you ever noticed that when you are fascinated by something, it gives more energy than it takes? Studying an interesting problem, for example, obviously takes energy, but when you anticipate that the solution is at hand, you begin to derive far more energy than you expend. This seems to defy the laws of physics which would suggest that systems producing work lose energy. What is it about the psyche that so frequently eludes this physical constraint?

2. Spirit gives rise to a sense of well being. We seem to elicit from certain words and experiences a sense of being "more alive," of being charged with the grandeur of a project or the beauty of the world. When we experience this being "more alive," we are filled with hope, aspirations, ideals; indeed, we feel at home in the totality of all that is—not merely that we have a place amidst it all, but that we have a significant place. This purpose gives rise to the power of goals and aspirations that can provide a drive in us far beyond any predictable physical model or equation.

3. Spirit opens the way to creativity. There is a capacity within us to achieve higher viewpoints, to not only get outside the box, but to stand above multiple boxes and unify them all with one grandiose mental superstructure. We see this in great geniuses like Plato, Aristotle, Newton, Einstein, and Heisenberg. But if we reflect for a moment, we will see it in ourselves. Virtually every positive form of change and adaptation requires a movement to such higher viewpoints. To move beyond the parameters of a previously established system, we need to stand above it—to see an old system in relation to a myriad of other analogous systems. These other systems might be similar or dissimilar to the old system, but the most creative insights come from dissimilar ones.

This desire to stand above a conventional practice and compare it to other practices through higher viewpoints, this desire to go beyond, to improve the conventional, and to be creative, is one of the key characteristics of spirit. What enables us to get beyond current methods and practices, to stand above ideas and systems, to unify huge complexes into even greater complexes? Sir Arthur Eddington, one of the greatest pioneers of contemporary physics and cosmology, phrased it this way:

> We all know that there are regions of the human spirit untrammeled by the world of physics. In the mystic sense of the creation around us, in the expression of art, in a yearning toward God, the soul rises upward and finds the fulfillment of something implanted in its nature. The sanction for this development is within us, a striving born with our consciousness or an Inner Light, proceeding from a power greater than ours. Science can scarcely question this sanction, for the pursuit of science springs from a striving which the mind is impelled to follow, a questioning that will not be suppressed. Whether in the intellectual pursuits of science or in the mystical pursuits of the spirit, the light beckons ahead and the purpose surging within our nature responds.[1]

4. Spirit heightens our ability to connect with one another, commit to a common cause, and achieve unity beyond material boundaries. A mere glance can convey collegiality, respect, care, acceptance, or even love. Through this capacity, we can impart to others a sense of well-being, hope, joy, aspiration, ideal, etc. We call some personalities "charismatic," which means that they are capable of not only energizing but galvanizing us, and even infusing in us a heightened sense of purpose. But we need not be charismatic. We can reach the "spirit" of another person in the subtlest of ways, producing tranquility, deep insight, and profound understanding. When we reach another person in this way, particularly when it is mutual, we say that we are "connecting" with one another. This connection is sufficiently life-enhancing to be a goal in its own right, but frequently, it goes beyond itself. We like to use our connections to accomplish a greater good beyond ourselves. Connectedness, then, seeks and revels in common cause, a joint purpose, a noble endeavor shared with another and achieved through others. This common cause attains to a synergy that achieves more and creates more than any physical system can explain.

5. Spirit magnifies our capacity for self-transcendence or self-sacrifice beyond normal physical limitations. We can see in our everyday lives that love and inspiration can move us to change old habits, to make incredible sacrifices, and even to transcend our very nature. This capacity to act against our instincts for a "higher good," to go beyond the seeming limitations of our nature for a "higher purpose," or for "common cause" betokens a curious energy that is difficult, if not impossible, to find in the physical world and the animal kingdom. What allows us to feel, think, and embrace a higher good at the expense of instinct and in-built nature? What is it about courage, heroism, and the noble pursuit that can move us to transform the seemingly fixed nature with which we were born? We frequently call it "spirit."

6. Spirit embraces the future as if it were the present. We have the wonderful ability to anticipate, to consider possibilities, to formulate options, and to actualize ourselves in accordance with these options. More wondrously still, we can derive energy from the goals we pursue and from the options we consider to be worthy of our time. Goals don't merely motivate, they incite the creative process. A goal moves us to create a path toward it. What allows a goal to be a horizon of hope, energy, creativity, and well-being? Again, we frequently call this self-transcendent power "spirit."

7. Spirit gives rise to peace, enthusiasm, inspiration, clear thought, good judgment, and efficient action. We have the capacity to modulate excitation. We do not have to proceed to a goal like a shot out of a cannon. We can proceed thoughtfully, methodically, carefully, calmly. We can consider tangents, other options, analogies, and associations. We can do all these things without compromising our speed or acceleration toward the goal. We can modify our actions at the spur of the moment. The psyche is like a school of fish that moves together and reacts to a stimulus as a single organism. Peace produces this effect—a peace that does not seem to come from any external stimulus, but rather from some state, condition, or energy within. When present, it allows us to consider an interconnected panoply of data. Peace is not limited to clear and comprehensive thinking. It gives the capacity for good judgment, which would seem to encompass a large array of subjective and objective data. Peace makes us more efficient. It helps us to not only see but actualize the path toward greatest efficacy. Peace does not limit energy, it makes it more productive and useful by removing agitation, exaggeration, and waste. When we spin our wheels, we are probably agitated. When we are effective and efficient, we are probably at peace. What can purify the use of energy and make most effective use of thought, action, and feeling? What allows us to live our lives with a sense of impeccable "timing?" Again, we call it "spirit."

I do not expect you to have an image of spirit, but rather a sense of it—a sense that will enable you to harness its power to move beyond, to act against instinct, to promote the higher good, to be emboldened, enlivened, to connect, to love, to achieve synergy, to create, and to transcend.

Given the changes in organizational environment and the ever-greater demands being made of leadership, we would be negligent indeed to ignore or waste these capacities of spirit.

Harnessing Spiritual Capacity

Can this capacity for multi-human, superhuman, and even multi-superhuman activity be harnessed? Yes, history is replete with examples of leaders who have done so. These leaders had a sense of purpose and destiny.

If today's leaders are to attain this quality of greatness, they will need this same spirit.

Inspired leaders produce "group ethos" (emotion that charges a culture). When group ethos is consistent and strong, sympathy, emotion, and even passion for spirit and common cause toward the common good are equally strong.

Conversely, weakness in group ethos produces weakness in sympathy, emotion, passion, spirit, and common cause.

Sociologists and anthropologists since Max Weber[2] have held that organizations go through three phases:

1) the phase of charismatic leaders (who possess charisma and spirit to impel new ideas, organizations, and institutions into being),
2) the phase of interpretation (where less charismatic leaders attempt to keep the spirit of the original charismatic leaders alive), and
3) the phase of codification (where spirit seems to disappear, and is replaced by structures, processes, systems, and laws that try to imitate and concretize the effects of the foregone spirit of the founders).

The third phase is tantamount to death in the highly changing, technocentric world of today. Spirit must be kept alive. It cannot be replaced by more static processes and entities. There will, of course, be a need for structures and processes, but these cannot be a replacement for spirit. Strong spirit (arising out of strong ethos) must stand above all processes and structures—adapting, controlling, changing, and growing them.

If leaders harness and convey this spirit, they will impart 12 measurable qualities to their products, processes, and people. I categorize these 12 qualities under four headings:

Capacity for change and growth

1) adaptability and openness to change,
2) increased ability to take reasonable risks,
3) increased creativity arising out of the increased openness to change and ability to take reasonable risks,

High-performance teaming

4) improved communication,
5) increased ability to work for a common good and a common cause (increased enthusiasm and synergy),
6) more internal motivation and *self-accountability* (less negative external motivations: fear, force, and bribe),
7) more *group* creativity arising out of increased high performance teaming and increased synergy,

Morale

8) decrease in fear, anger, blame, passive aggression, suspicion, and destructive compulsiveness in the workplace,
9) decreased absenteeism,
10) decreased turnover of top 25 percent of critical skills personnel,

Quality

11) increased good will among stakeholders to contribute to quality improvement,
12) breakthroughs in quality boundaries (improved design, decreased waste, decreased product defects, and improved processes).

When leaders add these 12 qualities to their products, processes, and people, they infuse their teams and organizations with a strong spirit—a sense of meaning, contribution, and common cause that imparts energy and inspires creativity and innovation.

3 Three Qualities of Inspired Leadership

How does a leader become inspired? How does she produce vision, trust, and spirit? What habits and attitudes are essential to moving a culture to exceptional synergy and creativity? What is the essential "mindset" for opportunity-seeking and avoidance of opportunity cost?

From my research, consultations, and experience as a CEO, I submit that three qualities are central: 1) vision and goals exemplifying both long-term organizational good and stakeholder good, 2) rational communication with stakeholders, and 3) personal, ethical, people-oriented, and leadership commitments evoking spirit and trust.

1. First Quality of Inspired Leadership: Vision

We have all heard the cliché, "the business of business is business," and the business of business is the maximization of shareholder wealth.[1] If we look at this adage from a comprehensive economic point of view, we can hardly dispute it. However, if we view it from a narrow point of view, we may be driven out of business. What differentiates the comprehensive from the narrow interpretation of this great economic formula? Two elements: 1) the definition of "shareholder," and 2) short term or long term?

"Shareholder" can be viewed in an extraordinarily narrow way, that is, as "stockholder," or in the comprehensive way as "stakeholder." Recall that "stakeholder" refers to any individual or group constitutive of the organization's success and development (e.g., stockholders, customers, suppliers, employees, managers, local community members, industrial community members, etc.).

Inasmuch as all stakeholders are vital to the success of the organization, they cannot be alienated from it. They ought to be treated fairly, indeed, as well as possible. The more satisfied they are, the more they will attach themselves to the long-term well-being of the organization. For example, customers who are treated well will likely pursue a more extensive relationship. Suppliers will be more prone to deliver equipment and inventory on time. Employees are more willing to change, pursue opportunities, share information, and go the extra mile.

Conversely, if stakeholders are alienated, they will detach themselves, giving rise to decreases in market share and the four quality objectives (product design, elimination of product defects, elimination of waste, and improvement of processes). Instead of pursuing new opportunities, discontented stakeholders will lose opportunities (opportunity costs). "Win-lose" relationships are directly correlatable with high opportunity costs. Thus, it is essential to pursue "win-win" relationships with all stakeholders.

This contention is merely a corollary of Ronald H. Coase's Theorem[2]. In brief, the theorem holds that two individuals with diverse interests will gain mutual advantage by replacing hard-bargaining ("win-lose") with what I term "soft-bargaining."

For example, if Organization A is polluting the air, forcing Organization B (next door to A) to invest in an expensive ventilation system to prevent the pollution from disturbing its employees, it would be better if A and B could soft-bargain their way to the least expensive solution. Let us suppose that cleaning up the pollution will cost X thousand dollars, but the ventilation system will cost 2X thousand dollars. It would be better for Organization A to clean up the pollution and have Organization B pay for one half of it (.5X thousand dollars), than to have Organization B take Organization A to court. Not only could Organizations A or B suffer substantial judgment against them, they will also compound the transactional costs by their hard-bargaining procedures. Such transactional costs would include legal fees, time lost in pursuing the court case, hostile neighbors after the court case, and possibly even future contingencies and costly punishments. These transactional costs seem intangible at first, but over time they become quite real, frequently doubling or even tripling the cost of an adequate solution. Because of these transactional costs, it is virtually always better to soft bargain and split the cost of an adequate solution, than to hard bargain and incur the long-term ramifications.

Transactional costs can increase significantly when the hard bargaining takes place not merely between neighbors with diverse interests, but stakeholders with a common cause. These transactional costs would entail not merely legal fees, time lost, hostility, future contingencies, and costly punishments, but could also include ongoing, unreasonable behavior on the part of both parties, high costs of monitoring a "win-lose" solution, destandardization of goods and services (leading to quality decline), not to mention the five debilitators. Among stakeholders, increased transactional costs alone produce incomprehensibly negative long-term relationships and opportunity costs. "Win-lose" is truly a "lose-lose."

Stakeholders have diverse interests. For example, employees will not have the same interests as managers; customers may not have the same interests as suppliers, etc. Thus, it is essential to fairly balance these diverse stakeholder interests.

Furthermore, stakeholder interests could be different from the interests of the organization. Employees may want to be paid more than an organization can realistically afford. Customers may want too good of a bargain. Suppliers may want too high a price. The community might have cumbersome and ineffective regulations. Thus, leaders must be conscious of both the long-term common good of the organization and pursuing the fair interests of the stakeholders.

How, then, can a leader best formulate a comprehensive vision and goals for an organization? By attending to three sets of issues: the long-term common good of the organization, the fair interests of individual stakeholders, and balance among the interests of various stakeholder groups.

1. The long-term common good of the organization. Leaders should solicit ideas from all stakeholder groups about possible opportunities for new markets, new revenues, reduction of waste and product defects, and improvement of product and process. After gathering all the "opportunity data," leaders should formulate long-term goals. The prioritization, timing, and strategic pursuit of these goals should be harmoniously and systemically arranged to avoid overlaps, time lags, repetitions, and fall backs.[3]

This first phase of strategic planning should be done with a view to optimizing potential. It should contain elements of reasonable risk and challenge for the stakeholders. Goals could be severely undermined or understated if leaders should pursue the path of "riskless realism." Besides, riskless realism does not charge anyone with spirit. Only challenge, anticipation of growth, pushing beyond the boundary, and the common cause necessary for these can awaken spirit.

2. Fair interests of individual stakeholders. Once leaders have elucidated the optimal long-term common good of the organization, they must turn their attention to the fair interests of individual stakeholders. No organization can give all stakeholders everything they want. It would be prohibitive from the viewpoint of net revenue and budget, and would also create unacceptable imbalances among various stakeholder groups. The best that can be done is to optimize the affordable good of the stakeholder groups while assuring that no stakeholder group is treated unfairly or negligently. If any stakeholder group is treated unfairly, that group will undermine the good of other stakeholders, and the good of the organization.[4] Knowing what is unfair, then, should be the starting point for understanding stakeholder interests.

Leaders need to ask, "What do our particular stakeholder groups mean by 'unfair?'" It is inadvisable for leaders to ask only themselves what stakeholder groups mean by "unfair." They should talk to objective, fair-minded representatives of particular stakeholder groups to ascertain the definition of "unfair." If leaders stay within the domain of fairness, they will avoid a multitude of counterproductive responses, including the five debilitators of culture (fear, anger, suspicion, passive aggression, and compulsive ego).

Some people believe that if businesses give more than what is fair to their stakeholders, they will needlessly decrease shareholder wealth, and therefore undermine the funds available for future growth and innovation. Others hold that business should go the extra mile, giving more than what is fair (so long as this does not undermine the common good or cause unfairness to other stakeholder groups). This practice, they contend, will build good will among stakeholders which will, in turn, allow businesses to ask more of their stakeholders in the future.

If stakeholders respond favorably, giving "more than fair" is clearly the way to go. However, if some stakeholders have a history of responding unfavorably, it might be better to err on the side of giving only what is fair. Leaders must judge for themselves what is fair to each stakeholder group. Customers cannot be lumped together with suppliers or employees. Indeed, one group of customers should not be lumped together with other distinct groups of customers. Hence, leaders should be aware of the responsiveness of each relevant group within each stakeholder group, and apportion their affordable funds accordingly.

3. Balance among the interests of various stakeholder groups. Once leaders have assessed the fair (or even optimal) interests of each relevant stakeholder group, they must now assure that one stakeholder group does not see itself as disadvantaged in comparison with the rest.

Suppose, for example, that there are three stakeholder groups who are equally responsive to an organization's generosity. If group A is treated fairly but not optimally, while stakeholder groups B and C are treated optimally (beyond fairness), stakeholder group A will view itself as relatively disadvantaged. Even though it is being treated fairly, it will exemplify the same anger, suspicion, passive aggression, and compulsion toward leadership that would be manifest in cases of outright unfairness. Hence, leaders need to assure balance among stakeholder groups. If there is a reason for imbalance among stakeholder groups (e.g., that one stakeholder group is integral to a growth initiative and will be asked to do more), this must be explained to the groups who might feel relatively disadvantaged. If it is not, the relatively disadvantaged group will begin to detach itself from the common good of the organization.

In sum, leaders must have double vision. They must set out an ambitious and challenging opportunity plan for the organization while recognizing the fair and balanced interests of all relevant stakeholder groups. These two sets of goals must be integrated into a single, multi-year plan that optimizes growth and stakeholder good will simultaneously. This plan will become the rational explanation for leadership's initiatives in the future. If this rational explanation is continually communicated to the relevant stakeholder groups, vision, trust, and spirit will burgeon.

2. Second Quality of Inspired Leadership: Rational Communication

There is no better way of heading off morale problems and internal conflicts than to give regular rational explanations of one's actions. I find that the levels of spirit and trust increase in direct proportion to rational communication.

The process of integrating rational communication into the organization is comprised of three steps: vehicles of communication, rational explanation of vision and goals, and status report: good and bad news.

Step 1: Vehicles of communication. At the very least, leaders should organize meeting times with various stakeholder groups to explain what they intend and why they intend it. These should be scheduled well in advance of the event, and should include time to answer questions from the audience. Questions can be submitted in writing during a break between a leader's presentation and the question-and-answer period, if leaders are not comfortable with responding to spontaneous questions. There are many other vehicles of explaining an organization's actions and directions, such as holding regularly scheduled meetings with designated representatives of stakeholder groups, opening appropriate books to those representatives, or holding large group strategy or feedback sessions.

The vehicle used to communicate is less important than the regularity of communication. Lack of regular communication causes rumors, and rumors are most often negative. When stakeholders are ignorant of what is happening, they begin to believe that there is a reason for their being kept in the dark. They ascribe intentionality to leadership instead of neglect. This belief incites the five debilitators which, in turn, cause the negative perception of leadership to be increasingly exaggerated. If leaders do not meet with a designated representative or speak directly to stakeholders, the level of trust and spirit (affecting willingness to change, be creative, openly communicate, and work in teams) can deteriorate rapidly. As a result, opportunity costs will increase dramatically. If stakeholders know that a designated representative will meet with leadership next Monday or that a meeting with the stakeholder group is scheduled three weeks from now, they will generally delimit the credibility of rumors, thus keeping the five debilitators in check.

Step 2: Rational explanation of vision and goals. The most important part of communication is to relate current actions to the vision and goal statement. If leaders have gone through strategic visioning and have integrated the long-term common good with the balanced, fair interests of relevant stakeholder groups, they have already done most of the work necessary for rational communication. Once stakeholders realize their role in the organization's future and where they stand relative to other stakeholders, they begin to feel valued and contribute to the momentum toward a better future. They begin to understand leadership's creative task of bringing together and balancing the long-term common good with their fair interests.

Most people do not want to grab for an unfair share of the pie. They want to be part of an organization that has a better future. Indeed, they want to be part of building that better future for both themselves and other stakeholders. People enjoy being part of a creative, winning, growing venture that makes the community, industry, and the world a better place. Hence, if leaders explain how their goals represent the best possible way of achieving both the common good and fair, balanced stakeholder interests, they will give an unassailable argument for their actions to stakeholders. This unassailable argument not only dispels the five debilitators, but also neutralizes the cynics and rumor mongers who frequent the hallowed halls of e-mail and Listservs. Most people will give greater credibility to rationality than rumor. Rational explanation of creative, winning goals not only crushes rumor, but also builds a sense of belonging with a momentum toward a better future. In short, rational explanation builds spirit.

Step 3: Status report: good and bad news. Leaders must connect the data of the current situation to the explanation of goals. Stakeholders need to know not only why the goals are the way they are, but also where the organization stands in the achievement of those goals. An honest status report (including both good and bad news) should be given to designated representatives of stakeholder groups at least once per quarter.

Good news is easy to report. It automatically builds spirit. Bad news need not have the opposite effect if it is treated as a vehicle for making rational adjustments to the strategy. When leaders notice that certain goals are not being reached, they need to avoid two pitfalls to change and growth: 1) hiding the bad news, or 2) blaming someone else for it. If bad news is hidden, no adjustment can be made to overcome it. It generally gets worse. When it does come to light, it can dramatically affect growth plans and morale. If leaders spend their time fixing blame, they will undermine the partnership needed to fix the problem.

A much better approach to unachieved goals is a problem-solving session with designated representatives of stakeholder groups. In such a meeting, leaders may want to begin by recounting some goals that have been achieved or exceeded, and then look at three or four areas that require some adjustment in strategy. They may then want to give some of their own suggestions, and invite the stakeholder representatives to give suggestions. The creative suggestions of stakeholders often enable formerly elusive goals to be achieved. Leaders need to respond to these suggestions. If the suggestions are utilizable, adequate time and monetary support must be given to actualize them. This will not only clear a new creative path toward the goal, it will create "buy on," ownership, common cause, and spirit. If the stakeholder's suggestions are not utilizable, leaders must rationally explain why (e.g., "We do not have adequate resources at this time," or "Your suggestion negatively impacts two other areas," etc.). The leader may then want to invite the stakeholder to make alternative suggestions that obviate the problems in the previous ones.

3. THIRD QUALITY OF INSPIRED LEADERSHIP: HEART

The heart of the leader is manifest in personal, ethical, people-centered, and leadership commitments that evoke spirit and build trust. Three statements form the foundation of trust and spirit in organizations: "We must respect each other," "We must appreciate the intrinsic dignity of our diverse work force," and "We must display appropriate concern for our people and not merely for their skill sets." No matter how many times they are uttered, these statements cannot be reduced to clichés because for those who have eyes to see and ears to hear they possess an almost infinite depth.

If leadership allows these statements to be reduced to clichés, they will undermine trust and spirit by rendering impotent the first two qualities of inspired leadership. An unconcerned heart can easily mitigate the noblest of visions and the most rational of communication processes. Mind is not enough. Stakeholders look to the heart of a leader to put their hearts into common vision and purpose; and heart, after all, is what will translate mentation into action. There is an old adage, "cor ad cor loquitur" (heart speaks to heart). The ancients looked at this from the vantage point of families and armies, but it is clearly applicable to organizations. If leaders forget this, they will fall on hard times.

4 Seven Myths of Mediocre Leadership

If ethical, caring, and committed leaders are more inspiring than those who are not, why is the "heart" so frequently ignored in leadership literature?

I attribute this gigantic error of omission to seven myths that have reached epic proportions in the mindset of international business. When examined, they can be seen to be an inevitable pathway to long-term decline, intransigence, turnover, bad morale, complacency, and the five debilitators. I mention them here because of their insidiousness. They seem to promote organizational welfare, but have precisely the opposite effect. If their destructive power is not exposed and faced by all well-intentioned leaders, they become the implicit creed of an organization, which would mean its imminent demise.

Myth 1: Resources are fixed.

Malthus' conjecture—that resources are fixed—grounded much of classical economic theory. Thus, as population grows, there will be less per capita wealth, causing shortages and famine worldwide. But, there is no evidence to support Malthus' conjecture, because per capita wealth has outdistanced the rapid increase in world population. What Malthus overlooked was the capacity of technology to multiply resources in remarkable ways. As we enter the age of hydroponic farming, solar and fusion power, and biophysical substrates of computer memory, the future of abundance amidst an increasing population seems hopeful.

Why is this myth of fixed resources so unhealthy for organizations? Because it creates an attitude of scarcity in a state of abundance. It focuses organizations on "protecting their position from enemies" instead of developing new markets, products, and processes. It makes businesses believe that stakeholders have to be controlled to prevent them from overconsuming the fixed resources of the organization. It also makes leadership focus on a world of hostility rather than opportunity. Instead of feeling the exhilaration of finding or creating something new, leaders only feel defensiveness toward enemies, leeches, and problems. People seem to be potential enemies instead of potential friends. New technology seems to be another problem instead of an opportunity to create new growth.

If leaders are to reduce opportunity costs, utilize new technologies, ask their people to contribute to teams, and explore new frontiers, they must have hope. Without hope, even the most reasonable risks and the most overt friends seem dangerous. The excitement and spirit of growth and creation are overshadowed by feelings of peril and defensiveness. Business is no longer fun, it is a labor of putting one's enemies in the grave—and everyone, including one's stakeholders, is a potential enemy.

If leaders believe in the probability of new resources, technology, and markets, they will view change and risk as vehicles of opportunity and growth, and therefore as blessings. However, if leaders do not believe in the probability of new resources, technology, and markets, they will view change and risk as vehicles of imminent danger, and try to avoid them. This avoidance will lead to sky-rocketing opportunity costs, abuse of the stakeholders, a culture filled with the five debilitators, and an eventual demise of the organization.

Leaders need not practice all of Martin Seligman's principles of learned optimism.[1] But an appropriation of hope based on an abundance mindset is absolutely requisite to the excitement of pursuing opportunity.[2]

Myth 2: The narrow view of maximizing shareholder wealth—to maximize stockholder wealth in the short term[3]—is a reasonable one.

This view seriously interferes with taking care of stakeholders' fair interests. The emphasis on short term could also interfere with proper investment in growth. Alienation of stakeholders and failure to invest in growth are prominent causes of opportunity cost, ethical problems, and the demise of organizations.

To avoid this serious misinterpretation of the primary prescript of capitalism, leaders should subscribe to the principle of optimal benefit: The business of business is to optimize shareholder wealth by seizing upon reasonable risks and opportunities through a network of satisfied stakeholders committed to the pursuit of long-term growth and quality improvement.

Myth 3: Three traditional financial statements—income statement, balance sheet, and cash flow statement—give a comprehensive report on organizational performance.

A belief in the comprehensiveness of these financial statements will lead to shallow and ineffective strategic planning. These statements tell us what did, in fact, happen; however they don't indicate what could have happened, but did not. In short, traditional accounting statements do not assess opportunity costs. They do not analyze customer's lost market share, new markets unseized, new customers unpursued, new technologies and efficiencies uninstalled, new opportunities unexploited, new processes undiscovered, waste uncurbed, or lawsuits unavoided.

Since financial statements do not record unexploited opportunity, their exclusive use for assessing performance leads to significant errors of omission. If net revenue is in decline, executives may simply cut costs. The battle cry goes up, "We have to cut deeper. There is too much waste. Too many superfluous support people. Too much...." This battle cry could be extraordinarily detrimental because those cuts could dissatisfy customers, suppliers, employees, and other stakeholders. In short, cuts can go too deep, can lead not to leanness, but to decline. Work simply doesn't get done. Customers don't get contacted. Suppliers can't be coordinated with the need for parts, equipment, and inventory.

Most CEO's are aware that the long-term solution to all business problems is new sources of net revenue, and that the cause of new revenue is generally growth and change. They are also aware that growth and change require investment in people, training, new products, etc. Hence, a strategy of cutting costs to gain net revenue, though sometimes appropriate, could also be suicidal.

I suggest that CPAs move into the business of opportunity cost, and help their clients to analyze the following eight opportunity cost areas: 1) new markets and opportunities; 2) potential revenues from these new markets; 3) competition in these new markets; 4) future customer base; 5) whether to lay off valued employees or reeducate them for work in new market areas; 6) whether to cut support, staff, and equipment or reapportion resources to new markets; 7) the opportunity costs of stakeholder dissatisfaction arising out of cutbacks; and 8) how quality objectives (product design, elimination of product defects, elimination of waste, and improvement of processes) are impeded by stakeholder dissatisfaction. I further suggest businesses design their own assessment of opportunity costs.

Myth 4: Consideration of people should come after consideration of product and process.

The three Ps (people, product, process) could be seen to have unequal importance. We might think that product must be far more important than process and people. After all, without a product there would be no use for the other two Ps. We might further conjecture that processes are more important than people because without the former, there would be no need for the latter. But we could also reason that without people, no process could be accomplished, and furthermore, without people accomplishing processes, no product can be made. The point is, product, process, and people are equally important, and they must all be attended to in their intimate relationship to one another.

If an organization has high goals and creative, inspired teams to actualize them, they will invent the right processes along the way. Similarly, creative, inspired people attract, solicit, and keep customers. Such people work well with vendors and establish relationships that bring in inventory when it is needed. Thus, leaders must be concerned with people issues at the same time they are designing new products and constructing new processes. The people system cannot be shunted off as an afterthought to product and process.

There is another reason why people are viewed in a tertiary way. Many creative, intelligent leaders tend to focus on quantifiable, analytical, and systematic data. Hard data is seen to be better controlled, more solid, even more prestigious than "soft" people data. When the boss asks, "What did you do to reach our goals this week?" it seems much better to report numbers than to say, "I inspired people to buy into our objectives," or "I decreased fear, anger, and suspicion," or "I encouraged the development of new ideas and co-participation in the X, Y, and Z workgroups."

As leaders think about new product lines, they must also think about stakeholder satisfaction, about ways of promoting co-participation, of creating a fun atmosphere, of helping people to be openly communicative, of decreasing blame and game-playing. The same four steps for building the heart of a leader are designed to help build stakeholder satisfaction. When these steps are combined with opportunistic visioning and rational communication, growth and quality of both products and processes will follow.

Myth 5: Leadership requires tough-mindedness—matters of the heart make one "soft" and should be avoided.

No doubt leaders need to be tough-minded. They must be courageous about the mission and hold firm to the common good. They cannot please all the people all the time. Even though a rational explanation can assuage the debilitators most of the time, it still requires strength to hold to a given direction. Any leader who needs to be "liked" will have some very hard days.

But most leaders do not spend most of their time on the tough decisions, standing firm, or taking the hit. The leader's job is to give direction, and most of the time, stakeholders appreciate challenging, meaningful, rational, well-communicated direction. Leaders spend most of their time creating visions and strategic plans, and forming teams to make these happen. Leaders, then, spend their time not so much on overseeing and administrating, but on making a vision of a better future come to life. Their job is to breathe spirit and life into vision. This job is fundamentally a matter of the heart.

Ethical, caring, committed leaders are simply more inspiring than those who are not. They incite people to move to bigger challenges and higher goals. They attract people to work closely with them, and they make people feel like winners whenever they are around. Their soul betokens common cause and trust. Inspired leaders, then, are not merely great visionaries and great planners, they know the ways of the heart. They know how to earn the trust, care, and even zeal of the people around them. Knowing the ways of the heart is just as important, if not more important, than being tough-minded. If "soft bargaining" (based on principled "win-win" negotiation) always wins more battles than hard bargaining, then leaders with a heart will always be more victorious than the merely tough-minded.

Myth 6: Principle-based ethics will make us less competitive; the best we can do is look at harms and benefits.

We are tempted to avoid principle-based ethics. It seems, at first glance, that principles will make us too rigid, will lock us in, and even lead to a loss of competitive position. We may think that if we have principles and our competitors don't, they will cut better deals and avail themselves of opportunities that our ethics would preclude.

Let's assess this proposition by starting from the opposite point of view. If we have no ethical principles, then we are reduced to so-called "situation ethics," that is, ethics based on emotions and intuition of the moment. This may not seem altogether undesirable until we consider our virtually infinite capacity to rationalize our behavior. Give me five minutes, and I can tell you why any action is beneficial, fair, and consistent with my word. Situation ethics easily become mere justification of convenience.

Now, you might think, "What's wrong with that? I like getting what's convenient." Unfortunately, our stakeholders will probably view the actualization of "my convenience" somewhat dimly. This may lead to disengagement of stakeholders from my goals, undermine my trustworthiness and reputation, lead to accusations of unfairness and irresponsibility, and even produce lawsuits. Remember: a lack of principles frequently means a lack of ethics, and this undermines trust, spirit, and stakeholder relationships.

Most organizations can buy into three master principles—minimize harm, keep promises, and be fair. These may be adapted to fit the needs of a particular organization. If they become part of the mindset of an organization, then processes for ethical decision making can be built around them, thus increasing trust, enhancing stakeholder satisfaction, and driving down opportunity costs.

Myth 7: Tangibles—money, equipment, and inventory—are more real than intangibles (ideas, ideals, trust, spirit, concern, and vision).

The first six myths cut a wide swath across the organization. Myth 1 concerns macro-economics; myth 2, micro-economics; myth 3, accounting and finance; myth 4, leadership; myth 5, leadership theory; and myth 6, ethics. The seventh myth is a metaphysical one that underlies all the other myths. Metaphysics—the science of ultimates (e.g., ultimate causes, ultimate grounds, ultimate principles)—frequently concerns itself with the definition of reality. Metaphysical assumptions can be carried around in the minds of virtually every member of a culture, but because they are so fundamental, they are almost never questioned.

The assumption that tangibles (money, structures, equipment) are more real and therefore more important than intangibles (care, trust, spirit, ideas, ideals, principles) has been ruining organizations for years. Tangible realities are more easily perceived and controlled, but this is hardly a reason to elevate their status.

Some 2,400 years ago Plato experienced a similar problem with his students. The quality of "justice" in a person seemed vague. It wasn't like height or weight. Plato kept insisting that vague, intangible qualities were more important than the tangible ones. "Justice" reached to the heart, indeed, to every action of a person; whereas height only described the surface. Slowly, Plato led his students through a series of questions to the realization that frequently the reality that is less obvious and less tangible is more enduring, effective, and pervasive. For this reason, Plato advocated a liberal education to help leaders see the importance of the intangibles so that they could actualize a world of higher ideals, ideas, principles, and opportunities. The more a person can sense the reality of an intangible, the more she can sense the reality of a better future. She has the capacity to see future ideals, ideas, systems, principles, and opportunities as if they were present now. These people would be the dreamers who would sense the presence of the future so strongly that they could not help but actualize it with every dimension of their being.

I too believe that the intangible qualities are frequently more enduring and more important than tangible qualities. Now the intangible technology of the future, a technology based more and more on intangible knowledge, may be viewed as far more relevant to the future than the fixed reality of tangible resources. Breakthroughs in computer memory, for example, may affect the world more than the fixity of fossil fuels.

The same would hold true for myth 2. If the intangibility of future vision (comprised of both the long-term common good of the organization and the fair and balanced interests of stakeholders) were valued as much as bricks and mortar, growth, adaptation to new technology, and the construction of a better future would occur with explosive acceleration. If the actualization of dreams were viewed as concretely as fixed structures, a better world would quickly emerge.

Myth 3 also loses validity when intangibles are given real status. Imagine what would happen if intangible opportunity costs were seen to be just as real as tangible, historical expenses. Missed opportunities for growth would be a thing of the past. Lay-offs might be superceded by new ventures and new markets.

Myth 4 would also be remedied, for intangible people concerns would now be valued as much as tangible products and processes. The intangible gifts of the heart, in myth 5, would be valued as much as tough-mindedness; and intangible ethical principles, in myth 6, would supercede the tangible emotions of the situation.

If the value of intangibles were given more credence by today's leaders, *esprit de corps* would be a foregone conclusion, and the human drive to invent, build, create, organize, and to integrate would be more fulfilling, giving rise to a culture characterized by principles, trust, care, and spirit.

5 Measuring the Effects of Spirit

Throughout this book, I make frequent mention of the many benefits of *esprit de corps*, ranging from decreased opportunity costs and transactional costs, to increased ability to change and to engage in cross-functional teaming.

You may be wondering, Can these benefits be measured? What is the bottom-line benefit of inspired leadership? What is the long-term profitability of counteracting the seven myths of mediocre leadership within our organizations? How will an investment in the three qualities of inspired leadership (vision, rational communication, and commitments toward trust and spirit) improve competitiveness, market share, and long-term profitability? An investment in inspired leadership will likely improve morale, but will it improve performance, productivity, and profitability?

Leaders must be sure that their actions not only benefit their people, but also the common good of all stakeholders. Every leader has fiduciary responsibility for the financial viability, productivity, and strength of the organization. Stakeholders not only must be happy, their happiness must translate into long-term efficacy, quality, and competitiveness.

Although Dr. W. Edwards Deming wrote the book on systemic and quantitative quality improvement, he was fully cognizant that we must go beyond those domains to the less clear and controllable areas of profound knowledge, leadership, and management of people.

An investment in vision, rational communication, and commitments toward spirit and trust will undoubtedly produce efficacious results. Any organization will enhance the four objectives of quality—improved product design, elimination of product defect, elimination of waste, and improved processes—by cultivating *esprit de corps*.

Quality improvement requires the goodwill, creativity, and unity of our people. Our people will not willingly pursue the elimination of waste or product defect if the five debilitators are markedly present in the culture. They will not, and even cannot pursue them if they are unable to take risks, open themselves to change, and be team players. They will be seriously hampered by a culture that shuns creativity, and that emphasizes inspection instead of inspiration.

If leaders want to take quality to the next step, they will have to reach the minds and hearts, indeed, the very spirit and freedom of their people. By helping people to come alive in their whole lives, leaders pave the way to the next level of change, self-efficacy, creativity, and teamwork. To cross the threshold to this new level, they have to look seriously at what was previously considered the intangible domain.

If leaders are to put this "investment in intangibles" on their radar screens, they will have to reveal the monetary consequences of not making such an investment. This is most easily done by constructing an opportunity cost analysis for each area (a team, a subdivision, a division).

An opportunity cost analysis measures *the cost of lost opportunity*. Such measurement is by nature inexact. It is difficult to predict how much an absence of enthusiasm or trust will affect the pursuit of new markets, relationships with vendors, or decreases in waste and product defects. Furthermore, it is even more difficult to put precise dollar figures on events that may not happen. Nevertheless, I encourage you to engage in opportunity cost assessment, for it reveals how investments in people (vision, trust, and spirit) can significantly reduce opportunity costs, and enhance long-term profitability. This, in turn, shows how an investment in intangibles is commensurate with a leader's responsibility to enhance long-term tangibles (e.g., market share, new markets, efficiency in inventory, decreased waste, and increased profit and return on investment).

We cannot escape qualitative analysis if we wish to pursue completeness. Hard metrics can only be applied to a narrow range of our decisions and intellectual endeavors.

We will be forced to go beyond what is "perfectly clear." The ambiguity of judgment is inescapable. It would be lovely if we could simply allow an equation, a formula, a thinking process, or a controlled interpretation of data to make judgments for us. But alas, they cannot. And if we try to make them do this, they will let us down by a string of errors of omission. Business judgment, decisions, and leadership are inescapably qualitative, interior, personalistic, and hazy.

In this book I try to lend qualitative clarity to essentially qualitative data to help you get as complete a picture as possible of the "people" domain of leadership, and to organize this picture so that you become uncomfortable with mere metrics and more at home with the domain of qualitative analysis.

In this increasingly fast-paced and complex world, positions of leadership require experts in both quantitative and qualitative analysis. It would be ideal if leaders could attend to both, and allow both to speak within their hearts and minds.

If qualitative strategies are to be effective, they must be measured, indexed, and evaluated in both the short and long term. All strategies—whether concerned with product, process, or people, or with the tangible or intangible—will manifest themselves in profitability and return on investment. These metrics are indispensable for measuring short and long-term success. Despite their efficacy, they frequently do not clearly indicate where success and failure come from.

If leaders want to know the sources of their success, they need to calculate the time a strategy takes to manifest itself in net profit and return on investment. For example, the profitability of a product innovation might be evidenced in one season. Investments in the people system not only take longer to enact, they also tend to affect intangibles like adaptability, teamwork, and creativity. These also have a lag time before being manifest in net profit and ROI.

Generally, people changes have a longer lag time than product or process changes because changes to the people system must go through about five stages before they can become manifest in the two core metrics.

Some aspects of these five stages are measurable, though these measurements will also take time to become manifest in the two core metrics. But the wait is worth it, for frequently this increased lag time produces far more perduring effects on the two core metrics than changes with shorter lag times.

I find that improvements in personal attitude and commitment manifest themselves first in improvements in leadership, ethos, and morale; those improvements, in turn, become manifest in improvements in adaptability, teamwork, self-motivation, and creativity; these, in turn, are manifest in improvements in quality, flow time, performance, market share, customer relations, opportunity costs, transactional costs, critical skills turnover, and production. These, in turn, are manifest in an improvement in both short-term and long-term profitability, and return on investment.

Expected Lag Time in and Measurability of People Changes

Difficult to measure — Easy to measure

Stage 1	Stage 2	Stage 3	Stage 4	Stage 5
Improvements in Personal Attitude and Commitment	Improvements in Leadership, Ethos and Morale	Improvements in Adaptability, Teamwork, Self-Motivation, Creativity	Improvements in Quality, Flow Time, Performance, Market Share, Customer Relations, Opportunity Costs, and Critical Skills Turnover result in Increases in Production	Improved Manifestation in Two Core Metrics

Long lag times and delayed measurability frequently lead to the capacity to improve continually. Such changes produce the internal fabric from which goodwill, unity, and creativity are generated. Enlightened leaders can maintain these elements of a people system, with minimum effort, indefinitely. Though products and processes must always change, the attitudes underlying the happiness, purpose, unity, integrity, and creativity of people are perennial. The more leaders recognize these perennial truths today, the more they can translate them into success in the future.

An Investment in People

How can you make an investment in people (vision, spirit, and trust)? By investing in the education, time, and reward structure necessary to implement four sets of commitments—personal, people, ethical, and leadership commitments (explained in the upcoming chapters).

The costs of investments in people can be estimated. Workshops and educational programs have specific price tags. The time and cost required to obtain education and to implement the four sets of commitments can be estimated. The rewards necessary to incentivize and thank people for the implementation of the commitments can also be estimated. Start-up costs for education and implementation of commitments are considerably higher than maintenance costs once vision, enthusiasm, and trust begin to manifest themselves. Once you calculate these start-up costs, you should compare them to the revenues generated by a decrease in the following 10 opportunity costs.

1. Opportunity Cost Category	2. Estimated Total Cost	3. High % of Total Cost Eliminated	4. Low % of Total Cost Eliminated
1. Waste in processes and materials			
2. Cost of product defects			
3. Lost market share from poor customer relations			
4. Lost market share from non-responsiveness to new markets			
5. Cost of inefficient flow times of process and delivery			
6. Cost of not having "just in time" inventory			
7. Cost of inability to change rapidly			
8. Cost of turnover in top 25% of critical skill personnel			
9. Cost of mediocre teaming and closed communication			
10. Transactional costs			
TOTAL			

How can a leader use this chart to assess opportunity costs? Column 1 lists the 10 major categories of opportunity costs. Column 2 seeks to define the total amount of each opportunity cost within an organization. Column 3 seeks a high side estimate of how much these opportunity costs could be decreased by an investment in the four sets of commitments leading to vision, trust, and spirit. Column 4 seeks a low side estimate of how much these opportunity costs could be decreased by such an investment. Leaders can use this chart to organize opportunity cost data.

Ten Categories of Costs

I will now briefly assess each category of opportunity cost. Leaders will know the specifics of these costs relative to their organizations much better than I. My purpose here is only to explore what should be included in the assessment of these costs. It is virtually impossible to make a perfect or complete assessment of these opportunity costs, but rough estimates underscore the importance of making an investment in the four sets of commitments leading to vision, spirit, and trust.

Row 1—Waste. Team leaders, administrators, managers, division leaders, and CEOs will want to estimate the amount of eliminatable waste in their processes and materials. Some of these costs will be hidden because a leader will not recognize what some of his line workers think is obvious. Nevertheless, about 60 percent of waste can be seen. This would include unnecessary steps in a process, unnecessary rungs of supervision, unnecessary interruptions in communication, poor sight lines in a process, poor data in setting up processes, etc. Materials waste includes inefficient use of by-products, processes which produce too much by-product, theft, and overuse of materials resulting from passive aggression and anger. Leaders who are already using a quality system may still see considerable room for improvement in all of these areas. Investments in inspired leadership (vision, spirit, and trust) can lead directly to these additional improvements. In any case, it would be well worth your while to make a rough estimate of the total amount of eliminatable waste in processes and materials (Column 2).

After you estimate your total costs, determine the *maximum* percentage of this waste you believe could be eliminated within the next two years by investing in vision, spirit, and trust within the organization (Column 3). After completing this, estimate the *minimum* amount of waste you think could be eliminated by increased morale, co participation, enthusiasm, creativity, self-accountability, and adaptability (Column 4).

Row 2—Product defects. Make an estimate of the costs of product defects, including lost market share, replacement of products, recalls of products, and restabalization of customer relationships (Column 2). These costs reveal that care for the customer and the product, pride in one's work, and respect for one's team (the effects of spirit) can be of equal or greater importance than monitoring and punishing.What is the maximum percentage of these costs which could be eliminated by an increase in moral, co-participation, enthusiasm, creativity, self-accountability, and adaptability (Column 3)? Finally, what is the minimum amount of this cost that could be eliminated by such an investment (Column 4)?

Row 3—Lost market share from non-responsiveness to customers or poor customer relations. Take a moment here to think of what poor morale and lack of enthusiasm, self-motivation, and adaptability can do to customer relations. Level 3 organizations care about their customers. They do not fix on merely minimum customer standards or even customer satisfaction, but on customer well being. They are concerned that their customers benefit from their product. They make efforts to deliver the product on time or early. They try to build the product to better than customer specification, and they solicit customer input during phases of the design and delivery process. Most poignantly, sales and customer relations personnel in Level 3 organizations are likely to make customers feel like real stakeholders or partners. They include their customers in their vision and aspirations. When customers sense their contributive mentality, their "win-win" attitude, and their desire to be trustworthy, they will usually respond in kind.

Customers can tell when organizations truly care, versus when they are just trying to close the sale. Their satisfaction is indicated by long-lasting relationships, referrals, expansion of inventory, and increased cooperation. All of these consequences affect sales and market share in both the short and long term.

Anything short of first-class treatment of customers is translatable into loss of future market share. Though the commission system can eliminate some of these opportunity costs, it tends to encourage sales and marketing personnel to find high paying, low maintenance customers instead of seeking all possible opportunities for customer satisfaction. Again, estimate the high side and low side percentages of this cost that can be eliminated through an investment in the four sets of commitments leading to vision, spirit, and trust.

Row 4—Lost market share from non-responsiveness to new markets. Environments in which the five debilitators dominate tend to be minimally creative, risk-averse, low drive, and dysfunctional. The ability of such a workforce to respond to change in market exigencies or to invent or market new products is minimal. They can be as much as one or two years behind their more enthusiastic and inspired competitors. A Level 3 organization is less likely to ignore new opportunities. The contributive mentality, the sense of excitement among team members, the heightened creativity, and the sense of contribution open the eyes of designers, marketers, production personnel, and sales personnel to market opportunities. If people become too satisfied with the familiar, if they are fearful or resentful, or if they have no entrepreneurial drive toward new opportunity, they tend to see far less than their counterparts who are not beleaguered by these states of mind.

This particular opportunity cost is the most serious. Slow responsiveness in two or three major product lines or customer segments can lead to an organization's non-viability within a few years. You might want to assess how quickly you seized new market possibilities compared to your competitors. Then, project it out into the future. Hence, if you missed one or two plausible, affordable opportunities last year (which your competitors exploited), project the cost of this lost opportunity into the next two years.

Row 5—Inefficient flow times. This category is not the same as waste within processes. Waste looks at the inefficiency of the process itself. This category is concerned with people's interaction with the process. It seeks to know the degree to which fear, anger, passive aggression, suspicion, and compulsive ego are causing slowdowns in the flow time of production and delivery. A Level 3 organization will show significant progress in decreasing the flow time of communication, decision making, design, administration, customer outreach, inventory and parts requisition from suppliers, production, and delivery of product.

Trust, unity, and spirit not only prevent a hoarding of information, but encourage a sharing of information to reach team objectives. They not only decrease the fear, compulsion, and resentment that sap energy, they encourage the enthusiasm, drive, common pride, joint appreciation, and joint cooperation that lend to a sense of well-being and heightened energy. All these improvements manifest themselves in decreased flow time.

Leaders should figure in a multiplier appropriate to the degree to which the fear, anger, etc. has become a cause celebre (a collective fear or anger). The costs of passive aggression should not be overlooked. Even though passive aggression is frequently not intentional, it still slows down production. It does not matter if a person is overtly angry (aggressive aggressive) or "subconsciously hates working for me" (passive aggressive) when she slows down production. Both kinds of anger are unnecessary, and both cause equal amounts of harm.

Row 6—Not having "just-in-time" inventory. Just-in-time inventory requires the cooperation of both vendors and employees in implementing highly complex, computerized systems. If our people do not want to cooperate, if they make the implementation process overly cumbersome, or if they plug shoddy data into the system, they can effectively force an organization to waste millions of dollars of investment in computers and systems. It is hard to blame these people for doing this, because the systems are generally very complex and require a high degree of attention and motivation to make them effective. If an organization has not invested in inspired leadership or the people system, and therefore, if morale is low, blame is high, and the atmosphere is risk-averse, it could take decades to implement such highly complex systems.

Vendor cooperation is equally important. If vendors find us unfair, unconcerned about their needs, or have reason to be fearful of or angry with us, they will simply not bother to make the extra effort to deliver the inventory "just in time."

Row 7—Inability to change rapidly. There is a direct correlation between the five debilitators and resistance to change. There is also a high correlation between the three qualities of inspired leadership and willingness to change creatively and rapidly. Cultures beleaguered by the five debilitators are risk averse and collectively negative. Change will be incredibly threatening to them, and hence they will collectively resist it. Leaders may want to hire a research team specializing in morale assessment to determine the amount of defensive aggressiveness or passive aggression within an organization. You may then want to correlate this with the amount of resistance to change in your environment. The cost of such resistance can be assessed in relation to competitors' capacities to change more rapidly. Again, past history is an excellent indicator of comparative response times to needed change.

Row 8—Turnover of top 25 percent of critical skills personnel. When organizations lose their most creative, self-motivated, adaptable, and co-participative team players, they cannot help but decrease in market share and quality. Aside from the cost of training new people, loss of talent, creativity, and experience will cause both short-term and long-term problems in efficiency, quality, and productivity. If these individuals are within 10 percent of the salary range of their colleagues, turnover or retention will not be attributable to salary. The culture of the organization then becomes the key cause of turnover or retention. If people feel uninspired, unappreciated, fearful, angry, or even depressed by coming to work, they will not stay if any other tenable position should manifest itself. Today's organization cannot count on employee loyalty or insecurity as motivators for retention. The organization that does not work through inspired leadership will lose its most valued people to other organizations. Frequently these "other organizations" are competitors.

The top 25 percent of individuals in this critical skills group have other opportunities. They are in contact with people who inform them of new, exciting, participative possibilities. These people desire co-participation and creativity because they want to use their intrinsic talents. When they feel that their contribution has helped, when they are recognized and rewarded for that contribution, they will participate and create all the more.

If organizations do "exit polls" of the top 25 percent of those people who leave for reasons other than family or external concerns, they will probably discover that this did not occur because of money, but rather, because of dissatisfaction with the culture, the lack of participation, the misuse of skills, superfluous oversight, and the five debilitators.

Row 9—Cost of mediocre teaming and closed communication. In an age of ever-increasing specialization, the presence of open communication and cross-functional teaming is more important than ever. If trust and spirit are not in a culture, there will not be open communication within that culture. Without open communication, teams (particularly cross-functional teams) will be ineffective. You may want to think back to the last time you were confronted with an ineffective or mediocre team. You may have brought in a personality inventory specialist, a conflict resolution specialist, or a communication specialist, but all of these skills and techniques seemed to fall upon deaf ears. I would wager that the problem was much deeper than personality and communication. It probably concerned the willingness of people to communicate and work out conflict. This willingness directly correlates with the degree of trust and inspiration in the culture. If these two intangibles are present, then the workshops on conflict resolution and communication will be extraordinarily fruitful. If the two intangibles are not present, all the workshops in the world will not bring people together to play the great game of business.

Row 10—Transactional costs. Organizations dominated by the five debilitators have skyrocketing transactional costs. You may want to total the costs of internal security, extra levels of supervision, monitoring costs, hard-bargaining costs, and legal costs concerned with internal employee and stakeholder matters. These costs can be significantly lowered, and the cost per transaction can likewise be significantly lowered by attentiveness to people's vision, spirit, and trust. Imagine for a moment, an organization where people give leaders the benefit of the doubt, and leaders feel comfortable with trusting their people in an atmosphere of minimum supervision. A large percent of this cost could be eliminated.

If transactional costs are high, they lead to considerable waste, conflict, superfluous supervisory structures, game-playing, delayed exchanges, additional contingencies, etc. These transactional costs may include: decreased standardization of goods and services, decreased clarity about roles, rights, privileges, and responsibilities, hostility among parties, unreasonable behavior, delays in exchange, high cost of monitoring, additional contingencies to protect from untrustworthy parties, and costly punishments.

When we take proper account of them, we can see that they could increase the cost of transactions up to 300 percent.

Total. Recognizing that this task can be completed only by means of the grossest estimates, it is still interesting to total the 10 categories of opportunity costs for your team, subdivision, division, or organization. More interesting still, is the total of Column 4 (the low estimate of opportunity costs that could be eliminated by an investment in inspired leadership and the four sets of commitments toward vision, spirit, and trust). I would wager that if your organization would reduce its opportunity costs *by one percent*, you will have paid for the entire cost of education, time, and reward structures for implementing a people system. If you find this to be true, you will want to proceed to the next section of this book concerned with the heart of the inspired leader, for this initiates the journey toward the four sets of commitments to vision, spirit, and trust.

If leaders find this simple opportunity cost chart helpful in their decision making, they may want to establish some long-term benchmarks in each of the 10 categories. This would allow them to check and follow up on data indicating continued problems. Some of these problems might be eliminated by improvements in processes or technology, but it must be remembered that people will have to implement these new processes and use these new technologies. It is likely that an investment in the people system will be integral to every solution for high-opportunity costs.

Three Steps and Consequences

By now my method for bringing inspirational leadership into the organization will be apparent.

Step 1. Vision. Leaders must develop a challenging, creative, engaging, and "noble" vision for their organization. This vision should be articulated with specific goals and the systems, processes, and action teams necessary for the achievement of these goals.

"Nobility" of vision goes beyond simply saying, "We're the best at this." (e.g., "We're the number one telecommunications company in the world."). Nobility picks up a deeper desire in human beings to make a positive difference in the world through their creativity and labor. It therefore gives dignity and purpose to the goals and processes of work. This "nobility" of the vision can be manifest through expressions like "We make life better through innovative communication technology," or "We are bringing the world closer together through innovative transportation technology," or "We are creating a better workplace through breakthroughs in the heart of leadership." People are responsive to noble purpose, and there is noble purpose in every area of product, process, and people development. This will become apparent in the next chapter with respect to the "third level of happiness."

Step 2. Development of systems and vehicles of rational communication. As noted in Chapter 3, the content of rational communication should always follow the format of "How have we achieved the highest common good for the organization, and the fairest and most balanced good for our stakeholders?"

Step 3. Implementing the four sets of commitment (personal, people, ethical, and leadership) ingredient to shared vision, spirit, and trust. This will be the purpose of the remainder of this book.

These three steps will produce three consequences:

Consequence 1—A movement from driven leadership to inspired leadership. Leaders will incorporate a healthy humility into their passion for the organization's noble vision (see the Introduction to this book).

Consequence 2—Optimal co-participation in organization's vision. After seeing leadership's humility and "buy in" to steps one through three, stakeholders will begin to freely enter into the noble vision of the organization. This will not only produce high morale, but also a feeling of partnership with leadership. This feeling of partnership will encourage stakeholders to more freely contribute creativity, knowledge, energy, good will, team behavior, and willingness to change in the achievement of the organization's vision. They will therefore be more self-motivated and team motivated, which will lead to the sense of common cause, group enthusiasm, group drive, and therefore spirit. This group spirit will ground resilience in times of challenge and downturn, and also enthusiasm to move to the next level in times of success and prosperity.

Consequence 3—Decreased opportunity costs. Nine characteristics—high morale, feeling of partnership, common cause, willingness to change, willingness to contribute creativity and knowledge to noble purpose, resilience in times of bad news, trustworthiness, trust, and a strong sense of team bonding around goals—will lead to sharp declines in the 10 categories of opportunity costs.

When these opportunity costs are added up, we see that they far exceed any investment that an organization might make in Level 3 education and leadership mentoring. An investment in vision, spirit, and trust, therefore, will enhance the two central metrics of profit-making organizations: profitability and return on investment. With proper care and maintenance, these measurable effects of spirit will continue into the far-reaching future.

The Effects of Spirit on Market Trends

Spirit not only leads to increases in morale and market share, while reducing transactional costs, opportunity costs, waste, and product defects, it also helps businesses in a downward trend to turn around, and prevents businesses in an upward trend from becoming stagnant.

If a Level 3 organization is having a tough year in the marketplace, the spirit of its stakeholders will produce quicker turnarounds because they will care about what is happening, be open to new opportunities for solutions, work together in actualizing these opportunities, and be less resistant to the required changes. They will have a spirit of resilience and hope. Downward trends can so easily discourage individuals and groups, they can cause a decrease in creativity and synergy at the very moment when that creativity and synergy is needed most. The resilient *turn* tough situations into blessings. The hopeful *gain* energy from the challenge of making light arise out of what appears to be darkness. Spirit can produce this quality within individuals and groups to such a degree that it can reverse a downward trend, and even create a boomerang effect.

The human spirit has a natural proclivity to respond to crisis when it is not impeded by the five debilitators. When it is "in the trim" spirit can gain upward momentum through the very downward pull of the crisis. This allows an organization to be more competitive, creative, vital, and viable after experiencing a crisis.

When spirit is not present in downward trends, the trends become both more prolonged and more pronounced (accelerated). Discouragement can lead to an attitude of "abandon hope all ye who enter here," which can push the trend even further downward at a much greater velocity.

When the organization "bottoms out," the absence of spirit will prevent a turnaround from coming quickly. Hence, there is a prolongation of the bottom plateau as the dispirited firm tries to "get its act together." Again reaction times are slower, creative solutions more difficult to locate, judgments less hopeful, and cooperation and team spirit difficult to muster. In a dispirited organization, crisis makes people get on one another's nerves. In a spirited organization, crisis engenders common cause.

With respect to upward trends, spirited organizations do not get overconfident. Though the sense of victory buoys confidence and energizes the organization, it does not fill people with overconfidence, smugness, contempt, and a sense of having reached the final goal. The contributive mentality and the humility of these organizations keeps people open to new opportunities, keeps them alert to possible pitfalls, and helps them attend to necessary details.

The peace intrinsic to spirit gives people staying power, helps them spot horizons beyond the horizon, and allows them to go the extra step without burning out. Hence, people do not have their hearts set on stopping at a particular goal and forever reveling in the victory. Rather, they enjoy the victory while keeping an eye peeled on the next opportunity to come. The excitement of continued progress is just as great as the excitement of past victory, and this makes all the difference. Level 3 people do not have to keep rewarding themselves as if the victory were the only thing that mattered to them in life. After a while, they turn their attention to opportunities for further good for an even greater number of people, and to a more distant future.

The difficulty with a purely competitive mentality (i.e., competitiveness without a contributive spirit) is that it treats victory as an end in itself. Instead of seeking to actualize the good beyond the victory, the person tends to stop at the victory and reap the immediate benefits. This creates plateaus and sometimes causes downturns because the marketplace reconfigures itself while one continues to celebrate past victories.

Conclusion

The history of organizations is replete with examples of dynamic, spirited leaders who have captured the spirit of their people. They not only decrease the five debilitators, they elicit a sense of contribution and the common good opening upon a unity and creativity that leaves their onlookers not only surprised, but stunned.

The rest of this book is concerned with the four sets of commitments (personal, people, ethical, and leadership), the foundation of vision, spirit, and trust.

THE HEART OF THE INSPIRED LEADER

The heart of a leader is as important as the mind in inspiring an organization toward greater change, growth, ethics, and team behavior. I have dealt with the leader's mind in four respects: 1) the creation of vision and goals, 2) rational communication, 3) fundamental attitudes and myths, and 4) the measurement of opportunity costs. The next 10 chapters deal more with the heart of a leader.

I do not mean to suggest by this weighting that heart is more important than mind, for they are of equal importance. When both are present, they complement and even liberate one another. Each becomes stronger through the guidance of the other. The weighting here suggests only that matters of the heart—dispositions, attitudes, ideals and commitments—are fraught with ambiguities that take time and space to clarify. Most leadership literature devotes less time to "heart" than to mind. In this book, I address matters of the heart without taking away from the importance of acute mental functioning in strategic visioning and rational communication.

The next four chapters deal with the personal commitments that leaders must make before they can commit to people, ethics, and team leadership.

6 Four Levels of Happiness

Esprit de corps arises out of the minds and hearts of inspired leaders, and inspired leadership in turn depends upon an internal disposition that allows for commitment, ethics, and team leadership. This essential internal disposition may be termed "freedom from ego-compulsion."

To help you understand this phenomenon, I need to describe the four main desires or drivers in the human personality. These four drivers have been called by different names: four kinds of happiness, four levels of meaning, four powers of people, four fulcrums of identity, dimensions of self-actualization, or markers of growth. Some theologians have identified them with phases in the journey of the soul, or levels of spiritual life. Philosophers, psychologists, sociologists, anthropologists, historians, and other writers have classified them under still different names. The different names simply reflect different perspectives on the same reality.

One can see these four drivers in the works of such diverse thinkers as Plato and Kierkegaard, Aristotle and Jaspers, Augustine and Sartre, Viktor Frankl and Abraham Maslow, Thomas Aquinas and Erik Erikson, Martin Heidegger and Gabriel Marcel, Karl Jung and Martin Buber, Edith Stein and Carol Gilligan, Bernard Lonergan and Lawrence Kohlberg, and Simone Weil and Max Scheler.[1] One may also see them in the scriptures of Christianity, Judaism, Islam, Hinduism, and Buddhism. Throughout the last 3,500 years, we see them recur again and again in the cultures of North and South, East and West. They are most deeply reflected upon, yet often most forgotten—the most obvious parts of our common heritage, and yet the most esoteric. They reflect not only what moves us in our heart of hearts, but the ideals toward which we aspire, the relationships we seek, the worth we attribute to ourselves and others, our sense of well being, of hope, and of groundedness. They are at once the sources of our sense of autonomy, self-possession, self-communication, love, self-transcendence, faith, and even our communion with a higher power or God. We return to them more often than any other concept or image. Our lives are imbued with them.

The four kinds of happiness are generally arranged as four levels of happiness.

Level 1 (H1)–Immediate physical gratification.

The first level of happiness (*laetus* in the Latin) refers to the pleasure produced by an external stimulus. The stimulus is normally concrete and tangible. The response is immediately gratifying and does not last very long. It could be produced by a material possession (e.g., a new computer), or by some kind of a sensorial pleasure (e.g., a café mocha). The senses are almost immediately engaged when the external stimulus is encountered; the external stimulus is pursued by the agent and brought under her possession. At the H1 level of happiness, there is immediate gratification from the pleasure or the possession of the external stimulus followed almost immediately by a desire for more.

Level 2 (H2)–Ego Gratification.

The second level of happiness (*felix* in the Latin) refers to ego-gratification. *Ego* (the Latin word for, "I") refers to one's inner world. The inner world is constituted by one's memories, choices, thoughts, and feelings. Whenever this private, inner world is built up and extended into the outer world, one feels gratified. Ego gratification generally comes in four forms: 1) achievement, 2) comparative advantage, 3) recognition and popularity, and 4) power and control.

For example, when I finished my doctoral dissertation I felt happy for I had achieved a new level of research and writing. Similarly, when I beat an opponent at chess, I feel happy (my opponent feels the opposite) for I have emerged as a "winner" in a game of comparative advantage. When people recognize and like me for doing good research, making an impressive presentation, or winning at chess I feel happy, for the recognition makes me feel more important. When I'm given a promotion, or an increase in power or control, I feel happy because the locus of control has shifted to my inner world. In all these cases, my inner world is somehow enhanced. Something has either come under my control or elevated my self-esteem. Imagine this form of happiness as elements from the outside spiraling into the control of my inner world.

This second level of happiness can be either healthy or compulsive. When it is complemented by other kinds of happiness, it is not only healthy but invaluable. After all, if we had no desire to achieve, we would still be cave dwellers. If we had no desire for comparative advantage, we would have no drive toward either self-improvement or improvement through competitiveness within a community. If we had no desire for recognition, we would not only have little self-esteem, we would likely be given little credibility from anyone else. If progress is to be made, if civilization is to continue, there must be a drive for achievement, competitiveness, self-esteem, and credibility. These drives all arise out of the fundamental drive to build one's inner world, and through it to bring the outer world under one's control.

H2 becomes compulsive when it is the *only* kind of happiness thought to be important or to give meaning to one's life. For example, though the desire for achievement is unqualifiedly necessary for the advancement of organizations and civilization, it can become quite negative and destructive if I view it as the *only* thing that will make me happy or give my life meaning.

If I view achievement as an end in itself, as the sole meaning and purpose in life, when I experience a time of little achievement or perceive myself to be slowing down in my achievements, or even anticipate a future time when such a slowing would occur, I will become quite desperate, because I have inadvertently made achievement the sole source of my meaning, identity, and happiness. In so doing, I have made my self-worth, goals in life, sense of belonging within the community and the world, and even my friendships dependent on these achievements. If the achieving should slow or, God forbid, stop, I would lose everything.

Can such desperation produce compulsion? Indeed, compulsion of the worst sort—a compulsion that will stop at nothing to maintain steady progress in achievements; compulsion capable of running over my family, friends, myself; capable of anger, jealousy, fear, suspicion, and contempt.

Could the same be true for competitiveness? Of course. Competitiveness is invaluable to the pursuit of excellence. However, it can also fall prey to the error of the "only." If I view competitiveness as the only thing that will give my life meaning or happiness, then again I stake my self-worth, goals, identity, meaning, friendships, and happiness on keeping up the winning pace. If this winning should slow or, God forbid, turn into losing, it would eradicate my very self. The mere anticipation of this self-eradication could cause a panoply of destructive emotions—fear, jealousy, suspicion, contempt, etc—and these, in turn, might induce a drive to do anything, "take out" anybody, even cheat or lie to keep up that winning status.

The same holds true for recognition, respect, admiration, and popularity. Though recognition is essential to a healthy sense of self-esteem, and to the establishment of credibility among stakeholders, it can also fall prey to the error of the "only." If I view recognition to be the *only* thing that will bring meaning and happiness, I will stop at nothing to get more of it. The same emotions and the same destructive behavior emerges to destroy family, friends, collegiality, organizational teams, and any other setting in which I am placed.

I emphasize that this problem does not stem from H2 itself, for H2 is necessary for achievement, self-improvement, self-esteem, and credibility. The problem arises with the word *only,* for the moment I believe that meaning and happiness are dependent *only* on H2, it will drive me to the brink of self destruction, opening upon a destruction of all the relationships around myself. Instead of being in control of myself, I am dispossessed, compulsive, and unreflective about what is happening to me. At the very moment I feel most self-possessed, I am really most out of control.

If H2 is to be healthy, then, it cannot be an end in itself. It must have an end beyond it. In a word, one cannot live for achievement alone. One must live for "achievement *for*...." One cannot live for competitiveness alone. One must live for "competitiveness *for*...." The "for..." refers to some positive effect beyond the achieving or competitiveness. If I am achieving *for* the betterment of my family, my organization, my colleagues, friends, or community, then my achieving will be healthy, for I will not have attached my self-worth, happiness, and meaning to mere achievement, but rather to some good that lies beyond the achievement. My self-worth and purpose does not depend on increasing the number of achievements in my life, but rather on attempting to do some good for my family, organization, or community around me. Hence, if my achievements should slow, but my contributions are maintained, I will not feel devoid of self-worth and meaning. I will not have to compulsively achieve to restore myself. Achievement will find its proper place—a place that frees me from compulsion. The same would apply to competitiveness and recognition.

Level 3 (H3)–Making a contribution.

The third level of happiness (*beatitudo* in Latin) refers to the contentment and exhilaration arising out of making some contribution to somebody or something beyond myself. It is, therefore, the converse of H2 that attempts to fill up the inner world and to bring people under the influence of the inner world. H3 is a giving away of what is in the inner world, giving one's energy, time, and talent to the outer world to make it a better place.

This level of happiness requires an investment of one's inner world in something bigger (the outer world), and it brings with it a sense of self-worth and self-value. When I believe I have made a difference to some person by my time, talent, or energy, or when I believe I have created something new in the world that could benefit someone, I believe that my life really matters, that it does make a difference to this bigger reality. In some small way, I have made the world a better place. I have made a net positive difference by my existence. My life, my existence, my talents, and my energies are objectively significant. The objective world around me is better because of my presence, and I know it. This sense of objective significance makes me feel more alive, more at home in the universe, exhilarated. It awakens my spirit. I feel connected to what is beyond my inner world through the positivity that I contribute to it.

One can also see this kind of happiness through its absence. If I do not believe that I am contributing anything to the world through my time, talent, presence, and energy, I feel devoid of life, like my life is somehow wasted, that I am not doing what I was somehow meant to do, that I am living beneath myself, underliving my life. I am not at home in the universe. This leads to a feeling of emptiness, aimlessness, and a kind of incipient depression. I know something is missing—there is an empty spot within me—but I may be confused about why I feel that way.

One can imagine a person arriving at a ripe old age and looking back upon his life, asking, "What was the difference between the contributions that I made throughout my life, and those of a rock?" If he is inclined to answer, "None," he will have arrived at incipient despair.

Throughout history great philosophers, theologians, and psychologists agree that we have an innate desire and tendency to make a net positive difference with our lives. We strive not merely to make the most out of ourselves, but to make the most for the world. There is something intrinsic to all of us that wants to make our time and energy positive and purposeful. It is not enough to be better than everyone at everything. When we reach our old age and ask the question, "What was the purpose of my life?" we know ahead of time that it will not be enough to say, "I had a better car than Joe and a better house than Mary. I was better at chess than Frank, and I had better grades than Sue. I had a better bottom line income than Harry, and I was more athletically gifted than...." I want more. I want my gifts to make the world a better place, to have a lasting effect. I want my life to be connected to what is bigger, more enduring. I want to live my life optimally. I want to make the greatest possible positive difference.

Please note that I can make a contribution not only by "doing," but also by "being." I do not necessarily have to write a book, give a lecture, start an organization, create a process, etc. Sometimes I can make a greater contribution by simply being present to someone who is suffering, listening to a child, giving time to a friend, or smiling and acknowledging another person's presence and goodness. "Being" like "doing" requires a decision and a concerted effort. If I do not focus on the child who is talking, she can be easily ignored. But if I do focus, and she does make that connection, much good can come from it and, as a result, I can feel that same "at homeness" with the universe, that same sense of exhilaration that comes from purpose and contribution, that same sense of being alive. This sense of spirit gives me energy, hope, horizon, a sense of opportunity, adventure, and positivity. I am happy.

Notice that my feeling of happiness here is different from the feeling connected with H2, and that these two feelings are different from the feeling connected with H1. H3 (spirit, hope, positivity, connectedness, horizon, etc.) feels quite different than H2 (self-possession, control, influence, being filled through achievement, winning, etc.), which, in turn, feels quite different than H1 (the café mocha). They feel different. They have different results. But in a generic way, we say that all of them make us "happy."

H3 can prevent H2 from becoming an end in itself. Recall that when H2 is my *only* form of meaning or happiness, it becomes quite compulsive, leading to negative emotions and undermining relationships and teams. If I focus on both H2 and H3, H3 can act as the horizon for H2. Thus, I do not have to worry about achievement becoming an end in itself if contributing to my family and my colleagues is the major purpose of my life. My achieving is now an achieving for my family and my colleagues, etc. My competitiveness is a competitiveness for my family and colleagues, etc. When I truly allow H3 to be the major purpose in my life, it will automatically make H2 healthy and productive.

Level 4 (H4)—Being involved with something of ultimate significance.

The fourth level of happiness (*gaude* or *sublimity* in Latin) is the joy that comes from being involved with something of *ultimate* significance. Philosophers since the time of Plato have noticed that human beings are "ultimatizers." They are not only interested in what is concrete and immediate, they want to be involved in something of ultimate, permanent, absolute, unconditional, and even infinite significance. It is not enough to experience a concrete truth. We would like to have a sense of ultimate Truth. It is not enough to have a concrete love—we would like perfect and unconditional

Love. It is not enough to have justice in relationships with family—we want perfect Justice for the world. We have a socratic, orphic and promethean urge for god-like Truth, Love, Goodness, Beauty, and Being.

If this is not clear to you from your own experience, look at children. They are likely not content with one or two factual truths. The moment you assert something, they are likely to ask, "Why?" to which you are likely to give a perfunctory answer. They will realize that your answer is perfunctory and ask you the further question, "Well, why is that?" to which you will have to give a more profound answer. The child will again recognize that you can't just assert this and, as a consequence, will ask again, "Well, why is that?" This has the potential to go on indefinitely, until you find yourself in the deepest modes of quantum theory, and have to retort, "Time out. You're overeducated." Children seem to want the *complete* set of correct answers to the *complete* set of questions. They have an unrestricted curiosity—an *unrestricted* desire to know.

Take a look, too, at children's desire for fairness (justice). Do you have to tell them when something is not fair? Believe me, they will know when something is not *perfectly* fair all on their own, as if they had had some precognition of perfect justice. In their idealistic moments, adolescents can thirst for perfect justice for the world. They can allow their desire for a "perfect world" to manifest itself almost transparently, because they have not yet learned how to mitigate that desire by their knowledge of the "real world." Their seeming naiveté should not be disdained, for it reveals the real ideal, the perfect ideal they seek. Their frustrated idealism and their disappointment at imperfection, are not simply manifestations of naiveté, they are revelations of a light within, a desire for perfection, goodness, and justice.

Do you have to tell your children to seek unconditional love? Do you have to train them to want your love to be authentic? Even though you have to make them aware of other people's feelings, or of the consequences of their actions, you do not have to "train" them to yearn for unconditional and perfectly authentic love. Literature is replete with stories of young adults discovering love, and the perfect and unconditional expectation they have of both love and their beloved. Love opens upon an unconditional horizon which allows lover and beloved to hope for a perfect and unconditional happiness. These stories usually end in tragedy because the expectation of unconditional happiness is usually dashed by the finitude, the humanity, and the creatureliness of the beloved.

I am, here, not so interested in the tragic component, as in our seemingly endless capacity to fall prey to the same problem. Haven't we all expected the perfect (as least implicitly) from our beloved? Haven't we all believed (at least implicitly) in the divine sublimity of love? Haven't we all been frustrated by these unconditional expectations? Why? Why did we believe this? What is it within us that makes us believe there is a perfection here, an *unconditional* awaiting us here? What objective incites our desire? Whatever it is, it makes us ultimatizers.

For those with faith, the human capacity to seek the ultimate, infinite, eternal, and unconditional in love, goodness, truth, beauty, and being, is rooted in the presence of God within us. Many religions have a sense of "God" as a perfect, interpersonal, and loving agent creating humanity in love and drawing humanity to the fullness of love by sharing divine life. In the Judeo-Christian tradition, human beings are believed to be made in the very image of God and drawn by God toward eternal life with Him. God calls human beings by being present to them in their consciousness. Once humans feel His presence, they want Him in His fullness. They want to enter into His divine life and love. That yearning can sometimes manifest itself as the desire for perfect Truth, Goodness, Love, or Beauty. In the heart of the believer, it is God who evokes them all.[2]

The yearning for ultimate happiness (at once the yearning to be at home with God) incites individuals to search for God and to participate in a relationship with Him. This generally takes the form of prayer, seeking God's self revelation in history and worship, and a seeking of God's will in one's life. This relationship with God brings a deep peace, which, in turn, gives greater freedom to love and to contribute to others in humility, patience, kindness, forgiveness, and joy.

For those without faith in a personal God, the same desire for ultimate happiness will manifest itself, and will be connected to the desire for perfect truth, perfect goodness, perfect love, perfect being, and perfect beauty. This capacity and desire for the ultimate and perfect impels us toward continual self-transcendence in a search for wisdom, harmony, and peace, that will have its effects in the way we love, contribute to others, achieve, and live.

The desire for ultimate happiness will continue to manifest itself even if we should ignore it or be unreflective about it. When this happens, we will try to extract ultimate significance, transcendent peace, and the perfect from something that is, by nature, imperfect, conditioned, or imminent. When this happens, we become at first dissatisfied, then frustrated, and, in the end, reject the very object that we thought could bring ultimate happiness.

For example, I might find myself growing in a friendship with another to the point where my desire for ultimate happiness, meaning, and love becomes incited. In the hope that this desire for ultimacy can be satisfied, my expectations begin to soar. I become an ungrounded idealist or romantic and begin to blind myself to even the possibility of flaw. Eventually, imperfection and finitude break through. Expectations are dashed, and amidst the disappointment a friendship is lost.

Without a healthy recognition of this desire for ultimate happiness and its proper source, we can wind up rejecting or even repudiating what we formerly thought to be good, lovable, beautiful, and true (namely, the beloved). The error was not believing in lovability, goodness, truth, and beauty in people or in the world; it was in trying to elicit *perfect* lovability, goodness, truth, and beauty from those imperfect sources. This error moves us from one false extreme to the other—first, leading us to believe that the perfect can be found in an imperfect source, then, after dashing our expectations, leading us to believe, almost cynically, that love or goodness or truth are not to be found in those sources at all.

Cynicism about the truth can easily arise out of trying to elicit perfect truth from an imperfect source, and consequently having one's expectations dashed. The dashed and cynical romantic has generally tried to elicit perfect love or lovability from an imperfect beloved. The dashed and cynical idealist has generally tried to elicit perfect goodness or justice from an imperfect source in the world. Tragedy seems to have this error at its root. We should, therefore, ensure that what we expect to fulfill our desire for ultimate happiness is really ultimate.

In sum, beware of seeking the ultimate in the imminent and concrete: "Let God be God and let creatures be creatures."

A Point About Priority

I draw two conclusions from this summary of 2,400 years of human reflection about happiness and the meaning of life. First, we can prioritize the kinds of happiness according to three criteria: 1) pervasiveness, 2) endurance, and 3) depth. In most philosophical traditions, the more *pervasive* a form of happiness, the better. For example, a form of happiness that positively affects many people around me (say, the joy of creating a product that could make life easier for people) would be considered more important than a form of happiness that affected only me (say, buying myself a new car). The same holds true for *endurance*. A form of happiness that lasts longer (say, working on a long-term friendship that produces good for decades for those touched by it) would be considered more important than a form of happiness that, though immediately gratifying, doesn't last very long (say, eating a bowl of linguini). Finally, the same would hold true for *depth*. A form of happiness that makes use of a large number of my powers (say, creativity, intellectual reflection, love, and moral agency), would be considered more important than those that made little use of these powers (say, watching TV).

It is, therefore, not surprising to see H2 with its achievements and competitiveness, frequently ranked above H1 with its possessions and pleasures; and to see H3 with its loves, depth of relationships, and entryway to the transcendentals (love, truth, goodness, and beauty) being ranked above H2. Finally, it is not surprising to see H4 with its concern for, and relationship to the unconditional, absolute, perfect, and infinite ranked above H3. Kierkegaard called this the metamorphosis from the aesthetic domain, to the ethical domain, to the transcendent domain.[3] Martin Buber termed it the movement from I-it, to I-thou, to I-Thou.[4] Many other philosophers have described these metamorphoses in different ways but with similar intent.

The second conclusion is, by far, more important, for it is a recipe for sanity, authentic relationships, and effective organizations: *If I allow a higher kind of happiness (more pervasive, enduring, and deep) to be the horizon of a lower form of happiness, the lower form will always be healthy and productive. However, failure to do this will result in compulsion, destructive emotions, and undermined relationships.*

For example, if H2, H3, or H4 (or any combination of them) is the horizon of H1, H1 will normally find its healthy, proper place. If I want to achieve and be competitive, I cannot allow my mind to be occupied by sensorial indulgence like an opiate. I'll have to wake up in the morning, curtail my eating and drinking, and delay gratification. Similarly, if I allow H3 or H4 to be the horizon of H2, I will not make achievement, competitiveness, or recognition ends in themselves. H3/4 will turn my desire for achievement into achievement for my family, colleagues, friends, organizations, and community. "Achievement *for*" not only puts an end to compulsion and destructive emotions, it builds our sense of hope and opportunity, giving rise to spirit and energy, allowing us to be far more creative, productive, adaptable, and team-centered. If we allow H4 to be the horizon of H3, then we will not be tempted to extract ultimate, unconditional, and perfect meaning out of people, human loves, human ideals, and human organizations. More than this, H4 can give rise to a peace and perspective allowing for a new freedom to lead, to love, to seek optimal truth and goodness with humility, patience, and deep respect. With the higher forms of happiness, the lower forms are liberated—they do not have to do what they are not designed to do. And the higher forms can open upon an optimally lived life with meaning, efficacy, and relationships that are pervasive, enduring, and deep.

Wherever we find happiness, we will also find the fulfillment of a desire; and wherever we find the fulfillment of a desire, we will find a power seeking a fulfillment. Hence, if there are four levels of happiness, there are at least four levels of desire: 1) the desire for pleasure and material possession, 2) the desire for ego-gratification—to build up one's inner world, 3) the desire to give away the fruit of one's inner world, to contribute to and connect with a reality larger than

Notions of Personal Fulfillment

Ultimate Good

Objective:	Participate in giving and receiving ultimate meaning, goodness, ideals and love.
Characteristics:	Good is ultimatized Principles include ultimate good, justice, love, and beauty. Methods are righteous
Gratification:	Eternal

Good Beyond Self

Objective:	Do good beyond self
Characteristics:	Principles include justice, love, and community Intrinsic goodness is an end in itself Decisions are focused on the greater good Methods are righteous Personal harmony
Gratification:	Long-term

Personal Achievement/Ego

Objective:	Ego centeredness, better than, gain advantage
Characteristics:	Promotion of self is primary Personal power and control are key Jealousy, fear of failure, contempt, isolation, loneliness, and cynicism.
Gratification:	Short-term

Immediate Gratification

Objective:	Maximize pleasure and minimize pain
Characteristics:	Obligation is to self alone No desire for common, intrinsic, or ultimate good Lack of self-worth, fear of tangible loss/harm, boredom
Gratification:	Immediate

oneself, and 4) the desire to connect with what has perfect, absolute, eternal, and unconditional meaning and reality.

Moreover, if there are four levels of desire, there are four kinds of human powers anticipating four levels of fulfillment: 1) the power of possession and pleasure, 2) the power of self-possession and self-appropriation, 3) the power of self-communication and love, and 4) the power of self-transcendence and faith. The more we attend to all four kinds of happiness, the happier and deeper we will be, and the more pervasive and enduring our effects on the world. We will also have a better appreciation of ourselves and our powers in that enduring, pervasive depth. This releases us from our bondage to gross self-underestimation, while giving us the freedom to pursue creativity, unity, and synergy.

7 The Comparison Game and its Resolution

The attitudes that frequently promote the five debilitators and undermine vision, trust, and spirit have their origin in a common dysfunction I call the comparison game. It arises out of grounding our identity almost exclusively in Happiness Levels 1 and 2. Recall the error of the "only" from the last chapter. If I say, "The only thing that will make my life worth living is achievement or popularity," I will act in a compulsive way. If left unchecked, this compulsion will lead to considerable unhappiness, breakdowns in relationships, an inability to act for common cause, and an incapacity for inspirational leadership.

The comparison game is generally not chosen. Most adolescents and adults turn to a Level 1 or 2 identity as a default system that causes them to subconsciously identify their entire self-worth with possessions and comparisons. If you were to ask them, "Do you believe that being better than Joe makes your life worth living?" they would say, "Of course not," but deep down they live as if this is all that counted. A panoply of emotions arises from this subconscious identity (e.g., jealousy, contempt, suspicion, fear, ego-sensitivity, etc.) that can cause considerable breakdown in business efficacy and family life. The objective of this chapter is to unmask this subconscious disposition, and to help all stakeholders in an organization to move beyond it.

The Identity Crisis

All of us need an identity. This identity reflects our reason for living, goals, sense of self-worth, sense of whether we are progressing in life, and the kinds of relationships we pursue. We make our conscious or subconscious selection of an identity by accenting one or more of the four levels of happiness. Hence, we are likely to select one or more of the following as our purpose in life: 1) material identity, 2) comparative identity, 3) contributive identity, or 4) transcendent identity.

We could try to ascertain who we are by our possessions (H1). We could also try to establish our identity in a more abstract, versatile way by making comparisons of ourselves to others, asking, "Who's achieving more? Who's achieving less? Who's likely to progress more? Who's likely to progress less? Who's more popular? Who's less popular? Who's a winner? Who's a loser?" (comparative identity — H2). We will likely make this a dominant mode for developing identity if we are unreflective about the third and fourth ways. We could ground our identity in contributions, loves, and ideals (H3). We could also ground our identity in faith, or some other transcendent principle (H4).

Finally, we could ground our identity in two or more of the four identity fulcrums. If this combination included some elements of H3 and H4, the comparison game could be averted. If not, the comparison crisis would be inevitable, inhibiting team efficacy, creativity, and flexibility (not to mention the capacity for intimacy, relationship, and depth).

How does this crisis arise, and why does it take hold in so many people? The comparison crisis arises when an H2 identity becomes so dominant that it leads to the exclusion of almost every element of H3/H4. How can this fulcrum become so dominant?

Two major reasons can be adduced. First, comparative identities are more concrete than contributive and transcendent ones. They are, therefore, easier to see and to hold. They give more immediate gratification than the contributive and the transcendent, and are, therefore, favored by a less disciplined, less experienced mind. Indeed, if we do not choose an H3 or H4 identity, then H1 or H2 will become dominant by default. Hence, I will refer to comparison and competition as our "default drive." Secondly, our cultures—by the media, peer pressure, and entertainment—favor a climate of winners and losers.

If we are not reminded of our potential for contribution, love, leadership, self-communication, self-transcendence, and faith, we can easily forget them and give ourselves over to the more insistent demands of our default drive. If we are not cognizant of how important our potential contributions and friendships are, and choose not to highlight them in our meaning and purpose in life, we will simply allow all this positive potential to fade away in our all-consuming effort to be a winner. A dominant comparative identity can become an exclusive comparative identity. When this happens, the comparison game is played with a vengeance. This game cannot be won. Let me explain why.

Personal Fulfillment and Related Crisis

1. Immediate Gratification

Identity Crisis (Crisis #1)

2. Personal Achievement/Ego

Comparison Game (Crisis #2)

3. Good Beyond Self

Dashed Idealism/Cynicism Seeking the ultimate and perfect in people and things (Crisis #3)

4. Ultimate, Perfect, Unconditional and Infinite

The Comparison Game and its Consequences

The comparison game arises out of a dominant, or exclusive H2 identity. When an adult vests her identity almost completely in H2, she will attempt to extract her self-worth, goals, ideals, friendships, and sense of belonging from being a "winner." If she believes she is achieving more, progressing more, becoming more, getting more, being better, looking better, and getting more recognition, she will get a *temporary* high, a *temporary* burst of self-worth, belonging, and meaning in life.

This temporary high will eventually be followed by a series of negative states ranging from contempt to anger to emptiness. If, however, she believes herself to be progressing less, slowing down, outshined by someone else, becoming less popular, or being less popular in relation to someone else, then she will feel a range of emotions resembling depression, jealousy, emptiness, fear, and inferiority. This should not be surprising, for after all, by simply believing herself to be losing she has in fact lost her sense of self-worth, meaning, friendships, belonging, and future. This would not have happened if she had complemented her H2 identity with elements of either H3, H4, or both.

The first sign that we have invested the dominant part of our identity in H2 is a narrowing of perspective. We begin to look at life in terms of the three possible outcomes of the comparison game: win, lose, or draw. All three of these outcomes produce extremely negative emotive states, undermine relationships, and undermine our ability to achieve the common good and organizational objectives. I will examine each outcome in turn.

Options of the Comparison Game		
Win	***Draw***	***Lose***
• Upping the stakes • Emptiness • Contempt ↳Isolation ↳Resentment	• Fear of Losing • Suspicion of others	• Depression • Jealousy, anger • Inferiority

1. Lose. With respect to losing, if I have my entire identity invested in winning, and I lose (or even slow down), I will feel a range of anxieties conglomerating in depression. I will feel anxious about my future, for the myth of ever-increasing progress and recognition will be challenged. I will also feel unmoored, unanchored, as if I don't belong, for the myth of acceptance through ever-increasing progress and recognition will again be challenged. I will also feel as if my friends think less of me or even are afraid to be around me, for I am no longer the winner they thought I was, and after all, in my view, friendship is based almost solely on whether or not I am maintaining the same degree of winning as those with whom I associate. Finally, I feel devoid of worth, for worth in my view is determined only by progress, achievement, competitiveness, and recognition. When these four feelings converge, I become depressed, anxious, fearful, and even desperate. I look at myself in the mirror and sense an emptiness.

Two other negative internal states begin to manifest themselves: jealousy and inferiority. In my depressed, fearful, and desperate condition, I ask the question, "Why?" which provokes blame. When I blame others for seemingly being "superior," I feel jealousy, envy, even hatred for them, though I secretly would like to be like them. I cannot transcend my feelings of anger: "It's not fair," I say to myself, concluding that I don't have to like the person who got more. Jealousy, of course, provokes judgments and self-hatred, for after all, I do feel "inferior" and therefore, as if I am worth less, have less meaning, and should expect less from life. Finally, if I have some belief in God, I am likely to blame Him for giving me a "raw deal," making me less worthy, and, therefore, less capable of having a meaningful and worthy life. Needless to say, my self-judgment is making both my life and the lives of others around me a self-created hell.

These negative emotions generally have one of two results. I could collapse into a kind of listlessness, aimlessness, darkness, inefficaciousness, and even cynicism; or, I could fight desperately, do anything, no matter what the cost to my ethics, my relationships, my commitments, and my responsibilities, to get out of my losing state. In either case, I am likely to negatively impact myself and the people around me.

2. *Win.* Winning ought to be better. Not really, for a similar complex of emotions arises here: the upping the stakes game, emptiness, and contempt.

• ***Raise the stakes.*** With respect to the "upping the stakes game," if winning is an end in itself, then to have a sense of progress I have to win more, and win more often. Even if I should be tremendously successful, say, the CEO of the tenth largest corporation in the world, I still have to achieve more to get a sense of self-worth, meaning, belonging, and friendship in my life. It is the "more" that gives me my sense of meaning and purpose. Hence, I raise the stakes (the expectations) of myself with each success. I am not indifferent to these expectations, I *must* meet them, or I get a sense that I am slowing down. This sense of slowing down vitiates my self-worth and meaning in life. I begin to think my life is no longer worth living. Hence, I either begin to collapse (unlikely), or I become a desperate fighter willing to compromise my ethics, cut corners, control, manipulate, and blame. As a consequence, my friendships, family life, and professional relationships begin to suffer and, ironically, I don't know why. My desperation blinds me to my inability to appreciate, recognize, and care for others.

Most people experiencing this desperation and decline in meaning and relationships are not malicious. They do not start off as selfish, uncaring, or arrogant people. They seem to slip into this mindset contrary to their true nature. Compulsion lies at the root of the decline of these good people. With each passing success, they make H2 an even more exclusive fulcrum of identity. Now, as they reach the pinnacle of success, they find themselves more desperate for continuous progress to be happy. If these good people are to recover, they will have to find another fulcrum for their identity—presumably H3 or H4.

A second consequence of this "upping the stakes" game is hyper-susceptibility and hypersensitivity to embarrassment. As the expectations for H2 success increase, so do the expectations of personal perfection. I begin to think that others are viewing me with the same grandiose expectations that I have of myself. After a while, I believe that people expect me to be perfect. If I am not perfect, they will think less of me; and if they think less of me, I will again lose my sense of self-worth, meaning in life, and friendships. If this is all that really matters to me, if I have lost all sense that my contributions, love, ideals, and faith are significant, then the slightest embarrassment, the slightest loss of face, the slightest decline in comparative advantage will produce excruciating psychological pain.

For example, as a manager I might think that my subordinates expect me to know more than they do in all things. If, one day, a subordinate corrects me, or even manifests knowledge that I do not have, I could become so embarrassed that after making some perfunctory excuse, I will return to my office, close the door, and wish some physical harm on myself to prevent the tape of that horrifying incident from playing in my mind once again. I could, of course, always abuse someone else to assuage my self-hatred and embarrassment, or I could simply wallow in a bottle of scotch. A further consequence might be heightened manipulation of and vengeance on my subordinates.

This little embarrassment matters little in the whole order of salvation. My subordinate could not have anticipated my reaction. He didn't know he was threatening me. He probably thought I would be proud of him, or grateful to have such a competent supporter. It's my perfectionistic expectations, resulting from the upping the stakes game, that have produced my pain, my self-hatred, my anger, blame, and self-destructiveness. Again, I find myself, not maliciously, but compulsively hurting both myself and others.

• ***Emptiness.*** A second negative interior condition resulting from winning is emptiness. The more I experience H2 success, the more I depend on it for identity. But I need more than H2 success, for I have internal drivers to make a difference (H3), and for ultimate significance (H4). As a result, I begin to feel that something is missing in my life. I'm not sure what it is, for after all, I am more successful than most people at most things. What could be wrong? The emptiness persists, and I begin to turn to H1 and H2 satisfactions to fill the interior emptiness. I might find myself eating more, drinking more, buying more, watching more television, or seeking more praise in a desperate attempt to make up for some unknown that seems to be missing. Failing this, I become somewhat confused and attempt to figure myself out. I look to my past and present circumstances and begin to assemble vast arrays of cause-effect sequences, retelling my story to myself again and again as I look for a direction. In the end it becomes all too complex, and I find myself sinking and feeling the same emptiness.

This generally has two consequences. First, I could become quite cynical about myself and life. I could advocate and try to drag others into a pessimistic or absurdist outlook (for misery loves company). Or I could content myself with a continual accumulation of H1 and H2 satisfactions to stave off this feeling. Generally, I run out of opportunities to continually enhance these distractions, or I simply find them utterly boring and will either have to face the fact that I am more than these H1 and H2 drivers, or simply lapse into a pessimistic or cynical worldview. The latter can be quite destructive of self and others.

• ***Contempt.*** The third negative interior condition arising out of winning is perhaps the most serious: contempt. Contempt is a lack of regard for another. The other is so far beneath me that I do not have to associate with him. I do not have to be concerned about him. He is imminently forgettable. Furthermore, I should not have prolonged contact with him because my friends may think me to be on his level (guilt by association). As with the upping the stakes game and emptiness, contempt begins with making H2 a dominant or exclusive fulcrum of my identity. Once such an identification is made and I happen to be winning, it stands to reason that others will have to be losing. The comparison game is a zero-sum game. For every superior there must be at least one inferior. For everyone progressing more, there must be at least one progressing less. For every winner there must be at least one loser. Since I identify self-worth with being a winner, I generally look at these inferiors as having little worth, which leads to contempt.

Contempt has a series of consequences for me and for others, which lead to the destruction of teams, friendships, associations, and families. The first consequence is isolation. Suppose I achieve more than some longtime friends. I begin to feel a contempt toward them out of comparative advantage. Because they are my friends, they notice my contempt and hint at it. But I take no notice of it because I "know" that comparative advantage is far more important than love. My friends have a sense of self-respect, and so they progressively distance themselves from me. I am left wondering, "Why have they done this? Why are they not giving me the kudos I deserve? Why aren't they groveling at my feet and acknowledging my natural superiority?" It does not occur to me that they have not elevated H2 to the level of an exclusive identity fulcrum. I, therefore, do not recognize that they are growing weary with my subtle "put downs," pandering for praise, and looks of superiority and contempt.

Isolation breeds loneliness. It is not my intention to dissolve my friendships, for I still have a need to enter into the experience, care, and responsiveness of other people. Even though these friends are inferior from the vantage point of comparative advantage (H2), I still *need* them on the level of the interpersonal and love (H3). I cannot, of course, acknowledge this need because I have completely confused lovability with esteemability. I need love, but all I think I need are esteem and admiration. In the end, despite my arrogance, I cannot help but feel lonely. I cannot stop the feelings of loneliness because that might entail bringing myself down to the level of those for whom I feel contempt. This results in either self-pity (blaming myself) or resentment (blaming others).

If my tendency is to blame myself, loneliness will result in a downward spiral of thinking myself to be unlovable, leading to progressive isolation, leading to greater feelings of unlovability, leading to greater isolation. I do not see that I am *not* unlovable and that it is my arrogance, contempt, and subtle put downs that are causing the isolation; so I attack myself instead of attacking the real cause of the isolation. If the cycle progresses, it can produce both social retardation and even self-destructive feelings, for the root of these feelings is an attack upon myself.

If, conversely, my tendency is to blame others, I will feel resentment toward those others for not acknowledging my natural superiority. I convince myself that they are purposely withholding much deserved praise from me because they are jealous of me. I do not understand that it is *not* jealousy that motivates them, but weariness of being put down. I want to push my natural superiority back into their consciousnesses by overcoming their petty jealousies. I will get them to see that they really need to make me the center of their lives to have any meaning at all. When, of course, they withdraw further, I blame them for the outrage, and take vengeance in a variety of ways: undercutting their reputations, insulting them among friends, undercutting their livelihood (if possible), or undercutting their beliefs, loves, hopes, and aspirations by some form of cynical or skeptical superiority. Needless to say, I will become a walking anathema, extending my resentment and rage to secretaries, colleagues, organizational teams, and even my family.

From an organizational point of view, this behavior is disastrous because talented people who exaggerate their H2 identities tend to undermine unity, objectives, openness to change, team spirit, and quality. But it need not be so, for these are not bad or malicious people. They do not start off this way. They arrive at this point through compulsion arising out of an exaggerated H2 identity. If organizations do not stem the tide of compulsive egoism, they will not combine talent with high performance teamwork, and thus they will lose competitiveness, quality, and long-term viability.

An exaggerated H2 identity will turn winning into the upping the stakes game with its sensitivity to embarrassment and self-hatred, emptiness, and contempt—all of which constitute a second form of self-created hell.

3. Draw. If both losing and winning result in negative interior conditions and relationships, perhaps *drawing* will be better. Unfortunately, drawing promotes similar problems, particularly anticipatory fear and suspicion. Anticipation is one of our greatest powers; but with an exaggerated H2 identity it can become one of our greatest adversaries.

If I elevate achievement, winning, and recognition to ends in themselves, if I make my self-worth, meaning, and friendships dependent almost exclusively on them, I cannot even bear to anticipate slowing down in achievement, progressing less, seeing another progressing more, or experiencing a net decrease in recognition. These anticipations, at the very least, produce debilitating anxiety and fear. I begin to view the world around me as cold and even threatening. Aside from sleeplessness, I begin to recontextualize my surroundings to ward off the "threats." I have to create façades, even lies, to make the world more hospitable to my continual progress. I have to control and manipulate, threaten and cajole those who have talent, and therefore could one day catch up to me, progress more than me, or, God forbid, overtake me.

As fear undermines relationships, suspicion overtakes trust. I suspect not only my colleagues, coworkers, and friends of elevating themselves to my status, basking in my glory, or even stealing some of the praise that I alone am worthy of—my best friends and family also become suspect. They, too, are trying to gain on me and bask unjustly in my glory. I now have to become very exacting in the rewards and recognition that I give. I become very sensitive to who gets praise and who does not. I spend sleepless nights worrying about potential and actual "injustices."

Drawing is no more of an effective strategy for the comparison game than winning or losing. It results in the same kind of self-created hell, the same inability to work with and be grateful to others, and the same kind of destroyed relationships. In essence, the comparison game cannot be won. Win, lose, or draw, everyone is a loser.

Some people can move from one set of anxieties to the next throughout the day depending upon the various circumstances confronting them. They may start the day feeling the fear and suspicion of drawing, and then have a positive experience leading to the contempt and sensitivity to embarrassment associated with winning. They may then have a bad experience leading to the fear, depression, jealously, inferiority, and self-hatred associated with losing. What a day!

If the comparison game cannot be won, it must be transcended by appropriating contributive (H3) and transcendent (H4) identities.

Escape from Crisis: Beyond the Comparison Game

There is a way to resolve the life crisis arising out of the comparison game. This method has proven to be effective in the lives of thousands of people working in organizations of every kind. I refer to this technique as the "Six Higher Viewpoints."[1]

What Am I Looking (Living) For?

Viewpoint	H2 Attitude Only	H3 Attitude Making H2 Healthy
1. View of Meaning	Better than others Comparison only	Good for others Contribution (making comparison healthy)
2. View of Others	Looking for the bad news in others	Looking for the good news in others
3. View of Relationships	Being over and against others Threat, manipulation/blame, suspicion	Being with and through others Common cause, enjoyment, team
4. View of Commitment	"Freedom from"—Keeping all options open; not committing	"Freedom for"—self determination; making long-term commitments
5. View of Self	Object self only: Treating people as objects, not as whole human beings	Subject self (making object self healthy) Appreciating people as human beings
6. Overall Viewpoint	Viewing people and life as problems	Viewing people and life as opportunity, mystery, and adventure

For each viewpoint, I can have an exclusively H2 attitude or an attitude comprised of H2, H3, and H4. My dominant attitudes will determine the way I look at life, meaning, self-worth, success, freedom, others, and relationships. H3 and H4 attitudes can mitigate the compulsiveness of the H2 viewpoint. So, for example, with respect to meaning in life, if I am looking for meaning exclusively in comparisons, I will become compulsive. But if I look to contributions to bring some meaning to my life, I will mitigate the compulsiveness of only looking to comparisons.

With respect to these six fundamental attitudes, *what I am looking for is what I am living for, and what I am living for is what I am looking for*. My attitudes can either enhance my relationships, optimize the value of my time, energy, and talents, and produce positive instead of negative interior conditions; but if I do not take custody of what I am looking for in life and at work, I will live for what fails to support deep relationships, optimal values, and positive interior conditions. The choice about what I am looking for is up to me, and therefore what I am living for is likewise up to me.

Because my attitudes influence my views and my views influence my attitudes, if I want to change my view of myself, I will first have to adjust my views and attitudes of meaning, others, relationships, and commitments.

I invite you to test these higher viewpoints for yourself. Once you see your life relationships, interior conditions, and contributions improving, you will possess the motivation to embrace the higher viewpoints that put an end to the comparison game and to help form a healthy H3 culture.

1. My view of meaning. The most important and fundamental viewpoint, is, *What am I looking for to obtain meaning and purpose in my life?* I can look to comparisons alone, or I can look to contributions as well as comparisons. If I look for contributions, my achievements, winning, competitiveness, and recognition will become achievements *for* some good for the world, winning *for* my family, friends, colleagues, and coworkers; my competitiveness will become competition *for* some form of self-improvement, product improvement, or community improvement; recognition will become recognition *for* credibility to open doors and to pursue new avenues.

Try it for yourself today. First, simply tell yourself, "The meaning of my life is to be better than Joe at XYZ..., and to achieve more, progress more, and be more recognized than Mary at ABC...." Fill in the XYZ and ABC with any strength or comparative advantage particular to you. Treat it as an end in itself. Watch what happens.

I predict four things will happen:

1) All the anxieties of the comparison game will arise and become acute, for all the reasons I have previously explained.
2) Your family members, friends, colleagues and coworkers will respond to you defensively. The reason people react defensively is because they sense what you are looking for in life. People are acutely intuitive and sensitive to the expectations of others. If you are comparing yourself to someone, she will likely intuit this in less than a second, and will respond by either defending herself or engaging in the battle. The net result will certainly not foster understanding, gratitude, unity, common cause, generosity, mutual concern, listening, commitment, or any other attribute likely to promote high performance teamwork.
3) Any sense of hope, opportunity, and adventure will turn into a sense of problem and pessimism. An exclusively comparative identity tends to promote a sense of fear, threat, and resentment. So, the people you meet during the day will not be viewed as opportunities for cooperative effort and friendship, but rather as potential threats and problems who need to be controlled, hemmed round, and manipulated to prevent them from "causing trouble." The various meetings and situations you encounter will not open new avenues of opportunity and adventure to create or achieve a worthy objective; but will likely be problem situations you will have to control to ensure your "best interests" are served. They will be time-consuming, energy-sapping hassles. You don't *want* to do them; you *have* to do them. You don't know why you feel so tired and uninspired at the end of the day. If this feeling pervades your work and family environment day after day, year

after year, you will eventually conclude that life is not an opportunity, mystery, or adventure. Life is a problem. Other people are problems. In fact, you are a problem to yourself.

4) You will experience increased suspicion and an increased desire to manipulate, blame, control, and judge. Your hyperawareness of threat in the comparison game will compel you to overcome increased fear by manipulation and control, to overcome potential mistakes by setting up others for blame, and to counter your own sense of inadequacy with negative judgments of others.

If your personal experience bears out these negative consequences of living only for comparison, then before it becomes overwhelming, switch to a contribution viewpoint and notice the difference. First, make a list of the various ways you could contribute to your family, friends, colleagues, coworkers, organization, community, church, etc. Be sure to include not only the "doing" and creative contributions, but also the "being" and relational contributions. You will want to include giving time to a child and being present to a friend, along with improving a process or finishing a project. Upon completing the list, try to associate your self-worth and meaning in life with these ways of making a difference, these net positive contributions. Try to sense how the world is a better place for your doing these things.

Now, look at the way you view achievements, competitiveness, and recognition. I suspect you will find that:

1) Since comparisons (in the form of achievements, winning, and recognition) can no longer be ends in themselves, the anxieties of the comparison game begin to diminish substantially,
2) People respond to you more positively, openly, and trustingly,
3) You feel more alive, more inspired, and see life again as an opportunity and adventure, and
4) As the urge to judge, blame, and manipulate subsides, you begin to feel a joy, gratitude, and concern for others as persons and colleagues.

You may not be able to maintain this contributive viewpoint or build a permanent attitude or habit at this time, but you should see that this change of attitude works to alleviate the anxieties of the comparison game, to change people's reactions to you, to increase your sense of opportunity and adventure in life, and to increase trust.

If this resonates with your experience, I would suggest making it a life-long pursuit, sharing it with your children, and making it a reality within your teams and organizations, for it will have a remarkable power to decrease fear, compulsion, and resentment while increasing commitment, trust, adaptability, common cause, and unity. This will not only make you happier and your relationships better, it will vastly improve your organizational life and spirit as well.

2. *My view of others.* What am I looking for in other people? I can either look predominantly for the bad news or the good news in others. Try the following experiment with a spouse, friend, or colleague. First, look for the bad news in the person. Look for what is irritating, insensitive, weak, and stupid. What do you notice? You will likely note:

1) An inability to see the good news in the person;
2) This person notices almost immediately that you are looking for the bad news and responds either defensively or by looking for the bad news in you,
3) A proclivity to be impatient, judgmental, and to associate this person's mistakes with his whole person,
4) The anxieties of the comparison game return with a vengence, and
5) When those anxieties emerge, your optimistic view of life and people as opportunities and adventures, shifts to the pessimistic view of life and people as problems.

After completing this experiment, I think you will agree that this seemingly small attitude shift can have a profound effect on your relationships with others, your view on life, and your emotions.

Why is this so? Looking for the negative—the bad news in others—tends to sap energy, making it difficult to see any good news. Trying to recognize one item of good news when I am looking for the bad news feels like a huge effort.

When I have no sense of the good news, I convey this to people through my detached, critical view manifest in my eyes, voice, and gestures. Again, people are not stupid. They are sensitive to my view and will adjust their response to me in accordance with what they perceive. The usual reaction of a person who feels my negative response is to defend herself against it by either withdrawing or building up a set of defensive barriers. She could also look for the bad news in me if she is inclined to play the comparison game. In either case, the relationship will be dominated by threat, one-upsmanship, hyperjudgment, and hypercriticism. Such relationships—whether they be between spouses, friends, colleagues, or coworkers—will likely either come to an end or become somewhat sadistic, as impatience, hyperjudgment, and hypercriticism flow through my whole disposition.

Again, most people experiencing these negative conditions are not malicious. They are normal, interpersonal persons who start off trying to make a difference with their lives, but now find themselves compulsing because of the comparison game. The tension in their interpersonal relationships causes considerable loneliness and resentment, giving rise to cynicism and pessimism, dragging them into various negative emotions associated with the comparison game, and causing a shift from the viewpoint that life and people are opportunities and adventures, to life and people as problems. Bad news irritates us and draws us to itself. It is therefore easier to see.

Now, before the negative side of this experiment becomes overwhelming, start adding in the positive point of view (the good news). Stop playing the comparison game by giving an accent to the contributive point of view. The question is not "what do I see?" but "what am I looking for?" To move beyond the bad news, you need to start looking for the good news.

Since looking for the good news is more difficult, you might begin by writing down a person's good qualities. Not writing these qualities down will probably result in their being unrecognized or forgotten amidst the continual influx of new data in your work and family life. So, look for the little good things this person tries to do, his ideals, what moves him in his heart, the goodness of his presence, the goodness of his friendship, his kindness, the good things he has done, even his delightful idiosyncrasies. You will likely discover that;

1) Even though you can see the bad news, it is contextualized by the good news.
2) The person notices that you are looking for the good news in him, and connects more deeply, responding with openness and trust.
3) The sense of threat and arrogance begins to subside, giving rise to increased patience and forgiveness.
4) The negative emotions associated with the comparison game begins to subside giving rise to an increased sense of being alive, a new purpose and meaning in life, and a brighter, lighter spirit.
5) A brighter outlook on life results in a shift from viewing life and others as problems, to life and others as adventures and opportunities.

Again, it may be difficult to maintain this positive outlook for long if you are new to this way of thinking. But, this experiment shows that temporary relief can be attained by shifting your focus from negative to positive.

Even though I cannot blind myself to the bad news, I can still look for the good news. The way the bad news effects me depends on what I am looking for. If I see the bad news when I am looking for it, I tend to be judgmental and pessimistic, and associate a person with his mistakes. If, however, I see the bad news when I am looking for the good news, I tend to be more detached, honest, and objective about a person's good and bad points; more proactive about ways to help this person; and less likely to associate a person with his mistakes.

No doubt you sometimes have to evaluate colleagues and coworkers. You will therefore notice the bad news when it emerges. You simply cannot become naive and turn a blind eye to obvious problems. However, the way you interpret the bad news will change considerably depending on whether you are looking for bad news or good news.

In addition to my work as a university president and business consultant, I continue to teach. Obviously, I have to make evaluations of my students, correcting papers and exams. If I see misplaced commas and incorrect equations when I am looking for the bad news, I get quite impatient, sometimes even angry. Instead of looking for ways to help the student, I tend to write him off, not only as a bad writer or poor mathematician, but also as a person. I devalue him—sometimes even feel contempt—and associate his personhood with his mistakes. However, if I see the bad news when I am looking for the good news, I tend to be more patient, rarely getting angry about such monumental matters as commas. I tend to notice the student's strong points, and I am attentive to ways to help him.

When I am looking for the good news in another, regardless of whether I *see* bad news or good news, the other person seems to intuitively recognize it. If he is not playing the comparison game himself, he will generally respond with openness and trust.

A connection between people naturally forms when their attitude is to seek the good news in one another. This is revealed by the old cliché that "love begins with the lovability of the other," and "liking begins with the likability of the other." Loving and liking are not merely stoic acts of will, they are recognitions of the other's goodness that draws me out of myself and makes me want to contribute to the other. Normally, when I experience a natural connection with someone, I find it almost effortless to like him because I allow his natural goodness to elicit friendship from me. The converse makes friendship difficult. Can you imagine looking for the bad news in someone and then trying to use a stoic act of will to overcome the repulsion that you feel? "Here comes Joe walking down the street. Despite the fact that I am fully cognizant of all his irritating features, his mistakes, his lack of talent and goodwill, and his stupidity, I *will* like him. I *will*. I really *will*!" Obviously, there is little genuine friendship in such acts of willpower.

Friendship is not the only quality induced by looking for the good news in others—colleagiality and win-win association also depend on this natural connection among persons, and on recognizing (and looking for) the good news.

So long as I look for the good news, unity will deepen (whether this be manifest in associations, colleagueships, friendships, or family relationships). This sense of unity, this natural connection, makes the boundary disappear between myself and others. After a while it becomes just as easy, if not easier, to do the good for another as to do the good for myself. When this occurs, I enjoy being with and around others. I look forward to their association and feel their presence to be life-giving, sometimes even inspiring. It makes it easier for me to work, muster energy, and be creative.

This unity makes "common cause" almost effortless. *You* and *I* are not working toward this common good. *We* are working toward this common good. When unity is present, the relationship has three components: you, me, and the connection between us that was not there before. This connection allows us to operate synergistically, to be more patient with one another, less judgmental, more willing to give one another a break, and to forgive one another. A feeling of mutual concern and enjoyment brings with it a freedom and tranquillity not only to bear with one another's humanity, but to cope with the ups and downs of everyday life. This general change in outlook makes us feel more alive. We are no longer depleted by relationship problems, we are energized by freedom and connection. Life again begins to look like an adventure and an opportunity with colleagues, associates, friends, and family.

The comparitive attitude leads directly to the negative, judgmental attitude. If I seek meaning in life through achievement, comparative advantage, and recognition alone, I likely won't look for the good news in others, for the good news will emerge as threat. If I see the good news in you, it could indicate that you are as popular as I am, or achieving and progressing as much. God forbid that you should be achieving more. In either case, the sense of threat forces me to look for the bad news.

Conversely, if I begin by seeking meaning through contribution, I will be free to look for the good news in others. The more I see the good in the person for whom I do the good, the more good I perceive myself doing. Upon seeing this good in others, I will want all the more to do good for them. Hence, if I want to correct a compulsive attitude with respect to another person, I will first need to correct my compulsive attitude with respect to meaning in life.

3. ***My view of relationships.*** If I am dominated by a sensorial (H1) or competitive (H2) viewpoint, I will look for potential threats from which I will have to defend myself. I will view relationships as *you against me*. If, however, I have elements of contribution (H3) or ultimacy (H4) in my outlook, I will look for complementarity and common cause in relationships.

Your outlook on relationships will, perhaps more than any other factor, determine whether your team is high performance or mediocre. High performance teams are constituted by three Ss: structure, skills, and spirit. Team spirit is linked to this view of relationships. If I am looking for the bad new in others, my viewpoint will prevent a high performance team from ever emerging.

If I am seeking achievement, popularity, and competitive advantage *alone* for my purpose in life, I will compulsively look for the bad news in others. If I look for the bad news in others, I will consider those others to be threats to everything I am, everything I'm worth, and even to my entire future. I must react defensively to such threats. I will have to control you or manipulate you. If manipulation is beyond my power, I will set you up for blame. If that is beyond my power, I can at least "badmouth" you to those in authority or to other team members.

Since others have an intuitive sense that they are being controlled, manipulated, set up for blame, or "badmouthed," they naturally react with counter-defense. The first step in counter-defense is, of course, suspicion. They feel they must be on the lookout for all the ways they could be put down. But most people eventually realize that the best defense is a good offense. They might have to plant a few seeds in the minds of authorities and team members to undermine the person who might otherwise undermine them. Of course, they are not doing this maliciously, but only in response to the person they believe will act likewise.

One dominant H2 team member can transform the atmosphere of an entire team into pure Byzantine intrigue. Other H2 people on the team will be only too willing to use counter-defensive tactics to undermine the initial offender. H3 people on the team will be dragged down, their energy sapped. They will not want to cooperate with H2 people on the team and will not know who to trust. In the long run, they will simply do what they have to do get the job done. Needless to say, attentiveness to quality improvement becomes virtually impossible. No one is looking at the product, process, or common objective of the team. They are all looking at one another with abject suspicion.

Without trust, open communication is virtually impossible. People will hoard information to defend themselves against the bad guy (and make sure he doesn't look too good). As trust and open communication decrease, project flow times increase. No one seems to have the energy to finish segments of the project. We find ourselves needing to redesign and restart processes again and again. We sometimes have to go outside the team to get vital information to know what we're supposed to do, let alone complete the project. The leadership style turns heavily extrinsic (fear, force, and bribe), to push the project to completion. At this point, the atmosphere within the team is so threatening that most team members shirk self-accountability and become completely dependent on the team leader to tell them what to do. Scared of blame and threatened by one another, they just want to get their orders. Extraordinarily creative, self-starting people are turned into drones. They won't extend themselves, offer good will, or take reasonable risks. They see their security being vested in knowing how to "milk" old processes and structures. Hence, they are fearful of, and resistant to, change.

To alleviate these problems, we must cultivate trust by attending to our view of relationships. We cannot start with this view, however. We must first move beyond compulsive views of the meaning of life. If we want a good team, we must begin by using the mentality of contribution to heal the mentality of exclusive comparison.

This shift will open the way to looking for the good news in others, allowing me to make a natural connection with others. This natural connection, in turn, enables me to enjoy others, derive life from them, and enter into common cause with them. Others are no longer seen as threats, but as opportunities for life, freedom, and joy.

My disposition will now be trust instead of suspicion. I will look for ways to get along with people, even if I disagree with them. To the extent that I feel connected with them, I will also share information. Mutual concern leads to a free flow of information. The creative enterprise seems less like work and more like fun. People will be more content with the truth about contribution rather than grabbing the glory, and will be more willing to share success with the whole team. This allows the team not only to pursue their common objective with enhanced energy and creativity, but also makes work fun, exhilarating, spirit-filled, and life-enhancing. Participating in a spirited team can be such a high that people can come away with more energy at the end of the day than they brought at the beginning. They have more to give back to their families after a day of high productivity with a spirited team than they would have after a day of low productivity on a bad team.

This may at first seem exaggerated, for the mechanistic view of people suggests that there is only a certain amount of energy per human being. Hence, if we want to know how much productivity or creativity a team is capable of, we simply add up the fixed amount for each member of the team.

Nothing could be further from the truth. Human energy and creativity are not fixed. They are enhanced or depleted by the team atmosphere. Working within a highly trusting, creative, communicative team does not deplete energy, but actually deploys and restores energy.

The psyche has peculiar effects upon our physical make up. If I were purely physical, I would feel a net decrease of energy per unit of time worked. However, the psyche allows me to gain energy per unit of time worked when that work contributes to something I believe in, to a sense of community, and to a sense of a life well-lived. Inasmuch as a spirited team contributes to all of these dimensions, it could enhance energy per unit time worked. This gives rise to synergy, where two people in a highly functioning team produce more than double what they could do by themselves. It is remarkable sometimes how little rest we need when we are excited about what we are doing.

If leaders hope to move to high performance teams and organizations, they must cultivate spirit, *esprit de corps*, positive connections that are fostered by our view of relationships, and influenced by our view of others (good news or bad news), and by our view of meaning in life (contributive or exclusively comparative). These fundamental attitudes are not only a foundation for sanity and good family life, they are absolutely requisite to high performance organizations.

4. My view of freedom describes my viewpoint on commitment. I can view freedom predominately, or even exclusively, as "freedom *from*." Or, conversely, I can view it as "freedom *for*." "Freedom from" refers to the view that freedom is either an escape from constraint or keeping options open. It is not merely what I think, it is what I feel. I *feel* free when I'm getting out of something, when I don't have to be disciplined, or when I have open options. I *feel* enslaved when I cannot be carefree, when I need to be disciplined, or when others are asking things of me. When I have to foreclose some options to actualize a particular one, I feel like a portion of my future has been annihilated.

"Freedom for," in contrast, refers to feeling free when I am accomplishing what I set out to do, becoming the person I want to become, pursuing the relationships I want to pursue. In the Jeffersonian sense, it is self-determination. From a religious point of view, it is determination of self through relationship with God. I *feel* free not when I'm dreaming about all my open possibilities, but when I'm actualizing possibilities in my life. Freedom then is the freedom to get things done, rather than statically avoiding constraint while merely dreaming about all my possibilities.

Our view of commitment will vary drastically according to our view of freedom, for "freedom from" (taken exclusively) must view commitment as an enemy, whereas "freedom for" must view it as a friend. Inasmuch as "freedom for" promotes the search to become a particular kind of person, achieve particular goals, contribute particular goods, and pursue deeper relationships, it must consider the long term.

When you think about the kind of person you want to become, the kinds of relationships that are worthy of you, or the kinds of goals you want to pursue, I would bet that they are high-minded enough to take at least 25 years to actualize. If this is true, you won't be able to actualize these good things without "stick-to-itness" or commitment. You need stick-to-itness to get through the hard times, the boring times, the stress-filled times, the confusing times. Without commitment, "freedom for" is impossible. Where there is "freedom for," there also must be a disposition to the goodness of commitment—even a love of commitment.

Conversely, "freedom from," in its attempt to escape constraint and dream about open options, will find commitment to be daunting. Commitment forces the foreclosure of options and annihilates whole portions of our future. It requires a discipline that constrains us or enslaves us. When we hear the "C" word, we may literally want to run!

But if we as persons and organizations want to pursue goals, relationships, and missions that are truly worthy of us, we must embrace the view of freedom that enables us to love commitment, the view that looks to actualization beyond mere dreams, the view that embraces discipline as desirable rather than a hardship to be endured. But how do we get to this notion of freedom?

The attitude of contribution opens the way to looking for the good news in the other, and these two attitudes, in turn, provide the foundation for trust and common cause in teamwork. When these three attitudes are combined, we begin to see what is truly worthy of us. We begin to hope for new friendships and greater contributions, seeing life with a new sense of adventure, opportunity, and mystery. We no longer want to avoid commitment with its discipline; we want to embrace it because we want to make our vision actual. It is the love not only of dreams, but of realities that creates a love of the means to make those realities: i.e., commitment through focus and discipline.

This commitment may at first engender fear because it seems difficult. In point of fact, it is difficult. But just as love enables us to do something difficult for family, so also can love allow us to transcend the difficulty of stick-to-itness. Love, of course, does not do its work instantly. It takes time to grow into a love of commitment opening upon the reality of the actualization of a contributive life.

5. My view of self. This concerns what I am looking for in myself—what I consider to be my essence or nature. I can view myself predominately as a function or thing (object self), or as having a personal presence that is inclusive of, but not reducible to, functions and things (subject self). For example, when someone asks, "Who are you?" my mind could immediately turn to what I have and what I do. I might just give you a summary of my resumé, or I might tell you about my job, my income, my degrees, my grades, my hobbies or other things about myself. If I take this view to be a comprehensive picture of myself, I will have "thingified" myself. Obviously, I can't get away from things and functions when I am applying for a job, volunteering for a team, or angling for a promotion. Without question, people need to know what I am in addition to who I am. "Thingification" occurs when I reduce who I am to what I am. I am nothing more than my resumé. This attitude makes deeper friendships almost impossible and creates a confusion between esteemability and lovability.

Alternatively, I could view myself as a personal presence. At first glance, this might seem intangible—difficult to see, hear, and touch. But exploration of some of its deeper characteristics will reveal it to be my authentic nature. In sum, the subject self is the particular way I, in my whole person, connect with others. It is "me-ness." It is the unique presence, friendship, kindness, connectedness, smile, commitment, ideals, values, and delight all woven together in one indivisible, interpersonal presence.

Recognition of the subject self prevents me from confusing my esteemable self with my lovable and likable self, from "thingifying" others, and from withholding love from my friends and family.

By "esteemable self," I mean that tangible part of me that is subject to comparative advantage. People can admire me for my academic degrees, or esteem me for my accomplishments or abilities. But esteem or admiration does not imply loving or liking. We don't say, "I love your academic degrees, your accomplishments, and your athletic ability." We love or like persons with whom we connect, whose presence, care, and response make us come alive, and through this give us a heightened sense of freedom. We like and love people whom we think will find a natural connection in our presence and will likewise feel more alive and free through that association. Obviously, liking and loving are vital parts of human life, even more important than esteem and admiration. And, therefore, if I should forget my lovable and likable self, and associate myself solely with my esteemable self, I will seek only esteem and admiration instead of connection, relationship, and friendship.

Seeking esteem *only* is not enough. I need to feel the vitality, spirit, and freedom of human friendship. When I am deprived of it, I feel something is missing or even dead within me. Furthermore, I will seek associations almost exclusively with people whom I admire and esteem, and who will likely admire and esteem me. I will look not so much for friends who will make me come alive through concern, care, and interpersonal connectedness, but rather for those whom I consider to be elegant company and whose recognition will enhance my esteemability—those who will praise and admire me. The result is not a relationship giving rise to mutual concern, appreciation, and common cause, but rather, a superficial relationship that may end whenever expected esteem and admiration levels decrease.

This forces me to play the comparison game with even greater intensity, for to lose comparative advantage is to lose esteemability or admirability, and to lose this is to lose my sense of self. As the cycle progresses and the need for continually enhanced comparative advantage increases, I can become desperate and find myself creating façades, exaggerating, and even lying to obtain the needed esteem and comparison so vital for friendships and self-worth.

The only way out of this cycle is the rediscovery of the goodness of liking and loving (friendships that go beyond mutual admiration societies). But how can we rediscover liking and loving after pursuing exclusive esteemability for so long? We must recognize or rediscover our subject selves.

How? We must broaden and deepen our vision of reality and life. By finding purpose in life through the contributions we make (H3), we no longer make achievement, comparisons, and recognition the sole source of our happiness, meaning, and identity. Achievements, comparisons, and recognition are far more interested in the esteemable, thingified, and admirable self than the naturally connecting, contributive, and lovable self.

Of course, I realize that we can turn contributions into a contest and thereby make our contributive self an object of comparison and thingification. But generally comparisons and achievement associate almost exclusively with the esteemable and thingified self, whereas contribution is open to the naturally connecting likable and lovable self.

So long as I am pursuing contribution out of the goodness it brings (without making it a contest) I will be open to the good news in others. That good news naturally includes the goodness of human presence, friendship, kindness, humor, delightfulness, openness, connectibility, affection, concern, and care. To be open to the good news in others naturally leads to an awareness of the other's subject self. As I begin to value the other's subject self because of its capacity to bring about something that the esteemable self cannot bring, I begin to value my own subject self. I begin to discover the goodness of my own unique, intangible presence, friendship, care, concern, and connectedness. I rediscover my true self. As I grow at home with this true self, the need to show off, brag, create façades, exaggerate, and lie decreases. I can see friendship as a good in itself (not requiring an additional jolt of admiration to make it worthwhile). These friendships open up my affective life which deepens not only my family life but also my organizational life. I can now appreciate people as people in the workplace and enjoy working with them without subordinating this friendship to getting admiration and esteem. As a leader, I do not have to subordinate my appreciation of people as people to my desire for esteem, recognition, and admiration. I am free to be a team member and a person at the same moment I am a leader.

6. My overall view of life. This summary category indicates my normal, day-to-day mindset. If I have an H1, H2 attitude, I am likely to view life, freedom, other people, and even myself as a problem. If I only see the bad news in others and view people as threats against which I must defend myself, if I view freedom as escape from constraint and recognize only my esteemable self (not availing myself of friendship and love), it will be difficult to view life, freedom, others, and myself in any way other than as a problem. With "problem" at the center of my inner world (the way I take in and give out data), I will find life to be tiresome, maddening, and unfulfilling. Pessimism begins to emerge and I become the champion of Murphy's Law.

Eventually, I content myself with being the class critic, the skeptic, the cynic who sits above everyone and everything and sees how bad it all is, disdaining people for being so naive not to notice. I point out to them how bad things are, but they don't seem to listen. Their naiveté maddens me all the more. Eventually, I realize that I have to distance myself from people and only give my "invaluable advice" when it is asked for. I devote the rest of my life to breaking through people's simple-minded, optimistic naiveté. I will use all my learning, energy, time, and talents to undermine people's beliefs, hopes, aspirations, good will, and optimism. My byline will be: "Joe, you're an optimist and I'm a pessimist. You'll be happier than me, but I'll be right more often." When I am not right more often, I simply detach more.

Conversely, if my overall view of life is based on commitment and contribution, my life will become more and more an adventure, opportunity, and mystery. If I see my life as really making a difference, my time, energy, and talent being well spent, that I am living my life to the full; if I am open to the good news in others and attend not only to my esteemability but to the goodness of my subject self, likability, and lovability; if I have a deep and fruitful family life, truly good friends, an excellent interpersonal life in the workplace; if I see my life as headed toward a new depth of contribution, new goals and achievements, new depth of personhood, and new quality of relationships ("freedom for"), it would be difficult to view my life as anything but an opportunity, adventure, and mystery. I will have the freedom to love life, others, and myself, desirous of the opportunity to be fully alive in this interpersonal world, and to give myself away.

I am not suggesting that I will be completely at home in the world. Friendships, loves, ideals, commitments, and contribution not only bring with them a sense of life, meaning, freedom, and joy, they also bring certain problems and alienations. Still, life as mystery, despite its potential problems, outshines life as problem.

The higher viewpoints provide us with a recipe for sanity, friendship, meaning, love, and mystery—a way of overcoming crisis, darkness, pessimism, cynicism, depression, and despair; a way of living life to the full. It builds trust and prevents those drivers that undermine teamwork: fear, compulsive ego, resentment, defensiveness, passive aggression, and cynicism. It is key to spirit in the family as well as in the organization and our larger culture.

I invite you to assimilate the attitudes that open upon happiness and meaning for ourselves and others. These attitudes and commitments are a foundation for lifelong learning.

The Resurgence of H2 in the Midst of H3

The journey toward a contributive lifestyle is filled with sidetracks back to comparison and competition. These manifest themselves in subtle ways, and undermine our pursuit of Level 3 happiness. The following three H2 problems are most frequently manifest in H3 neophytes.

1. THE CONTRIBUTION CONTEST ("I'M DOING MORE GOOD THAN YOU ARE.")

When I first move into H3, it enhances my life, giving rise to an enhanced sense of purpose, spirit, ideal, friendship, communication, effectiveness, and self-worth (while decreasing negative emotions associated with being exclusively H2). These positive dimensions are sometimes followed by a resurgence of H2 in the form of an "H3 contest." I begin to think, subtly at first, "I'm contributing more than other people. My life is more significant. It feels great having an extraordinarily significant life with an extraordinary effect on the world. I feel sorry for those other guys who lack meaning and have very little positive effect on the world. It's okay, though. I'll tolerate them."

Obviously, the comparison game has again made its influence felt. I am simply playing it according to a higher viewpoint with higher purpose and ideals. Instead of saying, "I'm a better chess player than you are," I can now claim that my whole life is more significant than yours.

What happened? The increased spirit, purpose, and contribution arising out of H3 became commingled with the comparison game. Then, the high associated with the comparison game became stronger than the one associated with H3. Eventually, it became a full blown elitism with full blown contempt ("Your life is not significant by comparison with mine, but I will tolerate you, nonetheless.").

Most people around me will react defensively, and some will try to fight back by shifting the ground of the contest: "You may think you're doing more good than I am, but you're a worse athlete, and I'll always be smarter than you."

Other H3 people can also be dragged into an H3 contest. When they begin to sense my feeling of superiority, they will suffer both discouragement and frustration. They might begin to believe that my life has more purpose than theirs. In making this judgment on themselves, they have effectively made the "more" more important than their contribution to others. What's important is not the contribution they're making to their family, friends, community, and organization, but how much contribution they are making by comparison to me. I have dragged them into my contest, and I feel great that I'm winning. The irony here is that despite having moved to the contributive level, I am now doing more harm than good. I am dragging other people into my game, discouraging them, frustrating and disempowering them. True, they didn't have to enter my contest, but people are vulnerable.

Therefore, we have to look out for one another when we get to H3. We have to guard our own vulnerability to return to H2, and we have to be even more vigilant about preying on others' vulnerabilities to return to H2.

It is sometimes easier to silently proclaim, "Loser," at the very moment I am living for contribution, for I am blinded to what I am doing precisely because I am trying to live for H3. I'm getting the high from being a "winner" without knowing that it's coming at others' expense. As I vitiate the good effects of living on H3 and undermine others' attempts to live on H3, I discover, to my surprise, that others are distancing themselves from me. They recognize my arrogance and contempt, and in self-defense they become cooler. The very people who once said, "He has really changed—something good has happened to him. He is a much better leader and contributor," now suspect that I am hypocritical.

The solution to this problem lies first in recognizing what's really happening. I'm undermining my contribution and others' contributions by my comparative contest and arrogant attitude. This recognition forces my real desire to the fore, namely, that I want to make a contribution more than be a winner. I want my contributions to be effective in the lives of others. I don't want them to be vitiated by the comparison game. In short, after recognizing the problem, I must again make a choice. H3 can only be effective by controlling H2. When I sense that tinge of arrogance, I will do my best to replace it by my desire for contribution, friendship, and cooperation with others.

Over time it becomes easier to recognize that tinge of arrogence amidst H3. At the same time, my desire for contribution, friendship, and cooperation with others intensifies. A healthy sense of humility begins to emerge. This is not humility for its own sake, nor is it a discouraged, false, or stoic humility. It is humility for contribution, friendship, and cooperation with others. Others are good. Contribution is good. That is what I want, not the contest. As this attitude becomes more dominant, the "we" becomes more important than the "you and I." I gain a freedom to have a shared sense of purpose with others. I no longer find it necessary to inquire, "Who has more purpose?" Frankly, I really don't care. What I want is shared purpose. As this sense of shared purpose intensifies, I begin to notice using "we" instead of "I." I welcome others in my purpose and am happy to be welcomed by others in their purpose. I do not sabotage this sense of welcoming by saying, "My purpose is too great for you," or "Your purpose is too little for me." I enjoy being part of their purpose and sharing the fullness of my purpose with them. This enjoyment of others for their own sake outweighs the "more." At this juncture, friendship, cooperation, teamwork, colleagueship and all other forms of interaction are enhanced. A little bit of this humility goes a long way.

In sum, the solution to the problem of the H3 contest has three steps: 1) recognizing that the contest is destroying contribution, friendship, and cooperation, 2) choosing contribution, friendship, and cooperation over the "high" coming from the contest, and 3) choosing to enter into shared purpose with others.

2. THE H3 UPPING THE STAKES GAME

The second H2 problem arising in the midst of H3 concerns a new form of the upping the stakes game. Let us suppose again that while living in H3, I begin to value "the more" more than my contributions. I begin to feel that I have to enhance "the more" with each passing day. If I do not, I feel as if my life is less significant. A sense of compulsion starts to arise. I must contribute more because the contributions I am now making are "old hat." I begin to think to myself, "If I have the capacity to save the whole organization, I'd better get started on it. Maybe I ought to set my sights on the culture—perhaps the world." (Note the missing "we").

This inflated sense of expectation has three effects:

First, I become discouraged over how little I can really do. This, of course, may not be "little" at all. It may be of immeasurable importance to particular individuals, families, organizations, or communities, but I think my feats are little because they do not measure up to my expectations: they're not saving the culture. In short, no matter how much good I do, I feel discouraged, for I am not doing enough; therefore my life is not significant enough.

The second negative effect of this feeling is a resurgence of the H3 contest. Because I feel capable of saving the culture, I don't need anyone's help in this undertaking. I feel a slight sense of resentment when I hear that other people are making similar contributions. It's almost as if they stole my idea. "I'm the point man on this. I had the idea first. What are you trying to do?" I don't want to admit that others are really there. I want to be the hero. I want to be the first. I don't stop at non-inclusion—if I have the power, I'll drop them into second place or even discourage them from participating in a good cause.

The third negative effect of the upping the stakes game might be called Messianism. At this point, my expectation for ever-increasing contribution has now extended to the world. I open the newspaper in the morning and feel helpless. "If I don't rectify this problem, who will? And I simply don't have the time to do it right now. What will happen to the world, to the culture, to my organization? It's all too overwhelming to think about." The ensuing discouragement begins to make me feel powerless and therefore cynical about myself and my purpose. This results in a bitterness about life, anger with the culture, and an undermining of my capacity to do good.

The solution to this new form of the upping the stakes game is first to recognize that I have come to believe that "the more" has become more important than contribution, friendship, or cooperation. This may take some doing, for the error is not in my mind, it is in the way that I am living. If someone were to ask me, "Do you really think that 'the more' is more important than the actual contribution that you make?" I would say, "Of course not." But any objective observer would say that this has become my priority.

We must rectify the core belief that led to the problem: "If some contribution makes my life significant, then more contribution must make my life more significant." This is only true to the extent that my situation, capabilities, and point of development permit. If I do not have this all-important caveat in the forefront of my mind, I am likely to believe that I have to keep making more contributions ad infinitum to do my best. What I must see is that if my expectations go far beyond what I am able to accomplish at a given point in my life, they will undermine the good that I am able to do. When exaggerated expectations start discouraging me, pushing me to resent like-minded others, or even embittering me toward myself and the culture, they undermine the good that I can do. I must see this error for what it is and content myself with the real.

This error is not the sole cause of my discontent. It gives rise to an exaggerated sense of heroic destiny. I implicitly believe that as God, or fate, would have it, I am meant for some great purpose without which the world would crumble. Of course, I am meant for a great purpose with respect to the people I can touch and the situations that I can help, but the resentment I feel about not being able to affect the whole world fills me with discouragement, non-cooperation, and bitterness. Therefore, recognition of the error is not enough. I must also choose real contribution and real self-estimation over the exaggerated sense of heroic destiny.

Finally, I must return to shared purpose. After recognizing that I cannot increasingly contribute ad infinitum, and after tempering my exaggerated sense of heroic destiny, it becomes possible to again appreciate and enjoy others who would have common cause with me. I don't have to be the leader or the hero unless this is what is needed to accomplish a particular task. Again, if I can content myself with others entering into my purpose and my entering into their purpose without regard for who has to be the hero, true leadership can emerge.

3. Judgmentalism

When I strive for H3 ideals and see others who do not, I could secretly grow resentful. Even though I know that if I return to H2 it will give rise to the negative attitudes and the destructive contests that make me underlive my purpose in relationships, I still feel a longing for the good old carefree days when I did not have to attend to higher level concerns. I look at Joe, and he's competing with me. I am trying to look for the common good, and I think to myself, "Who cares about the common good—I want to win. I particularly don't want to be put down by him." Either I can allow myself to be dragged back into the comparison game on Joe's level (a return to H2), or I can create a new comparison game that I'm guaranteed to win (an H3 comparison game), or I can resent the H2 person, judging him to be a leech on the organization, the society, and the world. His life is despicable, his personhood of little worth. How does the world endure him?

Notice here that I have moved from judgment of actions to judgment of a person. I can say with impunity that Joe's actions were not destined to contribute to the world, but I cannot say that Joe's personhood is essentially negative (almost implying that his demise would be no great loss to the world). I can never know why Joe performs some compulsive H2 actions. I do not know his family background or whether he simply was not exposed to any ideals when he was young, I certainly can't say he's malicious. He may just be going through a short, compulsive stage. I can't say that he can't be touched by education or some other means of improvement, because like me, he could. I cannot say that he will not achieve the heights of H3 in the future, for the human spirit is remarkably resilient. In short, to judge his personhood, negating his intrinsic goodness (and therefore implying that his life is somehow not valuable to humanity and to the world) is simply unwarranted. Such unwarranted judgments can do incredible damage, and even though I have not spoken them, people will know that I am thinking them.

We can stop the potential damage of judgmentalism by attacking it at its roots. If we remember that judgmentalism begins with resentment, and this resentment has its roots in a secret longing for the comparison game, we can temper it by recognizing that 1) the anxieties and problems associated with the comparison game will again emerge when H3 attitudes are undermined; 2) resentment and judgment will probably be noticed and therefore undermine fruitful relationships and contributions; and 3) we can choose the long-term efficaciousness and happiness of H3 over the short-term ego-gratification of H2.

In conclusion, contests, upping the stakes, and judgmentalism undermine progress in H3 and lead not only to a return to H2, but even a cynical regression to H1. It can have very negative effects on the very people, institutions, and ideals to which we are trying to contribute.

The remedy to all three problems revolves around recognition and choice. Recognition concerns truisms that may be obvious in the abstract, but difficult to see in our lives. It requires that we be open to this data and, therefore, that we really want to see it. How do we gain the desire to unmask self-deception? By valuing the contribution, relationships, efficacy, purpose, and happiness from H3 so much that we no longer want to be controlled by short-term, subconscious desires for H2. As time passes, this desire for H3 becomes a desire to see the truth about how we are living H3, which truth motivates choices toward a more authentic H3. As I explain in the next chapter, these choices can become a habitual disposition.

8 Forming Habits Toward a New Way of Life

Even though contributive attitudes can bring immediate relief from the negative emotions of the comparison game, they don't seem to have a lasting effect. Indeed, most people engage in these new attitudes and then revert back to the old ones in a matter of minutes. To them it seems almost impossible to maintain the new attitude. Rather than continue to work at something that seems to be a fruitless pursuit, they often give up. There is a reason why these new attitudes frequently do not have "sticking power." Most New Year's resolutions fail for the same reason.

When we attempt to change our viewpoint or attitude on something, the psyche becomes divided. Part of the psyche has cultivated a series of reflex attitudes and habitual reactions over the years and acts out of these old attitudes and reflexes. However, the conscious mind, which is not reflex or habit-based, desires to progress in relationships, contributions, self-efficacy, and vision. It wants the new set of attitudes. The psyche will thus appear to be at odds with itself, even at war with itself.

The conscious mind has most of its power when a person is refreshed, has slept well, is not under stress, feels good about life, and has a sense of hope and optimism. Psychic energy is high, and so also is the capacity for thinking, deciding, and willing. It is not necessary for the psyche to revert to virtually thoughtless reflex reactions.

When psychic energy is low, however—when a person is under stress, has not been sleeping well, has not been taking care of himself, or is mentally preoccupied—reflex reactions are necessary merely to get through life. Hence, the habitual subconscious mind takes over.

Moving from Tension and Proclivity to Habit

This bifurcation of the psyche means that significant changes in attitudes or behavior normally have to go through three stages before they become habits or reflex reactions: tension, proclivity, and habit.

STAGE 1: TENSION

In this first stage, which need last only about six weeks, the psyche is almost completely bifurcated. The conscious mind is adamantly saying "yes" to a set of attitudes that it thinks to be desirable for optimum meaning and happiness, while the subconscious mind is adamantly trying to hang on to the reflex reactions with which it feels at home. Hence, when we begin to change what we are looking and living for, we will not only revert back to the old attitudes quickly, but will also experience alienation, fear, boredom, anger, and even nightmares toward these new viewpoints. This can be overwhelming, leading us to give up only moments after we have just begun to change.

If we make it through the first six weeks, our psyche can become powerfully integrated, because the subconscious mind is brought to the point of replacing the old habit with the new habit. It is saying, "maybe" to the new habit (proclivity). Though the bifurcation of the psyche is not nearly as pronounced as it was in the first six weeks, it can fall prey to new problems preventing the formation of habits. Once the second stage (lasting about another six weeks) has been completed, a habit is formed that can literally transform our way of looking at life, indeed, our way of living life.

The following six suggestions can help you cope with tension. Adhering to them will increase your probability of success and shorten the time needed for a successful transition.

1. Getting expectations right. Habits cannot be formed overnight. It takes time to bring the habitual subconscious mind to a point where it's willing to both accept and act upon a new viewpoint, attitude, or behavior scheme. So, remind yourself that failure is likely to happen after three or four minutes. That's normal. Calmly react to this setback. Calm allows you to simply begin anew without a dashed expectation. If expectations are dashed, you will feel anxiety. The anxiety will, in turn, deplete psychic energy that will lend itself to giving up. If you react with calm, you must remember that a second, third, fourth, even fifth failure is likely to happen within hours. Again, if you react to multiple failures throughout the day with calm, you can start anew without the undermining anxieties that arise out of dashed expectations. In short, you must think, "I must give myself at least six weeks. I must expect that my first attempts to live according to these new attitudes will last only minutes, and that I will likely have multiple failures per day. No problem. That's normal."

2. ***Positive self-discourse.***[1] This suggestion is meant to impact the way you talk to yourself. If failure should bring with it a negative self-dialogue such as, "I always do this," or "I can't get anything right," or "I'm no good," then you will deplete the psychic energy necessary to make and hold onto a change. Negative self-dialogue not only produces anxiety, it reinforces ongoing anxieties about the self, undermines self-worth and self-image, and makes the psyche preoccupied with its problems at the very moment that it requires the most psychic energy. Thus, you need to replace these negative self-assessments with positive ones. When failure occurs, instead of saying, "That's just like me," say, "That's not like me. I'll do better next time." The second formulation believes that you are capable of changing for the better and intrinsically better than the failure just experienced. This positive belief creates hope and energy for both the present and the future. Again, instead of saying "I can't get anything right," you might say, "I will get things right. I am getting things right. I just need more time to tackle this one." This positive self-talk can give you the psychic energy and hope necessary to actualize significant changes in your life.

These positive self-affirmations are not tricky little fictions recited by Pollyannas. They are, in fact, the truth about ourselves. If we look at the great leaders who have affected the world, we will see that they started off with the same negative propensities, and that the one thing that enabled them to change was a belief about themselves—a true belief.

3. ***Repetition, repetition, repetition.*** The contibutive attitudes are both general and long-term, yet we are living in a

world that is becoming progressively more specific and short-term. We have to make two to three times as many decisions per day as people in previous generations. We are flooded with data from mass media, the Internet, and conventional modes of communication, and so we tend to defer decisions or data that are general and long-term. If we are not, as a culture, to become completely superficial, and, indeed, if we are to change any habits at all, we will have to make this general, long-term data more important and poignant. Daily contemplation or repetition is one good way to do this.

4. Keep slips or "failures" in perspective. You might recall the Greek myth of Sisyphus who, in Hades, is constrained to roll a rock up a hill. Just as he reaches the precipice, the rock rolls down and he has to begin all over again. Many people believe this ancient Greek rendition of Murphy's Law—namely, if you suffer a failure, you can't just start where you left off, you have to go back to the beginning. If this thought is well ingrained in your consciousness, it is likely to forestall any change, because you can't bear the thought of starting over.

Although people tend to absolutize failure, if you practice the first three suggestions, then your subconscious mind will become "etched" with this new attitude. The more you believe in yourself, affirm where you are going, and get your expectations right, the more your subconscious mind will accept a new attitude. This acceptance effects a change in all your reflex attitudes and reactions. This is very difficult to lose. Once the subconscious mind takes on new habits, it does not give them up easily. The more ingrained the habit, the more tenaciously the subconscious mind holds on to it. Hence, if you were to fail after 10 weeks of "etching," you would not need to start all over again. In the language of the myth, *you* will have rolled down the hill, but the rock (the etching) will have remained in place. Hence, you only need to brush off, walk back up to the rock, and continue where you left off. So long as you remember this while practicing the other three suggestions, you will eventually move to a well-formed, well-integrated habit. The way you view meaning, others, relationships, and life will eventually become a permanent change.

5. Do not give negative emotions absolute power over you. When you try to change a reflex reaction, your subconscious mind will not only react with resistance, but also with a panoply of emotions. The subconscious mind is so at home with the old attitude, the new attitude seems threatening. Fear is just the beginning of the subconscious mind's emotional reaction to new, fundamental attitudes. I, for example, have experienced fear toward new attitudes because they seemed not to be the "real me." I felt as if I was not being authentic to myself because the "real me" was what I felt at home with, and what I felt at home with was the old attitude. These feelings of fear and inauthenticity undermined my purpose and made me feel a little depressed. As my energy decreased in the midst of the depression, I became angry with this new pursuit that brought with it all this hardship. The anger soon turned into resentment and cynicism.

How can you deal with these emotions? First, don't give them any more credence than they deserve. Negative emotions are not a sign of impending doom, past failures, or divine judgment. They are merely manifestations of the subconscious mind's discomfort with the new attitudes. These emotions do not reflect long-term, perpetual states. You are not becoming a fearful person, a bored person, an angry person, etc. The moods are only transitional and should be given no more acknowledgment than these temporary states deserve. Negative transitional moods, therefore, should not be generalized, dwelt upon, or exaggerated. Of course, if they persist for more than a few weeks, then you might become increasingly concerned. If they continue and grow worse over the course of several weeks, they undoubtedly have other causes that should be checked into by professionals. By and large, most of us will not experience worsening anxiety from negative transitional moods. If we persist in our change pattern, the negative moods will eventually disappear and be replaced with a far more optimistic outlook.

6. Sleep and stress relief can do wonders. The conscious mind gets its power when we are awake, refreshed, and relatively free from stress. The subconscious mind gets its power when we are tired and feeling stress and preoccupation. We move immediately to the "non-thinking" reflex part of our mind when we don't have energy. This is why we can suffer temporary failures even after a habit has been formed. If we are completely exhausted or under enough stress, we seem to return to lower or base patterns of dealing with reality. This does not mean that we have permanently returned to the base pattern. After a good night's sleep, a relaxing vacation, or alleviation of stress, we can resume our higher attitudes and habits.

STAGE TWO: PROCLIVITY

After a brief time, you will notice a subtle but persistent change in your attitudes, marking the transition to proclivity. When you are fresh in the morning, you will look for ways to contribute to others and for the good news in others. It will seem instinctive to be attentive to others' strengths, to be grateful for their presence, to look for opportunities for trust and common cause, and to be free from the need for one-upsmanship. When you feel this new freedom and others begin to react positively to it, your expectations can sometimes get out of control. You begin to think, "I'm nearly there. In a few more days, this will be permanent." In reality, however, you are only partially there, and failure, which can easily happen at this juncture, could fill you with absolute resentment or sadness. The Myth of Sisyphus then seems to be the real truth about life, and so you begin to regress to your baser attitudes.

I must emphasize that the Myth of Sisyphus is false. Don't go into a negative self-diatribe: "I've known all along that this is the way I really am...." If you want to become a cynic, this is the surefire way to do it. Again, calm is the key to success. If you can look at the setback objectively and simply say, "This is what happens to 99 percent of the people 99 percent of the time. It's not like me—it's not like who I have become. I'll do better next time," you will likely move right through the setback to the higher level attitude.

STAGE THREE: HABIT

If you keep reinforcing this proclivity for six weeks, it will become more habitual, which will give way to a new reflex attitude affecting every dimension of life. This habit is one of the fullest manifestations of human freedom, for we are literally creating our second nature. We are born into the world with a "first nature." We have little to say about our physical features and genetic structures, but we can do much about our second nature, and this is what really matters. The second nature is all about how we relate to others, how we conduct ourselves publicly, what we contribute, how we create, and what we live and even die for. If we can make these attitudes a permanent part of ourselves, we will have done well with our freedom. The ancients called a good habit a "virtue." And so it is, for a virtue is precisely good. It is a consecration of life to the good. It is something of purpose and permanence.

Four States of Mind that Inhibit Change

Four states of mind can inhibit the best intended changes.

1. Fear. Fear can often block change and even the openness to change. You feel safer by not moving, by remaining in your comfort zone, by embracing what is old and familiar. Fear has various sources stemming from personality propensity, to childhood traumas, to attaching too much significance to competitive successes.

How can you get around fear to make your life more creative and efficacious? I suggest a four-pronged strategy.

First, cultivate the attitude of contribution. This removes the fear surrounding having to be a winner, having to have friends, to have self-worth, and a meaningful life. You gain immediate relief from the fear of having to progress or succeed more than others simply by reflecting upon the ways you can make a difference with your life to family, colleagues, community, etc.

Second, have back-up plans. Many people who feel fear most acutely have only one plan in mind. They frequently believe that success, and indeed their whole meaning in life, rides upon this one particular plan. The mere anticipation of failure can be debilitating. It can cloud your thinking and lead to erratic actions, even self-punishment. But if you think about it, you can see an optimal plan with less optimal default positions beneath it. These default positions may be quite positive, but obsessing on this one particular plan blinds you to the second, third, and fourth best options. If you have the propensity to obsess on a single optimal plan, you must train yourself to see positive secondary and tertiary positions. This will not only help you to alleviate fear when the best option does not come to pass (as it frequently does not), but will also help you to see and take advantage of opportunities that you may not have seen at first. These new opportunities may fit together better with the second or third plans than with the first. Hence, with back-up plans, you can be more fully adaptable and creative.

Third, keep perspective. When you are tempted to make a mountain out of a molehill, ask yourself: "What has this got to do with the whole order of salvation?" Most of the time, the answer is, "Not much." This answer gives you the freedom and objectivity to look at new ways to proceed in light of setbacks to your optimal plan.

Fourth, exercise your faith, and ask for God's help. This openness to God's grace has the power to help you see goodness in setbacks, opportunities in uncertainty, and a capacity to serve in the midst of "being hassled."

2. Resentment and inability to forgive. Anger, particularly resentment, is an inhibitor of all forms of change. You can lose the energy to improve yourself or your performance because of the belief that life is unfair: "Life is simply one injustice after the next. Why should I bother anymore?" This sense of being pushed around by forces outside of your control and the deep and abiding anger resulting from this assault on your freedom not only can cause hopelessness and haplessness, but passive aggression and cynicism. It can only be rectified through forgiveness and a restoration of your sense of contribution and self-efficacy.

The following suggestions may help to accomplish this.

First, adopt the attitude of contribution. Resentment frequently comes from a compulsive ego vesting too much self-worth, identity, and friendship in a comparison game. Worries about the game, or even being beaten at the game (whether justly or unjustly) can cause extraordinary bitterness and resentment. The attitude of contribution (defining my meaning in life in terms of the contributions I can make to family, friends, colleagues, organization, and community) brings the stakes of the comparison game into focus and removes the sting of debilitating bitterness and resentment.

Second, rectify "flare-ups"—times when you are inclined to spontaneously let loose. You may justify these flare-ups by saying: "I needed to pressure her to get the job done." "He was incompetent, so I had to draw the line and...." Although these justifications have a core of truth to them, they do not make negative emotional outbursts helpful to the recipient or the organization. These outbursts can make an instant passive aggressive out of the nicest person. Think of what these outbursts can do to "not so nice" people.

Such outbursts can also debilitate you, because embarrassment may set in, forcing you to excuse yourself or avoid contact with the other person involved in the incident. If embarrassment does not happen, bullying frequently does. You begin to think that you can get your way by simply becoming the proverbial emotional bull in the china shop: scream loud enough and they'll all succumb. Unfortunately, the opposite is really happening. The bully loses credibility, incites passive aggression, destroys team spirit, and, in the end, is an inhibitor to quality. It is one thing to be aggressive and to inspire other people to be aggressive in the positive sense (soliciting customers, being competitive, etc.), it's quite another to be a bully, which invariably undermines the whole organization.

There are many reasons for these flare-ups. Some people are, by nature, more inclined to be outwardly emotional; some have suffered real injustices and have never dealt with them; others are extraordinarily sensitive to "ego-challenges" and will simply destroy or overwhelm anyone who seems to be trying to catch up or even achieve more. The reasons for the flare-ups are not as significant as the discipline required to move beyond them. This would entail: not justifying flare-ups, becoming aware of flare-ups, asking people to indicate when they think you are flaring up (and not punishing them for it), looking for the good news in others, and being grateful for others' talents.

Third, practice forgiveness—the intention to let go of a just claim you may have against another. Forgiveness is not forgetting. Forgetting takes much longer. The more acute the injustice, the longer it takes to forget. Forgiveness is, however, necessary for forgetting, for without the intention to let go of a just claim, time becomes an enemy, resentments fester, and bitterness becomes so acute that you can predicate your whole life on hatred or vengeance. With forgiveness, however, time is your friend. By intending (in your mind) to let go of a just claim, you begin to be free of it, and this freedom, in turn, allows your subconscious mind to let it go as well.

Furthermore, forgiveness should not be confused with enduring continued abuse. You have a responsibility to protect yourself, your psychic health, and self-efficacy. Hence, even the most forgiving person must be ready to defend herself from enduring abuse. You can do this by avoiding precarious situations and by extricating yourself from precarious relationships. You do not do this to hurt the other person or to exact vengeance, but only for self-defense and self-protection. The person who can forgive, let go, and forget can live for something other than grievance and anger. This is true freedom, for it opens up whole realms of hitherto consumed psychic energy and imparts the capacity to connect in trust with others in the future. This trust is not naiveté, but rather a heightened awareness of the frailty of people amidst their fundamental trustworthiness. It is not cynicism, but a wisdom matured through experience and compassion.

Fourth, let God take care of the persons and situations causing hurt and injustice in your life. The grace of God is particularly efficacious with respect to forgiveness. If God is the just Judge, the merciful Judge, then you can, in peace, "let go and let God." As will be seen in Chapter 9, prayer can be particularly helpful for forgiving others and receiving God's healing calm in your life.

3. Unconditioned attachments to what is conditioned. Everyone has likes and dislikes, preferences in things ranging from food to cars. Nothing is wrong with these preferences until they become ends in themselves. When I cannot be happy without a particular kind of car or clothing, that thing has become an end in itself. I have, in essence, an unconditional desire for a conditioned thing. It does not matter whether this unconditional desire is oriented toward a particular car, a promotion, or a particular friendship; they will fail to satisfy me because they are conditioned, yet my desire is unconditional. I am seeking an ultimate happiness, a perfection from things that cannot by nature give it.

Several consequences arise out of these unconditional attachments. First, frustration arises when the object of my desire (say, a particular car) no longer makes me happy. Once I felt a sense of exhilaration; now I only feel an ordinariness. The object leaves me empty and sometimes bored. Since I do not understand the real problem, I infer from this emptiness that I need more cars, better cars, quality cars, etc. Even 30 Rolls Royces will eventually fail to satisfy me. This frustration and emptiness can have far greater consequences. I can become obsessed with a particular object or person and try to make them give me the fulfillment that I expect. When they cannot, I can grow to hate them and extend my unhappiness to my life in general. Because this car or person cannot, in the end, satisfy me, I assume that life in general must be unsatisfying, and I begin to lapse into a boredom, cynicism, or malaise which, if it does not lead to despair, can be perpetually distracting. This makes reflection and achievement of new habits extraordinarily difficult.

The following four suggestions can help you to move beyond unconditional attachments.

First, practice the attitude of contribution. If you list the various ways you can contribute to your family, friends, colleagues, and community, you will begin to value these contributions on a par with the attachments. By having this new objective of desire, you can progressively detach yourself from the car, the promotion, or other obsessive attachments.

Second, consider what these attachments are doing to you and to the quality of your relationships. As you become obsessed with a particular conditioned objective, you begin to make yourself a thing in the very image of the thing from which you seek unconditional happiness. This reduction of yourself to a thing (the loss of your subject self) leads to a devaluation of the subject self of others. These others, in turn, become pawns in the achievement of your goals, things to be admired or disdained, things that either benefit you or discredit you. Your capacity to care for others seems to slip away, and the matrix of comparative advantage seems to replace it.

If I care about my friendships, the only way I can let these attachments vitiate them is if I blind myself to the attachments' effects. I want both my friendships and my attachments, but they are mutually contradictory, so I blind myself to the effects of the attachments until they catch up with me. But why wait until they catch up with me? Why not let the truth set me free now? If I open my eyes to the incompatibility between good friends and these unconditional attachments to conditioned things, I empower myself through this truth to delimit the attachments. Empowerment toward detachment comes from allowing myself to see incompatibility where it really is, and then to act on what I really value and cherish.

Third, gain perspective about your obsession. As you become obsessed with, say, a particular car to the point where you simply cannot be happy without it, you might ask yourself, "What has this got to do with unconditional Truth, Goodness, Love, Beauty, and Being?" or, if you have faith, "What has this got to do with the whole order of salvation?" As you gain perspective, the object seems to lose its spell, thereby curbing the obsession.

Fourth, exercise your faith. When you allow God to come into your consciousness in prayer, you will find it very difficult to maintain even the most idealized and romantic attachments, for you become at least tacitly aware not only that these things cannot satisfy unconditionally, but that only one being can satisfy—an unconditional Being. Again, prayer can be very useful in moving beyond unconditional attachments.

4. Pride. As the sage says, "Pride cometh before the fall." This is so true because pride seems to be one of the more "acceptable" vices. It's a bit more uncomfortable to be caught stealing or lying. What I mean by *pride* is not simply a false sense of self-sufficiency, but self-idolatry. I believe that I can be the center of my own universe, that my successes alone allow me to be self-sufficient and even to be my own ultimate self-satisfaction. In so doing, I attribute a kind of ultimacy to myself, even if it's only for myself. Naturally, I believe that others should also recognize and acknowledge this "truth." To make this self-image "truthful," I must get other people to buy into it. It's not enough to have me as my own best witness. Public corroboration clearly indicates truth.

If people do not buy into my myth, I may try to convince them of my ultimacy through some kind of proof or even bravado. Or, I could try to convince them of this "truth" by a kind of façade or an outright lie. Or, I could grow angry with them for refusing to believe this "truth," and either separate myself from them or seek vengeance on them. Or, I could just simply withdraw, contenting myself with myself, and knowing full well that these unbelievers are beneath me and that their opinion is of little worth.

All four reactions adversely affect my relationships with others and produce very negative reactions. They also cause me to waste time on perpetuating a myth instead of pursuing a reality. This not only stands in the way of actualizing new habits and higher viewpoints, but also tends to exacerbate all the negative emotional conditions of the comparison game.

The insidious part about pride is that it is "acceptable" enough for me not to notice it until all of these negative effects are almost out of control—I get a glimmer of the myth just before I'm about to fall, and then I do fall.

I have four suggestions for moving beyond pride.

The first, again, is the attitude of contribution. By focusing on how I can make a difference to ideals and others beyond myself, I take my focus off myself thereby lessening my sense of self-ultimacy. I recognize others to be invaluable not only to my life project of making a contribution, I see others' presence, concern, feedback, and care to be essential to my life. Inasmuch as love is not only giving but accepting and recognizing my need for others, it conquers pride.

The second suggestion concerns reflection. When I open my eyes to what pride can do to my relationships, how it can waste my time, and how it can obscure my sense of reality, I will likely become wary, even worried about it; but I don't want to worry about it, and so I frequently prefer to remain blind. Pride's power comes with its acceptability, and self-blindness can persist to the last possible moment before the fall. The key to moving beyond pride, then, is not letting it be acceptable. I must say to myself, "I am not going to let myself be seduced and beaten by this seemingly harmless little vice. I am going to see it for what it is, and I want to see it as other people see it in me. I want to feel the shame of my self-idolatry fully manifest in the eyes of another person." This opens the way to truth, wariness, and worry, which in turn provides an impetus to move beyond.

The third suggestion concerns perspective. In this case, pride seems to be immune to the question "What has this got to do with the whole order of salvation?" Other questions are needed, "Can I really be the center of my own universe? Can I really be my own ultimate source of satisfaction? Am I really an ultimate?" These questions reveal what I am thinking (but not saying) when I try to get others to acknowledge my superiority and legendary stature. They reveal my excessive need for others' recognition. They expose my need for public corroboration to keep myself within the comfortable boundaries of superiority, self-sufficiency, and ultimacy. By taking these questions seriously, while acknowledging my need for others (not merely to corroborate the myth about myself, but in reciprocal concern and care), the answer, "No," can begin to resound in my mind, allowing me, for a brief moment, to acknowledge the goodness of others, the desirability of reciprocity, and the fulfillment intrinsic to love borne out of truth.

The fourth suggestion is to pray for God's grace. Pride seems to elude our control. When we try to be humble on our own, we become proud about our humility. When we try to implement the first three suggestions, we tend to idealize our capacity to move beyond pride out of concern for others: "I can't believe how truly authentic my love is. It is so authentic that I have opened myself up to others in a pure stance of reciprocity and truth." Deeper probing may reveal that this stance of "authentic" appreciation of others and desire for pure reciprocity can be toppled by their daring to make an observation that might burst our little "authenticity" bubble: "I'm not sure you've reached the state of pure authenticity and reciprocity, yet," provoking us to roar back, "How would you know?"

I make these observations only out of my own experience. I am not implying that you have or will do the same. However, if you feel a resonant chord, you might again try prayer, for it is through God's peace, informing us of who we really are and helping us to accept others whom we need, that we can come to truth. Love borne out of truth makes all the difference.

At this point, you might be wondering, "What has all this got to do with the heart of inspired leadership?" Everything. It is not enough to give the six attitudes to your stakeholders. You must explain why these attitudes are important, how they work, and how they can be fully integrated into their life and work. It is not enough to talk about your organizational life; you must tap into the drivers of your whole life (personal, family, team, etc.).

These four drivers are what I have termed "the four levels of happiness." To understand them is to understand what can fulfill us and what can make us unhappy, what can lead us to an optimally lived life and what can lead to an underlived life, what can enhance self-efficacy and what can hinder it, what can lead to inspired leadership, or merely driven leadership.

We now proceed to the fourth and final level of happiness and purpose in life—the pursuit of, and involvement in, the ultimate.

9 Indications of God's Presence in Human Consciousness

Before we consider the fourth level of happiness (concerned with the desire for the ultimate, the transcendent, the unconditional, and the perfect), we would do well to look for indications of this ultimate objective within the human psyche. Inasmuch as this unconditional objective has been termed "God" by many philosophers, thinkers and worshippers, I characterize this chapter as "indications of the presence of God in human consciousness."

Since the time of Plato, philosophers have set out considerable evidence for God's existence. Many have provided proofs from the vantage point of metaphysics, mathematics, physics, and even the dynamic structure of human consciousness. In this chaper, I briefly describe some evidence of God's presence in human consciousness and document the power of self-transcendence.

This power of self-transcendence is manifest in six areas. Although all six manifestations of self-transcendence give rise to every form of human striving in knowledge, love, art, justice, and spiritual life, they can lead to problems in living out the ideal, for they sometimes incite us to seek ultimacy, perfection, the absolute, the unconditioned, and even the infinite and eternal in things that are by nature imperfect, conditioned, finite, and transitory. This desire for the ultimate makes the level of happiness incomplete, and can lead to a host of problems ranging from dashed idealism to dashed romanticism. The result is generally an undermining of the attitudes of contribution and cooperation and a cynical return to comparison and competition.

SIX MANIFESTATIONS OF TRANCENDENCE

I will briefly discuss each of the six manifestations of self-transcendence that give rise to the fourth level of happiness and purpose in life.

1. The desire for unrestricted truth. The *unrestricted* desire to know is manifest in children who persistently query, "Why is that?" You give an answer, and they ask further, "Well, why is that?" You give another answer, and still they ask, "Well, why is that?" They are likely to go on forever until you say, "Be quiet now, you're overeducated." This endless process of querying shows that children recognize the inadequacy of answers. They see that a particular answer is not fully explanatory, and since they want a complete explanation, they ask yet another question.

This process will continue indefinitely, for we seek the complete set of correct answers to the complete set of questions. We seek not merely pragmatic knowledge, (e.g., "How can I get more food with which to live?"), we want to know just for the sake of knowing. We seem to be endowed with a desire for complete explanation. Since we recognize when we have not arrived at this point, we are always beyond any answer at which we have arrived. We have the remarkable capacity of knowing that we do not know. How is this possible unless we have some awareness of what is beyond what we already know?

Many contemporary philosophers (such as Emerich Coreth,[1] Bernard Lonergan,[2] and Karl Rahner[3]) have concluded that we can go beyond the limits of knowledge because we have a sense of "the beyond." Though we cannot conceptualize "the beyond," our sense of it causes us to recognize the inadequacy of any conditioned or finite answer. This sense of "the beyond," is like Eddington's light beckoning us ahead.[4] As this light shows the inadequacy of conditioned and finite answers (by pointing beyond them), it incites a desire within us to ask a further question.

If this light didn't exist, then we would have no sense of it; and if we had no sense of it, we would never get beyond the truth we currently know. If we never got beyond the truth we currently know, we would never see the limits of that truth (the truth's inadequacy). And if we never saw the truth's limits or inadequacy, we would never ask a question.

The apple would have fallen on Newton's head, and he would have simply eaten it.

These philosophers go one step further and assert that the "light that beckons ahead" is unrestricted. The fact that we have an unrestricted desire to know points to the existence of a light that is unrestricted by its nature. Without this unrestricted light, the conditioned and restricted nature of knowledge would not manifest itself indefinitely until we reach a completely intelligible answer (i.e., an answer that is unconditioned and unrestricted, and therefore leaves no question to be asked).

This light frequently goes by the names of "unconditioned Truth," "complete intelligibility," or an "unrestricted act of understanding," and is frequently associated with "God." Those with faith interpret this to be the human sense of God (given by God to human beings). Hence, they believe that their self-transcendent quest for knowledge comes from God and can only find fruition through union with God.[5]

2. The desire to love unconditionally and to receive unconditional love. Similarly, philosophers have long thought that human beings have a "sense" of perfect and unconditional love. Not only do we have the power to love (the power to be naturally connected to another human being in profound emotion, care, self-gift, concern, and acceptance), we have a "sense" of what this profound interpersonal connection would be like if it were perfect. This sense of perfect love has the positive effect of inciting us to pursue evermore perfect forms of love. However, it has the drawback of inciting us to expect evermore perfect love from others. This generally leads to dashed romanticism and to the slow decline of relationships that can never grow fast enough to match the perfect and unconditional expectations of its participants.

What is the origin of this "sense" of perfect, unconditional love? Many philosophers believe that a transcendent, unconditionally loving reality is tacitly present to human awareness, giving a sense of what love could be. It allows us to be beyond any imperfect manifestation of love, causing at once a striving for more, and a dissatisfaction with what is. This unconditionally loving reality goes by the names of "Love, itself," the "idea of Love itself," "perfect, interpersonal subjectivity," "the ground of perfect, interpersonal subjectivity," "the ground of interpersonal connectedness," and for those with faith, "God" or "the loving God."

3. The desire for perfect justice and goodness and to be perfectly just and good. As with the "sense" of perfect and unconditional Truth and Love, philosophers have long recognized the human desire for perfect justice or goodness. Not only do we have a sense of good and evil, a capacity for moral reflection, a profoundly negative felt awareness of cooperation with evil (guilt), and a profoundly positive felt awareness of cooperation with goodness (nobility); we also have a "sense" of what perfect, unconditioned goodness or justice would be like. We are not content to simply act in accordance with our conscience now, we are constantly striving for ways to achieve the more noble, the greater good, the higher ideal. We even pursue the perfectly good or just order.

This desire for perfect goodness and justice can also be seen in children. An imperfect manifestation of justice from parents will get the immediate retort, "That's not fair!" Adults do the same thing. We have a sense of what justice ought to be, and we believe others ought to know this. When this sense of justice has been violated, we respond in our minds with, "That's not fair!" A violation of this sort always seems acute. We seem to be in a state of shock. We expect that perfect justice ought to happen, and when it doesn't, it so profoundly disappoints us that it consumes us. We can feel the same outrage toward God, groups, and social structures.

As with our "sense" of perfect and unconditional Love, our sense of perfect and unconditional Goodness and Justice has both a positive and negative side. The positive side is it fuels all our strivings for an evermore perfect social order, a more just legal system, greater equity and equality. It even fuels our promethean idealism to bring the justice of God to earth. The negative side of this "sense" of perfect or unconditional Justice is that it incites our expectations for perfect Justice in a finite and conditioned world, which normally means that our promethean ideals will be dashed. This causes disappointments with the culture, the legal system, our organizations, and our families. We always expect more justice and goodness than the finite world can deliver, and when our expectations are dashed, we experience outrage, impatience, judgment of others, and even cynicism.

What is the source of this "sense" of perfect Justice and Goodness, even the promethean desire to save the world and to be the "ultimate hero?" As with perfect and unconditional Truth and Love, many philosophers believe that there is a transcendent, unconditionally good and just Reality present to our consciousness. It goes by the names of "Goodness, itself," "the ground of human social connectedness," "the idea of perfect Justice," and for those with faith, "God."

In the famous "allegory of the cave" in *The Republic*,[6] Plato likens this reality to the sun, which is the source of all light and all shadows. From the time of Plato, many philosophers have called this reality, "the really Real." It is more real than the world of changing things, and far more real than the world of the shadows. In any case, we have a "sense" of this perfectly just and good Reality that allows us to be beyond any imperfect manifestation of it. Inasmuch as we are aware of what is beyond any imperfect manifestation of justice, we continually strive for, and expect, the more perfect.

4. The desire for unrestricted or perfect beauty. We need not read the 19th Century Romantic poets or listen to the great Romantic composers, or view the works of Romantic artists to see the human capacity to idolize beauty. We only need look at the examples of simple dissatisfaction with beauty in our everyday life. We don't look good enough and neither do other people (will we/they ever?). The house is not perfect enough, the painting can never achieve perfection, and the musical composition, though beautiful beyond belief, could always be better.

Once in a great while, we think we have arrived at complete ecstasy. This might occur upon looking at a scene of natural beauty: a sunset over the water, majestic green and brown mountains against a horizon of blue sky. But even there, despite our desire to elevate it to the quasi-divine, we get bored and strive for a different or an even more perfect manifestation of natural beauty—a little better sunset, another vantage point of the Alps that's a little more perfect.

As with the other three transcendentals (perfect Truth, perfect Love, and perfect Goodness and Justice), we seem to always have an awareness of what is more beautiful. It incites us to the desire of this more perfect ideal. This desire has both a positive and a negative effect. The positive effect is that it incites the continuous striving for artistic, musical, and literary perfection. We do not passively desire to create; we passionately desire to create, to express in ever more beautiful forms, the perfection of beauty that we seem to carry within our consciousness. We do not simply want to say an idea; we want to express it beautifully, indeed, perfectly beautifully. We do not simply want to express a mood in music, we want to express it perfectly beautifully. This striving has left a legacy of architecture and art, music and drama, and of every form of high culture.

The negative effect is that we grow bored with any imperfect manifestation of beauty. This causes us to try to make perfectly beautiful what is imperfect by nature. It is true that a garden can achieve a certain perfection of beauty, but our continuous desire to improve it can make us grow terribly dissatisfied when we cannot perfect it indefinitely. Thus, we see tourists going through the gardens of Versailles exclaiming, "Enough garden, already. What's next?" or a very handsome man or beautiful woman, who despite tremendous vanity, harbors a secret knowledge and resentment of every imperfection in them, or the music lover who proclaims, "I've heard Brahms too many times."

Where does this sense of perfect beauty come from? Again, many philosophers suspect that there exists a perfectly beautiful transcendent reality that is present to our consciousness. This transcendent reality frequently goes by the names of "Beauty, itself," "the ground of the artistic muse," "the idea of perfect Beauty," "unconditioned Beauty," "Glory, itself (*herlichkeit*)," "the ground of perfect ecstasy," and for those with faith, "God." These philosophers also believe that we have a "sense" of this transcendent Reality that allows us to be aware of beauty beyond any of its imperfect manifestations. This causes at once the striving to create the beautiful and even the more beautiful. It also causes us to expect perfect beauty where it cannot be found.

5. The desire for unrestricted harmony with totality: to be at home in all that is. We also seek a perfect sense of harmony with all that is. We not only want to be at home in a particular environment, we want to be at home with the totality, at home in the cosmos. Have you ever felt, either as a child or an adult, a sense of alienation or discord—a deep sense of not belonging? You ask yourself, "What could be the source?" And you look around and see that at this particular time you have a good relationship with your friends and your family. Your work relationships seem to be going well, community involvements have produced some interesting friends and contexts in which to work. Yet, something is missing. You don't quite feel at home in a *general* sense. Although you do feel at home with family, friends, and coworkers, you feel like you are out of kilter with, and don't belong to, the *totality*. And yet, all the specific contexts seem just fine. You feel an emptiness, a lack of peace, yet there is absolutely nothing you can put your finger on.

Many philosophers would identify this feeling with our "sense" not only of the totality, but some initial sense of harmony or peace with the totality—a "sense" of perfect home, a sense of home amidst the whole of reality without any taint of alienation. The contrary sense of alienation from the totality has both a positive side and a negative side. The positive side is that it presents a call to seek ever greater and deeper forms of harmony (peace within the world). The negative side is the confusion and discontent that it brings.

I do not understand why I feel this lack of peace, this emptiness, this sense of not belonging, and so I tend to feel animosity toward those groups who can do nothing for me when I'm feeling it. A man may look at his wife and think, "Although I feel at home with her, she can do nothing for my sense of emptiness." Her helplessness induces frustration in him, and she is baffled by this seemingly inexplicable frustration. Again, I realize that my best friend, who seems to bring comfort in so many situations, cannot help me to belong, to fit in, to feel at home in this universal sense. And so, I display my frustration and restlessness at his powerlessness. Relationships have a way of taking a downward turn in these circumstances because we are trying to extract from them what they cannot give. The only way out, seemingly, is to find perfect home and harmony with all that is.

What gives rise to this "sense" of perfect home in the totality? Again, many philosophers would assert that there exists a transcendent Reality that is itself perfect Peace (perfect home). This Reality goes by the name of "perfect Harmony," "Harmony, itself," "the idea of perfect home," "the

Eternal Order," "unconditional Love," "Love, itself," and "the ground of interpersonal connectedness." Again, many philosophers associate this transcendent reality with "God." They further believe that we have a "sense" of this transcendent Reality that enables us to go beyond any particular or imperfect feeling of home or peace that we feel in any specific context. This gives rise to a striving for more perfect peace. In some religions, this "sense" of perfect peace is identified with the unitive experience or the mystical experience.

6. Faith—a relationship with a personal God. The first five manifestations of self-transcendence provide the basis for human faith. If our "sense" of the perfect and unconditioned comes from a transcendent Reality that is perfect and unconditional Truth, Love, Goodness/Justice, Beauty, and Home/Peace, then our proclivity toward faith seems quite natural, for despite the different tenors of Truth, Love, Goodness/Justice, Beauty, and Home/Peace, they are all held together by one similarity: they seem to be perfect and unconditioned by nature. Long before philosophers attempted to prove that all these transcendentals were one and the same reality, we tended to blend them all together because of the perfection and unconditionedness we "sensed" in them. We felt that all reality participated in this perfect, transcendent Reality that is Truth, Love, Goodness/Justice, Beauty, and Home/Peace by its nature, and we identified this sense of perfection with "God."

We associated the perfect and unconditioned with the unrestricted and infinite. We began to sense, and later to prove, that an actual infinity of past time (an "achieved infinity") was contradictory and therefore impossible.[7] Therefore, a Creator of finite past time which would have to be outside of time, was associated with this unrestricted, unconditioned, perfect, transcendent reality.

These various attributes were then seen to be intrinsically interrelated, which gave rise to a host of proofs for God's existence beginning with Plato,[8] Aristotle,[9] Augustine[10] and Aquinas,[11] until the current day (Etienne Gilson,[12] Jacques Maritain,[13] Bernard Lonergan,[14] Mortimer Adler,[15] James Ross,[16] Alvin Plantinga,[17] and even mathematicians such as G.J. Whitrow,[18] to name only a few.) It therefore took on various names given by theologians, philosophers, physicists, mathematicians, and simple people of faith: "the Creator," "Pure Being," "Unconditioned Existence," "Being itself," "Power itself," "Unconditioned Power," "Timeless Power," "the First Cause," "Ultimate Ground of Being," "Creator of Being," etc.

The followers of Plato referred to the objective of this desire as Being itself, Goodness itself, Truth itself, and Beauty itself. They further imply that these perfections are one in the same being. Augustine and his followers view Plato's transcendentals as attributes of an infinite, absolutely unique, ultimate ground of being (God).

Physicists since the time of Aristotle have frequently associated this Being with an Uncaused Cause, a First Cause, an Unmoved Mover, a First Mover, a Creator. The creation event has been configured in a multiplicity of ways throughout the ages, and now is particularly rich in light of the possibilities suggested by quantum and big bang cosmology.[19]

Obviously, this ultimate reality has been reflected on by others besides philosophers and physicists. Its most wide ranging reflection takes place in faith and religion. Though not all religions personalize the Ultimate, most do, because love, goodness, justice, and home have an interpersonal quality and seem to reveal, therefore, an interpersonal dimension of the perfect, unconditioned, unrestricted Creator. Hence, faith not only sees this Being as a perfect, unconditioned Cause of all else that is, it attributes consciousness, self-consciousness, intelligence, personal identity, and even interpersonal identity to it.

Most faith traditions go beyond this. They associate love with the interpersonal consciousness of the Ultimate. This results from an intuitive awareness that love is one of the highest powers, if not *the* highest power, in human beings, making it likely that the Creator could not be completely devoid of it.[20] If the Creator created human beings to be ultimately fulfilled through love (through interpersonal personhood), it seems likely that the Creator would not only have to be cognizant of this ultimate form of fulfillment, but in some way possess it. This loving, interpersonal, unconditional Creator is normally given a name such as "God, " or "the Lord."

In many faith perspectives, God is recognized to be more than loving Creator. God is interested in our lives, for we are thought in some way to be made in the image of God, or to share in some finite way in a divine power (e.g., creative intelligence, the cognizance of good and evil, love, freedom, even the very desire and recognition of infinity and eternity). God's love is manifest not only in sharing God's power and life with us, but also in leading us to the fullness of life, including eternal life in the divine domain. We respond to God's loving initiative through prayer, worship, knowledge of Sacred texts, and trying to live a life commensurate with God's will. This constitutes a relationship that philosophers characterize in a variety of ways: the infinite passion of faith (Soren Kiergegaard), creative fidelity (Gabriel Marcelle), I-Thou (Martin Buber), etc.

Whether or not we call the Ultimate a "Higher Power," "Unconditioned Power," "Uncaused Cause," "Timeless Being," "Infinite Being," "the Creator," a "Conscious Deity," "Limitlessness," "Unrestricted Being," the "Loving God," the "Triune God;" or even if we do not believe in an Ultimate, we all seem to have one thing in common: a *desire* for the unconditional, perfect, absolute, and ultimate, which makes all finite and transitory beings incapable of fulfilling it.

10 The Role of Faith in Inspired Leadership

We may now return to the subject of human happiness, specifically, the fourth level of happiness. Though the desire for ultimacy/God is present to us (even as children), it is most poignantly recognized when we are forced to confront the inadequacy of H1, H2, and H3. This chapter is devoted to revealing the inadequacy of H3 when our desire for H4 (the desire for perfect, unconditional, and even unrestricted Truth, Love, Fairness, Beauty, and Home—i.e., God) is most active.

At first glance, it seems as if a Level 3 disposition can eliminate the anxieties of the comparison game. However, rooting our attitudes in contribution does not mean that the journey is over. Our desire for the ultimate gives rise to the problems mentioned in Chapter 9. The central problem is: if we do not recognize H4 and its needs, we will try to satisfy our desire for H4 (the ultimate, unconditional, and perfect) with the fruits of H3. Despite their goodness, the fruits of H3 cannot satisfy H4 desire for the ultimate, unconditional, and perfect; therefore, H3 will seem inadequate, frustrating, or even a betrayal. Since every cynic is born out of dashed idealism, this crisis might be entitled, "from idealism to cynicism."

Problems Arising out of H3, and their Resolutions

Again I emphasize a general principle about fulfillment, meaning, and happiness: If you allow H2, H3, or H4 to be the horizon for H1, then H1 will be healthy (non-compulsive) because it will not become an end in itself. Similarly, if you allow H3 or H4 to be the horizon of H2, then H2 will remain healthy because achievements, comparative advantage, and recognition will not become ends in themselves. Finally, if H4 is the horizon of H3, then H3 will be healthy because finite and conditioned goods, loves, and ideals will not become ends in themselves and, therefore, will not be mistaken for perfect, absolute, unconditional, ultimate, and even infinite and eternal goods, loves, and ideals. Just as H2 can be kept healthy with H3 as its horizon, H3 can be kept healthy with H4 as its horizon.

The human desire for unconditional truth, love, goodness, beauty, and home/peace at once inspires our creativity and striving (positive effect) while inciting us to expect perfect satisfaction from imperfect realities (negative effect). Sometimes we can carry this negative effect to an extreme by expecting a human being to be the perfect satisfaction of all five desires for the unconditional (e.g., "Would you please be perfect and unconditioned Truth, Love, Goodness, Justice, Beauty, and Home for me? And I will do my best to be the same for you, because my love is true.") Obviously, true love has been confused with perfect and unconditional Love, which will sow the seeds of its own destruction.

We do not stop there. If you can supply all these things to me and I can do likewise, why not just sum it all up and ask, "Would you please be perfect and unconditional happiness, meaning in life, and being for me? And I will do my best to be perfect and unconditional happiness, meaning in life, and being for you." The annals of human love, thereby, are transformed into the annals of human tragedy.

By the time I begin to sort out this misidentification between true love and perfect and unconditional love, a relationship once filled with care, natural connection, kindness, delight, self-gift, and joy has turned into dashed expectations, frustration, disappointment, and sorrow. This, of course, only gradually manifests itself to me.

As the first signs of imperfection, conditionedness, and finitude begin to emerge in the beloved, I show slight irritation but have hopes that the ideal will soon be recaptured (as if it were ever captured to begin with). But as the fallibility of the beloved begins to be more acutely manifest (the other is not perfectly humble, gentle, kind, forgiving, self-giving, and concerned with me in all my interests) the irritation becomes frustration, which, in turn, becomes dashed expectation: "I can't believe I thought she was really the 'one.' " Of course, she wasn't the One, because she is not perfect and unconditioned. Nevertheless, the dashed expectation becomes either quiet hurt or overt demands, both aimed at extracting a higher level of performance from the beloved. When she does not comply, alas, perhaps the relationship should be terminated.

I, for my part, also have a rather large responsibility to live up to, for I have implicitly promised that I would do my best to be perfect and unconditional Truth, Love, Goodness, Justice, Home, Peace, Happiness, and Meaning in life for my beloved. I have found myself experiencing certain shortcomings in this regard, requiring that some rather elaborate façades be constructed. These could turn into outright lies if need be, or if I'm good at it, I could just continue to hide the real me from my beloved. "One day I can get rid of all those imperfections in the real me, and then she can see me as I am; but right now, I'd better let the me I want her to see be the real me." Regrettably, I slip up. She inexorably finds out little details leading to other little details that open the way to self-exposure. "I hate her nosiness...her prying into my subjectivity. Her incessant desire to want to get in and see my weakness. It will not happen. Yet, I think she might see it."

Clearly enough, this relationship is not going to grow, if it is able to last beyond five tumultuous years. The root problem was not with the authenticity of this couple's love for one another. It did not arise out of a lack of concern, care, and responsiveness, a desire to be self-giving, responsible, self-disciplined, and true. Rather, it arose out of a false expectation: "Would you be the perfect and unconditioned for me? And I'll be the perfect and unconditioned for you." In the words of faith, "Would you be god for me? And I'll be god for you."

Why do we fall prey to what seems to be such an obvious error? Because our *desire* to love and to be loved is unconditional, but our actuality is conditioned. Our desire is for the perfect, but our *actuality* is imperfect. We, therefore, cannot satisfy one anothers' desire for the unconditional and the perfect. If we do not have a *real* unconditional and perfect Being to satisfy this desire, we start looking around us to find a surrogate. Other human beings at first seem like a very good surrogate, because they display qualities of self-transcendence. Hence, we confuse one another for the perfect and unconditioned, and undermine the very relationships that hold out opportunities for growth, depth, joy, common cause, and mutual bondedness.

We do not stop at trying to extract all six aspects of transcendentality from other human beings, we also attempt to extract them from imperfect and conditioned manifestations of truth, goodness/justice, beauty, and home/peace. With respect to truth, history is replete with examples of brilliant men and women trying to find the Perfect and Unconditioned in philosophy, science, mathematics, and literature, but there always seems to be some unanswered question that gets in the way of perfect intelligibility being fully manifest. There always seems to be some flaw in what could otherwise have been a perfect system. These disenchantments have, on many occasions, brought the brilliant from the heights of complete self-confidence, to the depths of dashed rationalism causing them to protect invalid ideas and systems beyond their time. Something has gone awry in these authentic and dedicated seekers of truth. Again, the problem is not with the thirst for truth and knowledge, and the love of the process of inquiry, but rather with trying to extract perfect and unconditioned truth from an imperfect and conditioned world.

With respect to goodness/justice, we need only look at last year's newspapers to find a host of well-meaning, dedicated and generous men and women who have tried to extract the perfect and unconditioned from the legal system, the ideals of social justice, and social institutions dedicated to the common good. The despairing rhetoric of dashed idealism and cynicism does not belong solely to early Marxism; it can be found in public defenders who decry the legal system for prosecuting the innocent, and victims who vilify the very same system for letting the guilty go free. It can also be found in educators who criticize the educational system for not setting strong enough standards, and in community advocates who tear down the very same system for making the standards too high and too exclusive. Who is right? Aren't both parties well-intentioned, committed, looking out for the good of society, trying to help? Again, the problem seems not to be so much one of searching for justice and goodness, but rather for seeking perfect and unconditioned Justice and Goodness in an imperfect, conditioned world.

We can see the same problem manifest in the artistic community. When we read the biographies of great artists, musicians, and poets we sense the tragedy with which art is frequently imbued. What causes these extraordinarily gifted men and women to abuse themselves, to judge themselves so harshly, to so totally pour themselves into their art? Perhaps it's because their art becomes their god, which makes them try to extract perfect and unconditional Beauty from imperfect and conditioned minds and forms.

Myriad cases manifest the problems arising out of talented people trying to extract the perfect and unconditioned from an imperfect and conditioned world. If we are to stop torturing ourselves, to cease becoming cynical about what is most precious in our lives—our beloveds, ideals, knowledge, and creativity—if we are to stop undermining ourselves in every pursuit that holds out the potential for self-transcendence, we must make sure that the objective for which we are searching can be found in the domain in which we are looking. We cannot be looking for the unconditioned in the domain of the conditioned.

For those with faith in a personal God, this would mean, quite simply, "Let God be God, let creatures be creatures, and let things be things." The way to overcome the problems associated with self-transcendence is to pray to the loving God, to establish a deeper relationship with God, and to include God in every aspect of our journey. Not only will God be the Ultimate that we really seek, God will be the source of grace and love drawing people of faith to the divine life—the only life that can ultimately satisfy.

If you do not believe in God, you still encounter the same problems, but you cannot call upon God or faith to help resolve them. These problems could, however, be mitigated by an act of negation: "I will not make anything that is imperfect, conditioned, or finite into an unconditioned, perfect Ultimate."

Reaching Happiness 4 is only the *beginning* of human transcendence. The life of faith and prayer brings Level 4 to its long-term completion. Faith and prayer can lead to a fulfillment of our desire for the perfect and unconditional by bringing us to habits that will transform our lives and organizations. Merely embracing the truth of Happiness 4 is not enough. We must *live* this truth. Different faith traditions give guidance for how to pursue the life of prayer, worship, journeying with God, and letting God's love for us flow through to the community, and God's love for the community flow into us. The deepening of this relationship with God and the consequent deepening of properly construed self-transcendent love is a lifetime project, but as we pursue it, the fruits do emerge. As these fruits emerge in love, our faith becomes deeper and more certain, and we come to the experiential conclusion that God does not disappoint.

The Role of Faith in Human Transformation

Faith is a choice to enter into a relationship with God. God has invited us to this relationship with the intention of allowing us to participate in the divine life and love forever. Hence, we should fully expect that God wants to help us move into habits that will enable us not only to contribute more to others, but to deepen our relationships, thereby bringing about the unity, peace, hope, generosity, and joy God intends for the world.

Faith and prayer can help bring about the higher viewpoints. The main obstacles to making these higher viewpoints into habits are fear, resentment, attachment, and pride. Prayer and grace (God's response to prayer) help us to move beyond these obstacles in our freedom by introducing peace into situations of fear, forgiveness into situations of resentment, detachment into situations of attachment, and humble love into situations of pride.

Spontaneous prayers (short prayers of petition) can help us focus our spiritual life on what God is willing to offer us in our times of need. These prayers open us to God's free and loving grace. We can be made aware of God's peace in the midst of fear, God's forgiving love in the midst of resentment, etc. These prayers help us bring faith into every aspect of our lives and relationships.

FAITH IN TIMES OF FEAR

Fear and uncertainty frequently undermine inspired leadership and *esprit de corps*. As you confront a possible negative effect in your career, or assume risks on behalf of your team or organization, you can allow fear or stress to erode your judgment. This, in turn, can affect your perception of the dignity of others, your ethical principles, and your leadership style. It is best to avail yourself of your faith life as quickly as possible in such situations, for the harmful effects of bad judgment may not be immediately apparent.

I recommend the following spontaneous prayer as an incisive way of allowing God's peace to take over a precarious situation.

> Help! Lord, please make some good come out of this potentially bad situation: good for myself, my family, my employees, organization, and stakeholders. Lord, snatch victory from the jaws of defeat.

This prayer is particularly helpful when the world seems to be collapsing around you. Sometimes it seems as if everything that can go wrong is going wrong, and darkness instead of light seems to be at the end of the tunnel.

When I prayed this prayer in particularly hard times, I began to see opportunities amidst what was formerly foreboding and gloom. Prior to saying this prayer, I did not see these opportunities because I was focused on being alone in the darkness. Once the opportunities became manifest, I began to think of strategies for moving toward these opportunities. Even if I was not completely successful, I normally found myself far ahead of where I was before the challenge. Even failures became learning experiences and lent themselves to effective fall-back positions. Of course, I believed that God was helping me in these situations, that His Spirit was present to the minds and hearts of those with whom I worked, and that He was orchestrating the events around me to optimize goodness and love. But more than this, God provided peace that opened upon the judgment to actualize opportunity and the common good in this situation. God not only pushed the gloom back, He made the peace of good judgment a reality.

Another prayer that can be helpful in a situation where you are worried about a potential harm you could have caused to another is:

> Lord, make good come out of whatever harm I might have caused.

Of course, it is important to apologize when you believe you have caused harm to another, but sometimes you might be uncertain, yet worried. Instead of rolling around on your bed at night, feeling guilty and overwhelmed, put the matter into God's hands and let the Lord of love, who works in mysterious ways in the hearts of every person, assist those who may have been hurt by your actions. This prayer has helped me and those with whom I work many times. The power of grace cannot be underestimated.

Another prayer that can be helpful when you are feeling confusion or malaise is:

> Lord, I give up on this particular situation. Please, You take care of it.

You are not giving up on life; you are giving up to God. This prayer is useful when you are trying to "figure yourself out." As you look at all the things that might have caused a negative propensity, you might trace it to causes A, B, and C. These, in turn, may have been caused by X, Y, and Z. These, in turn, may have been caused by D, E, and F, etc. After a while, most people begin to feel overwhelmed because they know they do not have perfect control over who they are, what will happen, or even what has happened to them. But it is not necessary to have complete control. Let God take care of it. God wants to take care of it.

This prayer is also useful at moments when you are feeling acutely overwhelmed. Once I was sent to study in Italy. After six weeks of language courses, I was expected to take all of my classes in Italian. After about 15 minutes of my first class, I realized that I was not able to understand the professor as he spoke rapidly in Italian. I sat there overwhelmed, thinking, "I'm going to flunk this class. I have never flunked a class before in my life." It provoked a bit of panic within me, until I prayed, "Lord, I am powerless. I give up. You take care of it." In that moment, I felt as if steam were coming out of my ears. I sensed God's grace, and I began to calm down. So much so, that I began to understand about one-fourth of what the professor was saying. After a week of calm in the Lord, I understood two-thirds of what he was saying, and eventually the class turned out just fine.

God's peace is far more powerful than the peace we can produce on our own, because it is grounded in His grace that extends far into a future over which we have little control. When He gives us this peace, we need to take it, abide in it, and live our lives in trust of that grace. Rough times could still be ahead, but by trusting in this grace, we can be sure that God's will is bringing good out of this fearful situation.

FAITH AND FORGIVENESS

Faith can be extraordinarily helpful to forgiveness. There have been times in my life when I have been powerless to forgive another human being by myself—times when I have been deeply resentful. This resentment severely inhibited my ability to live for a contributive identity, to see the good news in others, and to enter into common cause. As a consequence, it not only affected my personal growth and happiness, but also my ability to help my stakeholders, optimize my talent in the workplace, and practice the principles of inspired leadership.

My inability to forgive prevented me from forgetting. I would go home at night and play the tape of hurt and injustice again and again. This brooding enervated me, and perhaps worse, caused me to enter into a cycle of feuding and self-destruction. We have all heard the expression, "violence begets violence." It might be also said, "vengeance begets vengeance." No matter how viscerally satisfying vengeance might be, it never produces a personal, interpersonal, communal, or societal good. If personal lives and organizational cultures are not to fall prey to its ever-increasing destructive force, vengeance must be brought to a halt.

The *only* way of putting an end to vengeance is forgiveness. Forgiveness is not forgetting. It is an intention to let go of a just claim against another. Forgetting is far more than this. It is not merely the *intention* to let go, it is the *reality* of letting go. This takes much longer. The greater the hurt, the longer the time required for forgetting. But forgiveness can begin right away.

If you do not forgive, you will not forget. The memory of injustice will fester, resentment will grow, and the desire for vengeance and violence will increase. As you exact your vengeful penalty, the other will surely respond in kind, and the cycle will continue. However, if you do forgive, you will eventually forget, and the destructive cycle will be put to rest. Frequently, growth and self-transformation arise out of this self-sacrificially loving act, and this growth cannot help but lead to a deep appropriation of the principles of inspired leadership.

How can you forgive (intend to let go) of a truly unjust action perpetrated against you? How do you let go of betrayal and cruel insensitivity?

I can only answer for myself that I have been unable to do so without the help of God. Whenever I have tried to will myself to forgiveness, I wind up thinking about the outrageous nature of the cruel action all the more. Instead of helping me to forget, I find myself remembering with greater acuity. I sometimes even exaggerate the other's offense, adding little nuances to his intentions far beyond what was really there. The only way I have been able to overcome the tendency to hold on to the hurt and outrage is to give it to God with this prayer:

> Lord, You are the just and merciful Judge. You take care of that person and situation. I don't want to be dominated by this anymore.

These prayers become vehicles for a peace that I cannot bring to myself or the situation. I know beyond my limited reason, that God will take care of the outrage in His unlimited love and reason. I know I can entrust the grievous offense and its remediation to His wisdom. There is an assurance in the prayer that I cannot give myself, or talk myself into. Prayer is truly a vehicle, a conduit, a pipeline for the peace that enables me to intend letting go, and this intention opens the way not only to forgetting, but also to a transformation of my identity from a comparative focus to a contributive one. Forgiveness, in my life, always brings about a deeper understanding of "looking for the good news in the other," and "seeking common cause that is worthy of us." In my view, the fastest way to achieve these ideals is to forgive deeply and frequently.

The Prayer of All Prayers: "Thy Will be Done"

In the end, all spontaneous prayers are reducible to one underlying prayer:

Thy will be done.

In the vast majority of religious traditions, God is looked upon as loving and good. God's will is likewise viewed as loving and good. Indeed, God's infinite providence orchestrates the panoply of human activities toward the good of all.

Since God's will respects human freedom, human beings can act against what is loving and good; yet God will work through even this to bring out the most loving and good result. This activity of God's is so complex no person or group could even begin to fathom how and why it moves to its unconditionally loving end; yet, people of faith know that in the long term, this is precisely where it will lead. All suffering, in the long term, will lead to growth toward the good; all bleakness will, in the long term, be turned into light. God will not give us trials that His grace will not help us to endure. Indeed, that grace will always bring about a growth, peace, goodness, love, unity, and joy.

After many years of living a life of faith, I can say without question that God's will is not only trustworthy, but beautiful. Even though my trials are not immediately resolved in the ways that I would like, they are eventually resolved in ways much better than I could ever imagine.

I am often inclined to tell God, "Here's how to resolve this fearful situation. I took the liberty of outlining a 14-step plan so You could clearly see how best to make good come out of this situation. I also thought You wouldn't mind my including a timetable for the plan along with it." Needless to say, God's plan leads to places that I cannot lead and respects other people's freedom and needs. Not being God myself, I am unable to accommodate all of this, and so God sometimes allows my plans to fall on hard times (thank God).

God's will is not impending doom. It is not a hardship that I cannot endure. God is not a stoic, thinking to Himself, "I'm going to load some more suffering on Spitzer because he needs to get tougher." God is not a sadist who says, "What does not kill him will make him stronger." God is not waiting around to get even with people for things that they have done 15 years before. God is gentle and humble of heart. That is what it means to be unconditionally good and loving. We do not have to run away from God's will. We need to trust in it; trust in its awesome beauty, its unconditional power to bring goodness out of the seeming limitless diversity of so many people's lives; trust in the affection that the Hebrew prophets termed, *"hesed we emet"*—a parent's love for a child. If we know what unconditional love is for our children, how much more does God manifest this love for all of us who turn to God?

Living the life of faith will bring deep experiential conviction about the truth of trusting in God's unconditionally loving will, and it makes the essential prayer, "Thy will be done," an even more efficacious conduit of grace in our lives.

I say this prayer before I give talks or write books, indeed, before I even look in my calendar. It gives me peace, for I do not want to be successful at something that is not God's will. I would, quite frankly, rather have it crash and burn. But I do want to be successful at whatever is God's will, for then I know that I will be a conduit for goodness, love, and truth in the world. The third and fourth levels of happiness simultaneously come into my life through the coincidence of God's grace and this little prayer, made in faith. This prayer brings peace, and with peace comes the power to do much and to do much well, to have a net positive effect on the world while at the same time being competent, efficacious, and competitive. It is a prayer that brings all four levels of happiness together through the peace that is beyond all understanding.

PRAYER AND ATTACHMENTS

Since we naturally seek the unconditional and perfect (Level 4), we can become attached to conditioned objectives as if they were unconditional. When we do this, we try to derive ultimate meaning and purpose in life from what is conditioned or imperfect. This complete attachment to the conditioned can occur within the domain of Level 1 (e.g., a car), or Level 2 (e.g., getting a promotion), or even Level 3 (e.g., trying to obtain perfect meaning from a human beloved). When this conditioned objective fails to satisfy our desire for the unconditioned, it could produce frustration and even obsession, leading to a general dissatisfaction and malaise about life. Prayer can help us to move beyond such attachments by revealing that the only reality capable of satisfying our desire for the unconditioned is an unconditioned reality, namely, God.

How does prayer work to overcome attachment and obsession? Suppose that I am desirous of a promotion to a particular position, and that I have made this promotion an ultimate purpose of my life. I do not want to recognize this because it goes against my conscious desire to live for contribution and to recognize the intrinsic dignity of others. Nevertheless, the effects of my choice are beginning to manifest themselves. Frustration at little set-backs, guilt about indiscretions caused by my obsession, suspicion of colleagues, the need to obsessively make my strengths and accomplishments known, little put downs of others, unfair politicking, jealousy of others being recognized, lapses in good judgment, and general unrest are causing people to distance themselves from me. I am even feeling alienated from myself. I mask my discomfort with myself and continue my push toward my supposed "ultimate meaning" (my promotion). Things are worsening, but I'm not aware of it.

Prayer is perhaps the easiest and most profound way to recognize blindness toward attachments and obsessions. Generally, overcoming blindness does not arise out of a moment of lucid inspiration in prayer, but rather, in an acute desire to avoid prayer. My first clue that an attachment has become obsessive is my desire to avoid prayer. I will have difficulties praying in the morning. As I try to compose myself in contemplation, I feel a strong compulsion to bolt. I am tacitly aware that my prayer could unleash a host of negative feelings lying just beneath the surface of my active life. As a result, I do not let myself enter this state before God. "I'm just too busy to pray today," "I have to make some phone calls—right now," "Three important insights just occurred to me, and I have to write them down—right now," or, in a moment of lucidity, "I gotta get outa here."

Whenever I think such things before prayer, I am alerted to the probability of an attachment making me go out of control. I don't want to remember my indiscretions because I feel guilty. I don't want to think about my comparative disadvantage because it makes me feel inferior. I do not want to remember another person's hinting at my obsession because I do not want to feel the humiliation of being thought a fool or a hypocrite. Ironically, the very moment when I don't want to think about the negative effects of my attachments, is the moment when I need to think about them most. The point at which I most want to escape from prayer, is the point I need it most. From experience, I know that at this critical juncture, I must ask the Lord of love to reveal my attachment. I need to see this attachment in God's peace and perspective, for this is the only way I can confront and redress it. To look at the attachment without this peace, without being held up by God, would force me to endure virtually endless guilt, fear, anger, frustration, jealousy, and ego-sensitivity. Without peace, I have but one recourse: run.

At the moment when I want to run from prayer I ought to ask the Lord to reveal the attachment that controls me. Once this is done, I can ask the Lord to help me redress it, perhaps by using some of the prayers: "Lord, make good come out of whatever harm I might have caused," "Lord, snatch victory from the jaws of defeat," or "I give up, Lord, You take care of it." These prayers are the conduit of peace that allows me to look at my obsession and its consequences. I can then follow up with "Thy will be done." I can now ask for forgiveness for the times I have offended others, and to begin the long process of letting God's will for my ultimate meaning, purpose, and contribution take precedence over my momentary obsessions. To the extent that I let His peace lead me, I can begin to take on the heart of a truly contributive and inspired leader.

In sum, I suggest the following procedure for moving beyond the destructive, uncontrollable, and hidden attachments that inhibit the process toward inspired leadership:

1) Do not run from prayer. When the impetus to run seems strongest, ask the Lord for clarity and peace to confront the effects of attachment and obsession.

2) Use spontaneous prayers as vehicles for God's peace.
3) Bring that peace into the workplace to redress errors of judgment, to ask for forgiveness, and to reconnect with colleagues and employees.

PRIDE AND PRAYER

Pride is perhaps the most insidious and problematic impediment to positive change. We need new habits to get beyond the pride that inhibits us from making them. This vicious circle bespeaks the need for grace to move beyond the pride that so frequently leads to a fall.

Though there are many suggestions that can be made, ranging from listening to God's word in the Scriptures to worshipping within a faith community, I will here focus on only one, the prayer of prayers—"Thy will be done." This prayer brings God's peace, and enables us to move beyond attachments and fear, by letting go into God's providential hands. This peace leads to the freedom to see myself as I am. I don't have to be the Messiah; I don't have to be the greatest; I don't have to be an ultimate; and I don't have to make other people think that I am—because God is at the center of my universe, and God is taking care of what I cannot do for myself. When people confront me and ask, "Spitzer, how worthy are you?" I can simply respond, "As worthy as God wants me to be, and I suppose that's enough." I don't have to worry about being more worthy, or most worthy.

"Thy will be done," does not vitiate my desire to make contributions; rather, it frees me to see clearly what is true and false, what is worthy of pursuit and what is not, what will lead to life and to death. Peace does not kill ambition or zeal, it purifies it. Calm does not enervate, it energizes. The peace of which I speak does not come from an absence of pressure or fear, it is a peace filled with Truth that is so grounding, I no longer need to trumpet my success, to build a myth, or to garner others' approval of it.

"Thy will be done," said at the beginning of the day and frequently throughout the day, is God's peace filled with grounding Truth, energizing me to contribute, befriend, achieve, compete, and create.

11 Personal Commitments

The more we and our stakeholders embrace attitudes of cooperation and contribution, the more these attitudes will be transported into the culture, and the more an organization will feel, and act out of *esprit de corps*.

Three Action Steps

To move these Level 3 attitudes into the life of the organization, leaders must take three innovative action steps:

1. Move from a "training mentality" to an education mentality. "Training mentality" means "imparting a practical, immediately utilizable skill or skill set." "Education" means "conveying a higher viewpoint to become an empowered, inspired, independent goal-seeker and problem-solver in both the work place and personal life."

By now you know that Chapters 6 to 9 constitute a crash course in character education. They empower and liberate inspired leadership, because they concern the most important questions we can ever ask ourselves, namely, "What is happiness?" and "What is the meaning of life?" These two questions ground every decision we make, every judgement about our self-worth and progress, every goal and vision we construct, every friendship and association we pursue, and, as a result, every thought, passion, dream, conviction, and inspiration we muster as leaders.

Now, you might think that organizations should not be concerned with education because "higher viewpoints toward empowered goal-seeking and problem-solving" are not directly concerned with the manufacturing or delivery of products. Whereas, training *is* directly concerned with the manufacturing and delivery of products. This attitude leads to unbelievable opportunity costs, because it undermines "thinking implementers;" process management; creative, opportunistic, and entrepreneurial thinking; and effective teamwork. It forces leaders to assume a supervisory rather than an inspirational role, and forces stakeholders to be non-thinking drones who simply implement orders and await training for the prescribed new skill set.

The indirect benefits of education are the only antidote to these opportunity costs, for education can be transformed into vision, trust, and spirit—the three intangible characteristics that release creativity, synergy, and entrepreneurial opportunity-seeking. The "training mentality" seems to produce more *esprit de corps,* but a second glance indicates that it only gives the most short-term bang for the buck. If the "high performance" organization is to get long-term bang for its training buck and seize upon every realistic opportunity, it will have to move toward an "education mentality," imparting an educational curriculum such as this text) not merely to leaders, but to all employees.

2. Facilitate assimilative learning. Leaders must also provide assimilative education. The more intangible the content of education, the more it must be repeatedly assimilated. For example, you may require four repetitions with this material before you have sufficient familiarity with it to act on it. Such repetition might come through multiple readings, multiple exposure to video and audio tapes, or some combination of these.

Assimilative education is required for intangible content because most people focus on understanding the general picture in the first exposure, the specific parts in the second exposure, applications of the material in the third exposure, and finally on ways to implement it in their lives in the fourth exposure. We achieve an incremental increase in memory when we achieve an incremental increase in understanding. Hence, our memory curve increases dramatically with each exposure to the material.[1]

Level of Understanding=Level of Utilizable (Active Memory)

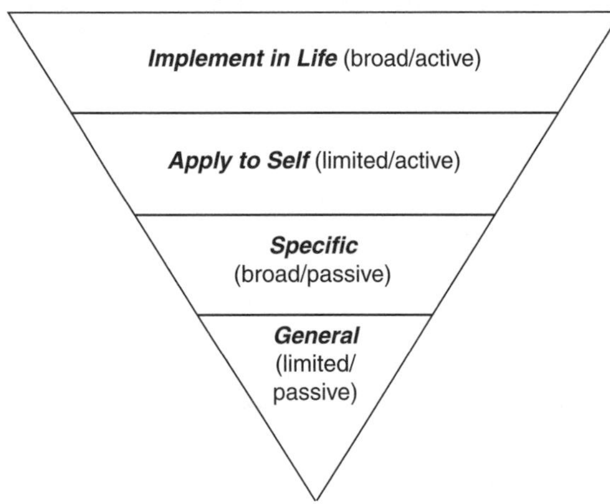

3. Make mutual commitments. In making mutual commitments, we move from transformation of personal attitudes to transformation of organizational culture. These mutual commitments should be public, reciprocal, and formative of group consciousness (ethos).

I now address two kinds of commitments: 1) commitments made to individuals within the culture (e.g., "I commit to you..., and hope that you will commit to me...."), and 2) commitments made to the group about how we do business (e.g., how we look at people, ethics, and leadership). The public nature of commitments makes them the indispensable intermediary between changing one's personal disposition, and changing the organizational culture.

Five Individual Commitments

I have identified five commitments made to individuals within the culture that have the capacity to transform teams almost immediately into high performance, highly communicative, synergistic, quality-driven unities of trust and work.

The Five Commitments for Increasing Trust

I commit that I will...
1) Look for contribution to you and to our common cause before I make any comparisons.
2) Look for the good news in you even if I should see the bad news.
3) Connect with you as a whole person before looking at your skill set and utility function.
4) Look for the "win-win" before settling for the "win-lose."
5) Trust you until you give me ample reason to do otherwise, and I will "cut you plenty of slack" because I realize that, like me, you are not perfect.

1. I commit that I will look for contribution to you and to our common cause before I make any comparisons. This commitment is the foundation for replacing compulsive ego with an attitude of mutual concern. Recall that H2 becomes compulsive when it is thought to be the *only* thing that can bring happiness or meaning in life. Even if this thought is implicit, it can still affect every action, attitude, and relationship within an organization. This commitment can mitigate the "only" that causes compulsive ego and resentment, thereby opening the way to trust. If made authentically and mutually, and modeled by the leadership, this commitment can cause a rapid decrease in the five cultural debilitators (fear, anger, suspicion, passive aggression, and compulsive ego).

How do we make such a commitment? Publicly, mutually, and without expectation of perfection. Commitments must first be public. If we commit "contribution before comparison," our intention is public. We can now call one another to the objective, and help one another to reach the objective. We can make humorous allusions to it when we fail, and use it as the core of common cause.

To be effective, public commitments must be mutual. A one-way commitment is like putting my head on the chopping block. If I commit to you that I will put contribution ahead of comparison, but you do not commit the same back to me, I would effectively be setting myself up to be used or taken for granted. The person taking advantage of me could then say, "Well, I never agreed to look for the common cause before looking out for myself. If that poor fool wants to be generous, that's his problem."

If these commitments are not mutual, and are not expected to be mutual by leadership, they should not be advocated. They will simply give license to compulsive people to annihilate contributory, common cause people. In the end, they could do more harm than good.

Hence, the proper form of the first commitment should be: "I commit to you that I will look for contribution to you and to our common cause before I make a comparison. I expect that you will do the same for me, because that's how we do business."

In making this commitment, we must also allow for imperfection. We cannot expect people to be perfect when they first make a commitment. Indeed, we cannot expect them to be perfect two years from now. There are simply too many situational stresses, marketplace exigencies, personal crises, and lapses in discipline that prevent perfection in any commitment. However, we can pledge to do our best, and we can expect others, within reason, to pledge to do their best. This expectation of "good intent" and "best effort" must recognize human frailty and finitude. We must be prepared for times of exhaustion, stress, personal concerns, and other difficulties that can negatively affect human behavior. This requires yet another rephrasing of the commitment:

> I commit to you that I will look for contribution to you and to our common cause before I make a comparison. I expect that you will do the same for me, because that's how we do business. In making this expectation, I will allow for imperfection and weakness, and hope that you will do the same for me.

2. I commit that I will look for the good news in you even if I should see the bad news. This commitment is a pledge to avoid associating others with their mistakes and failings. When we look for the bad news in others and see it, we become irritated, impatient, judgmental and inclined to associate these others with their mistakes. Since others will notice that we are looking for the bad news, they will respond with defensiveness. This means that most energy will be spent on devising techniques to prevent blame instead of getting a task done. People become indecisive. They need to "check everything with the boss." Creativity reaches an all-time low, and paranoia replaces openness to change. In short, people are unable to take risks and are even closed to thinking about taking risks.

Furthermore, evaluations become quite negative. The accent is no longer on helping people to improve or moving people into areas where they can perform well, but on venting my frustration about mistakes. Because I am looking for the bad news, I become more frustrated and impatient with that mistake than I really need to be. I start associating this mistake with the person, and eventually find myself almost compulsively indicating to her (by my frustrated looks, sighs, or harsh words) that she cannot do anything right. I feel contempt for her, and I have to let her know that she's making my life miserable. If I were to put this in perspective, however, I would see that this person is really not making my life miserable. Her mistakes are inconvenient, little blips on a huge radar screen. By "looking for the bad news" I reduce the person to her mistakes, and make the mistakes far more negative than they really are. I get unduly perturbed and lose psychic energy. She is crestfallen and more defensive than ever.

These negative consequences can be avoided by a simple shift in attitude to seek the good news in a person before making a judgment, to focus on her strengths, her goodwill, her personal qualities and ideals, her whole personhood before I allow myself to be filled with unnecessary impatience and indignation.

This second commitment must also be made publicly, mutually, and without expectation of perfection. It may be rephrased as follows:

> I commit to you that I will look for the good news in you even if I should see the bad news. I expect that you will do the same for me, because that's the way we do business. In making this expectation, I will allow for imperfection and weakness, and hope that you will do the same for me.

If this commitment is made and modeled by leadership to all stakeholders, all stakeholders will feel free to make this commitment back to leadership. Resentment, passive aggression, and negative morale will decrease as leadership credibility increases.

3. I commit that I will connect with you as a whole person before looking at your skill set and utility function. It is easy to focus on a person's skill set or job functions. We look at these skill sets and competencies when we hire people, make evaluations, and put people on teams. Unfortunately, it is easy to overlook the personhood of a colleague or co-worker because of the emphasis we put on skill sets. When we do this, people silently resent it. They don't like being reduced to things or functions. This resentment leads to uneasiness, then to passive aggression, and eventually to bad will. Even people who don't want to manifest discontent or aggression (who avoid conflict) can still be caught up in passive aggression.

Passive aggression is an indirect way of pushing back when we feel oppressed, disrespected, or undervalued. Normally, an employee cannot overtly manifest anger or frustration at being disrespected, so these emotions pop out in "acceptable," ways. "Is that in my job description?" "I don't think I'll have time to do that this week—Mary and Joe have already made requests of me." Even though Mary and Joe's requests may be far less urgent than yours, the employee's negative attitude makes him want to put your request on the bottom of the pile. He will, however, do this with a look of concern and even a "sincere" apology. Again, we can feel the passive aggression as a co-worker says, "I simply don't have the time to do this," or "I don't have the skills or competencies; Bob is much better at this than I am...." Creative avoidance, jobs poorly done, and incessant excusable delays not only slow down performance and production, they lead to a tense atmosphere.

Passive aggression is a key response to continual impatience on the part of the boss, a common response to fear in the workplace, and a major response to feeling undervalued or disrespected. The third commitment is meant to head off this undervaluation and disrespect without diminishing competency in skills and functions—to add respect and dignity to the atmosphere of competency so that the alleviation of passive aggression can help people to become even more self-accountable and competent.

Respecting one's personhood includes valuing the others' subject self (the goodness of their unique presence), their life outside the organization, their ability to be team players, and the goodwill and enthusiasm they offer to their colleagues and co-workers. By attending to these intangible elements of persons, I connect with them as whole human beings. This connection communicates trustworthiness and respect, allowing them to respond more openly and personally.

This human "connection" puts skill sets and function into proportion. I realize that I am not looking at a mere skill set, but at the skill set of a dignified, respectable, familial, connectable human being. This will not only head off passive aggression, it will help others to respect and feel respected in return. The atmosphere of "things under control," can now be replaced by an atmosphere of "people in mutual respect." Self-accountability, creativity, and increased competency grow hand in hand with enhanced respect and dignity.

Since commitments in organizations must be made publicly, mutually, and without expectation of perfection, the third commitment may be rephrased as follows:

> I commit to you that I will connect with you as a person before looking at skill sets and utility functions. I expect that you will do the same for me, because that's the way we do business. In making this expectation, I will allow for imperfection and weakness, and hope that you will do the same for me.

4. I commit that I will look for the "win-win" before settling for the "win-lose." This commitment is the key to converting the first three commitments into an organizational vision. A "win-win" atmosphere decreases the five debilitators by creating an atmosphere of equity and generativity. It also alleviates the problems of "win-lose" relationships that generally become "lose-lose" relationships.

If one stakeholder gets the impression that another is winning at his expense, he will believe that an injustice has been committed. This sense of injustice will lead to passive aggression, and frequently to aggressive aggression. Daily we see examples of employees taking aggressive action against leadership when they feel their leaders are getting rich at their expense. The same holds true for customers feeling slighted by suppliers or suppliers by customers. Even though all are stakeholders, the sense of resentment at injustice will lead the slighted party to seek retribution rather than the common good. This feeling of being slighted will increase the cost of doing business.[2] Absenteeism (in the case of employees), lost market share (in the case of customers), and delays in inventory (in the case of suppliers), all add to opportunity costs. But more than this, indignation or retributive thinking can add significantly to legal costs, monitoring costs, security costs, and flow-time problems. "Win-lose" today generally becomes "lose-lose" tomorrow.

One way to look at this fourth commitment is through "dynamic optimization," the attempt to optimize an ideal in imperfect situations. For example, suppose that you and I belong to distinct groups of stakeholders. You are a manager and I am an employee, or you represent the organization and I represent a vendor. Since a "win" for one stakeholder will become a "win" for all stakeholders over time, a win for employees will become a win for managers, customers, and suppliers. Likewise, a win for customers will, in the long run, be a win for stockholders, managers, employees, and suppliers. Even though stakeholders belong to different groups, they cannot afford to be at odds with one another. If they are, all stakeholders, and the organization as a whole, will suffer.

Now, even though you and I belong to distinct groups of stakeholders and hence our interests are, in some sense, opposed, by implementing dynamic optimization, we can turn a potential "win-lose" situation into a long-term "win-win." Dynamic optimization works by treating the "win-win" as an ideal, while realizing that imperfect situations will not allow the ideal to be actualized every time. So, we must consider four "fall back" positions that are preferable to "win-lose":

1) Win-win: You and I both win more or less equivalently. If the exigencies of a particular situation will not permit an equivalent "win-win," then we default to—

2) Win-less win: one party wins more than the other, but both parties are better off than they were before, and so both parties win. This position will not be effective in the long term

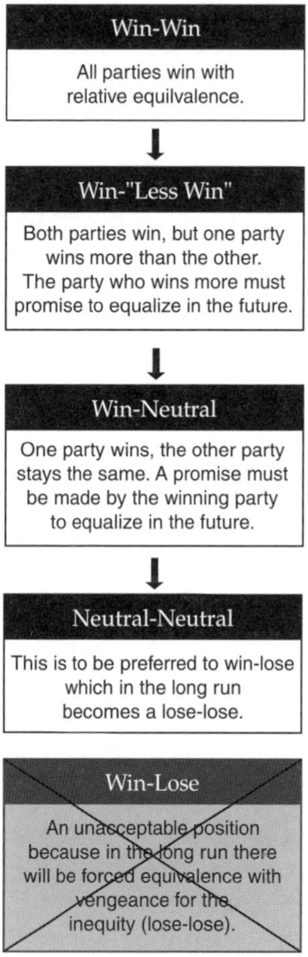

Win-Win
All parties win with relative equilvalence.

↓

Win-"Less Win"
Both parties win, but one party wins more than the other. The party who wins more must promise to equalize in the future.

↓

Win-Neutral
One party wins, the other party stays the same. A promise must be made by the winning party to equalize in the future.

↓

Neutral-Neutral
This is to be preferred to win-lose which in the long run becomes a lose-lose.

~~Win-Lose~~
~~An unacceptable position because in the long run there will be forced equivalence with vengeance for the inequity (lose-lose).~~

unless the relatively advantaged party gives some compensatory reward to the relatively disadvantaged party in the future. If the exigencies of a particular situation will not permit a "win-less win," then we default to—

3) Win-neutral: one party is better off than before while the other party is left about the same. One of the parties has to settle for the status quo so that the other might gain. This position cannot be effective in the long term if the neutral party is not given a compensatory reward in the future. Again, if the exigencies of a particular situation do not permit a "win-neutral" position, we default to—

4) Neutral-neutral: both parties have agreed to stay relatively the same to prevent one party from winning at the other party's loss. "Neutral-neutral" is preferable to "win-lose," for "win-lose" creates resentment on the part of the losing party who may find a way to get even, thereby turning the "win-lose" into "lose-lose" in the long run.

This commitment is an agreement to seek the highest degree of mutual advantage possible, but it also recognizes that the real world frequently does not permit this ideal. Hence, it acknowledges four fall back positions that give parties the freedom to seek the most realistically achievable advantage. As long as advantaged parties attempt to give future compensatory rewards to parties who are relatively disadvantaged in the present, this strategy will bring about long-term benefits to morale, cooperation, team synergy, productivity, adaptability, and quality.

This commitment is not simply a bargaining procedure—it is an attitude that can pervade all stakeholders, thereby maximizing interaction, creativity, and team spirit.

The first three commitments are integral to the fourth, for if both parties pledge contribution to the other and to the common good before comparative advantage, if they pledge to look for the good news in the other even if there is bad news to be seen, if they pledge to see them with dignity and concern before seeing them as functions toward their own separate ends, then the promise of a "win-win" attitude can be believed. If the first three commitments are not made, the fourth commitment will not be believed. The first three commitments only set the stage for the fourth commitment. Once they are made, all concerned parties must follow up in three ways:

1) Agree to dynamic optimization according to the four-step default program,
2) Proactively listen—try to make the other party's concern your own concern when negotiating, and
3) Walking the talk—give the relatively disadvantaged party some future compensatory reward. History and action speak louder than words.

This strategy may at first appear to be overly gratuitous, but in the long run, it will prove to be remarkably effective in building trust, team unity, co-ownership, openness to change, and the capacity to take reasonable risks.

It will allow all stakeholders to work together, make implementers into thinking implementers, convert opposed interests into common cause, and make the workplace something to look forward to instead of a rat's nest of blame, politicking, manipulation, retribution, and hurt. If we can unite the first three commitments to the fourth commitment, and follow through on our promises, we create a maximally efficacious people system and a maximally quality-driven organization.

Like the first three commitments, the fourth commitment must be made publicly, mutually, and without expectation of perfection. Hence, it may be rephrased as follows:

> I commit to you that I will look for the "win-win" before the "win-lose." I expect that you will do the same for me, because that is the way we do business. In making this

expectation, I will allow for imperfection and weakness, and hope that you will do the same for me.

5. "I will trust you until you give me ample reason to do otherwise, and I will 'cut you plenty of slack' because I realize that, like me, you are not perfect." This commitment is the culmination of the first four commitments. If both parties make the first four commitments to one another, they are declaring themselves to be trustworthy. This movement from threat to trustworthiness allows people to take risks for common cause. Sticking your neck out is no longer likely to result in getting it chopped off, but in helping the whole body to move forward to a position of mutual advantage. Most people want to be competent. They want to do a good job and to make a vital contribution to a common enterprise. This is a normal human instinct.

If the commitment to trust is to take hold, it cannot be based on a standard of perfect trustworthiness. People will make mistakes. They will succumb to pressure, egoism, and fear. They will be tired, stressed, and experience bad moods. So, we can only condition trust on realistic trustworthiness. This means trying to understand another person's possible failings, and making allowance for the pressures and exhaustion in their lives. It even means allowing for mistakes in judgment, (even ethical judgments).

I do not mean to suggest here that we should not seek accountability and responsibility from others, but only that if someone should appear irresponsible, we should first temper our dashed expectations; second, inquire into the possible reasons for the seeming irresponsibility; and third, allow the other to regain his dignity in the least costly way. If the irresponsible party is not given the chance to regain dignity, he will no longer be allowed to be self-accountable, and self-accountability, after all, is what we are seeking. "Cutting slack," forgiveness, and even bending over backwards to allow another to regain fallen dignity are essential for the promotion of long-term trust. Without these tools, self-righteousness is likely to replace trust, undermining the spirit of unity, common cause, and humane interdependence.

Five Questions for Cultivating Trust
1) Am I looking for contribution to others and the common good before making comparisons and seeking ego-gratification?
2) Am I looking for the good news in others, even when I see the bad news?
3) Am I connecting with people as dignified, whole persons (the "who") before looking at their skill sets and utility functions (the "what")? Am I connecting with their subject selves (empathy) before looking at their object selves?
4) Am I looking for fairness and contribution to my stakeholders ("win-win") before looking for advantage over my stakeholders ("win-lose")? Am I doing this at work? In my family? In my community?
5) If people have not given me a reason to be suspicious, do I give them the trust they deserve? Do I expect people to be human or perfect before I give them my trust?

Like the other four commitments, the fifth commitment must be made publicly, mutually, and without expectation of perfection. Hence, it may be rephrased as follows:

> I will trust you until you give me ample reason to do otherwise, and I will "cut you plenty of slack" because I realize that, like me, you are not perfect. I expect that you will do the same for me, because that is the way we do business. In making this expectation, I will not only allow for imperfection and weakness, but will also excuse you when possible, and forgive you always as a person. I hope that you will do the same for me.

By producing the trust necessary for people to take risks, these five commitments allow people to set higher goals, and put themselves out on the line without fearing the repercussions of blame, politics, and manipulation. These commitments allow an organization not only to formulate, but to live according to a higher vision.

These five personal commitments are good business. Why? Because they are good in themselves—good for colleagues and employees, and good for their families. They give rise to a culture filled with hope, fun, spirit, energy, and creativity. They open the way to growth, change, adaptability, and synergies with customers, suppliers, and community.

At first glance, such positive attitudes may seem too "nice" to be profitable. It may seem as if profitability needs to have a blunt edge. Hundreds of clichés imply this ("Nice guys finish last," "No one can afford to be generous...." etc.). But such clichés are generally misleading, because they do not take into consideration opportunity costs and negative transaction costs among sensitive and educated populations.

When leaders consider the cost of lost opportunity, then humane and generative attitudes translate directly into "bottom line" profitability. Personal commitments decrease waste, absenteeism, turnover, product defects, transactional costs, and opportunity costs. They therefore lead to better quality, larger market share, more efficient inventory control, and more exploited opportunities. In short, these commitments are not simply good for people; they're good for growth, new revenue, and therefore, return on investment. Contributive attitudes are simultaneously good for people and for business. Leaders can afford to have a heart. Indeed, they can't afford not to have one.

PEOPLE COMMITMENTS

In the previous chapter, I discussed five personal commitments integral to the heart of inspired leaders. The more these commitments are embraced by all stakeholders, the more adaptable, team-oriented, and growth-oriented the organization will be. Once most leaders and employees buy into these commitments, they will pave the way for an extraordinarily powerful group ethos that lies at the foundation of *esprit de corps*. When this group ethos is strong, the sympathy, emotion, and even passion for spirit and common cause toward the common good is equally strong. Conversely, weakness in group ethos produces weakness in sympathy, emotion, passion, spirit, and common cause.

If spirit and ethos are to be kept alive and strong, they must be nurtured not only by individual or personal commitments, but also by group commitments. Group ethos needs not only to be defined, but given a life of its own. This is done through a series of group beliefs or commitments. The next three sections outline three sets of group commitments that strengthen group ethos and lead to the sympathy, emotion, and passion of true *esprit de corps*:

1) commitments about people (Chapter 12),
2) commitments about ethics (Chapter 13), and
3) commitments about leadership (Chapters 14-18)

12 Commitments About People

How can you help form a view of people that will not only adapt to the highly complex and rapidly changing environment, but also to the increased need for inspiration, teamwork, trust, and spirit? I recommend a three-step strategy:

1) Note the changed work environment;
2) Challenge outdated cliches; and
3) Encourage growth in competency and personhood.

1. Note the Changed Work Environment

The way that the work environment has changed in the last 20 years may be summed up in seven points:

1) Higher education is becoming more prolific, as an increasing percentage of our work force needs to be college educated.
2) Theory Y management is more successful than Theory X, and modifications to Theory Y (sometimes called "Theory Z") are even more successful.
3) The quality movement required greater self-accountability and team accountability.
4) The movement from "stockholders" to "stakeholders" revealed the need for a "win-win" attitude. Even if stakeholders have different needs and expectations, making sure that all stakeholders are in a relatively equal winning position will optimize benefit in the long run.
5) Advances in industrial psychology showed, among other things, the effects of passive aggression, suspicion, and personality differentiation in the workplace.

6) Empowerment became essential. Increasing complexity required leaders to organize into smaller, local units with sight lines through all parts of the process. Management had to come closer to where the production and services were being accomplished to respond to customer needs. This meant relying on the knowledge and creativity of those closest to the sources of work and customer relations. The heightened need for "thinking implementers" gave rise to the so-called "empowerment" movement. The first attempts at empowerment were unsuccessful because managers tried to empower autonomous individuals. This revealed the need to empower through teams.
7) Attempts to achieve high-performance teaming have had their ups and downs. Some initial attempts led to mediocrity, causing several observers to criticize teams. Nevertheless, teams are the only way organizations can become more complex yet more adaptable. They are the only way we can get increased specialization of labor, self-motivation, and individual creativity while achieving increased *group* motivation, creativity, and energy.

2. *Challenge Outdated Clichés*

Once leaders experience the new working environment, they will see the counterproductivity of well-known clichés. Before examining these clichés, let's recall the most fundamental principle about people: "People want to be treated as people. When they are not, they become defensive, passive aggressive, and sometimes even aggressive aggressive." If people are not treated as people, morale suffers, the atmosphere in the firm is "unhappy," energy is depleted, and people start playing games. Therefore, spirit wanes.

People feel as if they are not being respected and treated as people when we treat them callously (i.e., without regard for their feelings), when we use them without compensating or thanking them, when we blame them for our failings, when we manipulate them, when we deliberately pursue the "win-lose," when we feel, because of our position, that we are superior to them as people, and when we overreact to mistakes and judge them by reducing them to those mistakes.

People always know when we are not operating in their best interests, and they can even pick up "vibes" about our negative intentions. When we disrespect people, they will disrespect us as people. This disrespect has consequences ranging from extreme defensiveness to passive aggressiveness and aggressive aggressiveness. Eventually, everyone becomes a loser.

When we treat people as things, as mere units of production, as skill sets, as units of labor, as things without beliefs, emotions, integrity, family, and commitments—as if they are only concerned with comparison and competition—we insult them and deprive them of personhood. These signs of disrespect produce the same effects in the long run.

Tacit signals of disrespect are far more dangerous than overt ones for they seem more excusable. The more tacit signs are protected by clichés such as, "I hired this person for her skills, that's the only thing that matters," or "When it comes to evaluations, personal qualities are insignificant. What really matters is, can they get the job done well?" or "If I'm going to make an objective assessment of costs and the efficiency of processes, I have to treat people as units of production, labor, and cost." or "What really matters is a decent return on investment. Everything else is icing on the cake." The insidious part of these clichés is that they are all at least 50 percent true, but they all contain false dichotomies which, in the end, amount to serious errors of omission. These undermine our businesses.

Let's examine four clichés up close.

1. "A person is hired for her skills." Of course, no one wants an incompetent person to be carrying out a vital job function. Indeed, we want the most competent person. But when we hire, we hire a person, not a skill set. The falsity in the cliché is to leap from our interest in a person's competency and skills, to having to be disinterested in her personhood. For some reason, good and fair employers think that they have to ignore the personal dimensions of their employees. They think those dimensions will cloud their objectivity about evaluation and planning. When most leaders reduce people to skill sets, they do it not out of malice or selfishness, but out of loyalty and the desire for objectivity.

Leaders will have to change this cliché radically. Rather than think, "I must keep my attention fixed on person X's skill sets and competencies by ignoring her personal characteristics," a leader might substitute, "I want to attend to my employees' skills and competencies by attending to their personal characteristics. I want to know them as persons because I want to know how to reach and inspire them, how to connect with and thank them, so that I can help them to form spirited and synergistic teams grounded in trust. If I do not attend to their personal qualities, I cannot free them to use their skills and competencies in the most creative, self-accountable, spirited, and team-oriented way."

Organizations cannot afford to hire on the basis of skills and competencies alone. As the complexity and changeability of the workplace increase, as quality margins get tighter, as teamwork becomes more essential, as passive aggressive behavior becomes more destructive, we must hire people not only for their skills, but for their personal characteristics. To hire a skill set instead of a person would severely undermine morale. It would make process management, systems management, and high-performance teaming virtually unattainable in the future.

2. ***"When it comes to evaluations, personal qualities are insignificant. What really matters is, can they get the job done well?"*** Anybody involved in high-performance teaming knows that many individuals can get the job done, but they destroy the unity, trust, and cohesiveness of the team. Their contempt and arrogance, followed by their fear and aggression, followed by resentment and emptiness, makes everyone leery and defensive. One minute of their presence is enough to drive every other team member into complacency ("All right, you do it. We have nothing to offer. You go ahead. You win."). The team suddenly begins to think of passing the buck, protecting themselves, or pleasing the superstar, instead of thinking like a team and offering particular competencies to the team in a spirit of self-sacrifice and common cause. Consequently, teaming leads to mediocrity because it never rises above the level of one or two individuals. Nevertheless, none of us can do as much as all of us. Hence, skills are not the only thing that matters in a job interview. The capacity to be a contributing team player is just as important. The important thing is not so much that "he gets the job done,"

but that "we can get the job done with him." The failure to recognize personal qualities undermines the capacity to adapt, to tackle complex problems that are beyond one or two people, to operate as a team, and to be creative.

Competitive behaviors that once seemed appropriate might destroy our organizations. We cannot turn the clock back; we cannot make the world less complex; we cannot slow down the pace of change; we can't make people less sensitive. Organizations need leaders who can adapt to highly complex environments.

3. "To make an objective assessment of costs and the efficiency of processes, I have to treat people as units of production, labor, and cost." At first glance, this cliché is as true as the others. Whenever we use quantitative scales or metrics to assess certain processes, we are forced to treat people as units. There is simply no way around this. But this does not justify treating them like units of production or labor when we are not making quantitative assessments. Indeed, when we do so people feel it. They know they are being reduced to a unit of something. They will probably not react with hurt feelings or anger because that's likely to get them in trouble. But they will react to the assault on their worth through passive aggression which undermines the organization. Again, the solution lies in assessing a person's skills and competencies by attending to her personal qualities.

4. "What really matters is a decent return on investment. That's what keeps our organization alive. Everything else is icing on the cake." This cliché is perhaps the most limiting and dangerous. Return on investment is essential. It not only provides for shareholder value, it also provides the financial momentum to continue operations in the future. If it is ignored, the organization will surely meet an early demise. However, if return on investment is seen to be the only bottom line—if everything else is seen to be mere "icing on the cake"—then the organization will not have the team unity and thinking implementers to adapt to change. An organization's capacity to change in relation to its environment is directly proportional to the capacity of its people to adapt, and its teams to achieve synergy. If an organization fails in its "people system," it will fail. By calling "everything else" icing on the cake, leaders relegate the adaptability and teaming capacity of people to secondary importance—a grave error, for it allows competitors with a higher capacity for adaptation to take over the market.

We see in biology how more adaptable organisms take over the environment of less adaptable ones. Organizations are subject to these same laws, though in a social context. If they cannot adapt, they will die. What is the adapting mechanism of an organization? Its product? Its processes? Its structures? Its policies? Obviously not. These things are all conditioned by time. The means of adaptation must be a creative, willful, synergistic, spirited person.

In short, people are the only source of adaptation. If they are encouraged to be compulsive instead of self-accountable, to be defensive instead of synergistic, to be autonomous instead of team-oriented, the creative means of adaptation will suffer, and so will the organization, leaving it prey to any upstart or mutant that would take over its habitat. In organizations, survival is dependent on spirit, because survival requires adaptability; adaptability requires creativity, unity, and self-efficaciousness; and all these depend on spirit. If people are only the "icing on the cake," then future return on investment is seriously in question. The only way out is to educate leaders to take account of both return on investment and the people system simultaneously.

Once leaders fully appreciate the need for good people to adapt to ever-increasing change, they must challenge the clichés that drag the environment back into comparitive and competitive thinking. These clichés must be exposed for the destructive partial truths that they express. Instead of laughing with them, leaders must laugh at them.

3. Encourage Growth in Competency and Personhood

To account for the atmosphere, morale, unity, team synergy, self-accountability, and creativity of their stakeholders, leaders need to look beyond competencies and skill sets to personal characteristics. Unfortunately, competencies and skill sets are much easier to recognize and value, because leaders are trained to evaluate them, and skills are easily subjected to quantitative metrics. Leaders must now be educated to help foster characteristics that are rarely recognized or valued.

Forming a people strategy is to take account of characteristics and strengths of stakeholders that will help the organization to adapt to the changed environment. Seven characteristics are relevant here.

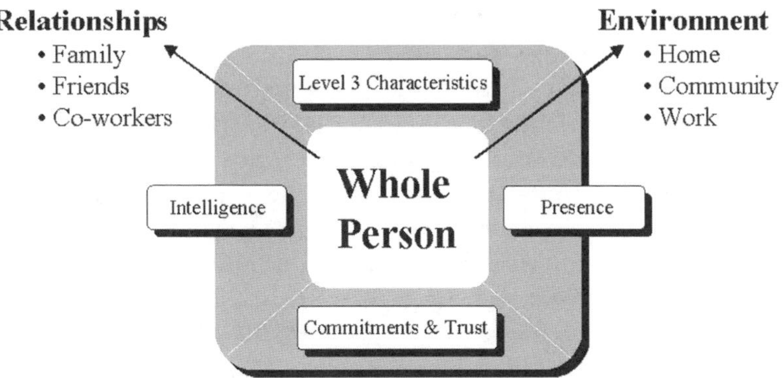

1. Characteristics of stakeholders. To move toward a cohesive team, leaders will have to be attentive to competitive compulsions both in themselves and in their stakeholders. This means not only being aware of the fear, blame, resentment, and passive aggression in the culture, but also the sources of these conditions within people and reward structures. Since these conditions are unpleasant, it is all too easy to turn a blind eye to them. Hence, leaders must act counterintuitively. They must take a good look at these unpleasant conditions, and formulate strategies to move beyond them.

Leaders must also note the positive attitudes and qualities in the culture. When they see stakeholders wanting to contribute, to look for the good news, to act for common cause, they must recognize the intrinsic value of these characteristics and encourage them within the group. Public encouragement of these characteristics, giving special recognition to certain individuals, is extraordinarily useful. Leaders must also help their stakeholders to see these characteristics in one another so that they become less reliant on leadership to foster them within teams.

2. Presence of the individual (the subject self). People have both an object self and a subject self. The "object self" refers to degrees, skill sets, competencies, position, and income. The "subject self" refers to a core of the individual that is not reducible to any particular thing or characteristic. Inasmuch as it is not an overt characteristic, it is somewhat intangible and difficult to classify. And, because it is unique to each individual, it is almost impossible to quantify. It is a unique way of connecting with others; a unique bonding in friendship; a unique smile, gaze, glance; a unique history, ideal, decision—all bound together in a unique, indivisible presence. This unique, indivisible presence is what we connect with and enjoy about one another. It is therefore the source of common cause, and the source of synergy.

Synergy is that connectedness and enjoyment of others that enhances creativity and energy within individuals. It allows 1 + 1 to equal 5 (more than double what individuals could do by themselves). It circumvents the laws of physics by allowing us to gain energy from work instead of losing it. It is, therefore, the key to teamwork, risk-taking, energy, creativity, and quality. If presence truly is the key to synergy, and synergy is the key to teamwork and quality, leaders must not only take account of it, but also foster it. Even though it is intangible and difficult to quantify, leadership must take pains to integrate it into their overall vision of people.

3. Commitments and trust. How committed are stakeholders? Do they operate out of "freedom from" or "freedom for?" Do they exude trustworthiness? Do they trust others? Are they capable of looking for the "win-win," or are they mired in the "win-lose?" Leaders cannot answer these questions unless they are attuned to them. Since these characteristics are vital to highly adaptable, team-oriented organizations, the faster leaders recognize them as valuable and foster them among stakeholders, the more their capability to adapt will be developed.

4. Intelligence. What are their dominant learning styles? Thinking styles are evidenced by learning styles. Four kinds of learning styles are required for outstanding adaptability and teamwork: 1) learning by ideas, 2) learning by observation, 3) learning by doing, and 4) learning by feeling. I purposely do not use the phrase "learning by experience" because it could refer to any or all of the four learning styles. Most people have two dominant styles and two recessive styles, though some can have one extremely dominant style leading to three recessive styles. People possess all four styles either as dominants or recessives.

Those who think and learn by ideas tend to be integrative. They enjoy having a superstructure on which to hang and interrelate all their units of thought and learning. They tend to be theoretical, systemic, and complex. They enjoy professions like mathematics, physics, philosophy, and logic because they put the world of thought into a highly integrated and systematic whole.

Those who think and learn by observation allow the world to reveal itself. They enjoy probing the world for a new piece of data, taking a machine apart to discover how it works, finding a new road to get to the same place. Novelty, surprise, and discovery excite them just as integration, foundation, and systemization excite the "idea" people. This group is more interested in the concreteness of the world than in its theoretical underpinnings. They tend to enjoy professions such as engineering, sociology, behavioral psychology, chemistry, and research biology. In business, they frequently mediate and translate between the "idea thinkers" (theoreticians) and the "doing thinkers" (the thinking implementers). They provide data to the theoreticians and provide concreteness to the doers.

Those who think and learn by doing enjoy practical tasks that can rarely be learned by any other means than "hands on." They enjoy putting their hands to the keyboard, getting behind the wheel, or trying out a new machine. These people rarely read directions. They would rather figure it out by pushing the button or pulling the lever. They are fascinated at seeing how things work by working with them. They have a knack for figuring out new ways of doing things. They enjoy technical professions and working with machines. They frequently pursue engineering, line managing, computing, and other critical skills professions.

Those who think and learn by feeling are fascinated by people. They have an intuition of what makes people tick, people's moods, and who would work well with whom. They are fascinated with the subject self, and are accustomed to using metaphor to express the intangible. They are attentive to the feelings of others and can feel the atmosphere of a group. They pursue literature, fine arts, poetry, music, psychology, and human resources. They become increasingly more important to the organization as teaming, adaptability, and communications become increasingly important.[1]

Since most people have two dominant and two recessive styles, there are many combinations of thinking styles that can help with every problem imaginable. Unfortunately, each individual tends to value his or her learning style the most. Groups can be even more prejudicial about their dominant learning style. This prejudice has two negative effects. It leads to a devaluation of a person with a different dominant learning style, and it undermines adaptability and team behavior because all four learning styles are necessary for optimal adaptability and team unity. Therefore, leaders need to recognize the value of all four learning styles, to overcome prejudices against their own recessive styles, and to organize teams to best use all four.

5. Relationships with co-workers, friends, and family. Leaders need to recognize that people are fundamentally interpersonal. Even though this interpersonal dimension requires autonomy, self-appropriation, and independence, most persons' actions arise out of, and go back to, interdependence with others. We need one another's feedback, concern, understanding, and presence to get the energy and purpose necessary for both happiness and efficacy. The better grounded our relationships, the more energy and creativity we have. Leaders will want to recognize and support the three fundamental relationships: family, friends, and co-workers. When leaders are supportive of good family relationships and family time, stakeholders not only gain energy and creativity, they willingly help when crunch time comes at work. By facilitating connection and friendship among co-workers, leaders can decrease fear, resentment, and compulsion in the workplace, and foster the trust and synergy necessary for adaptability and teaming.

6. Environment. Ironically, if leaders want to move the organization to a more cohesive and adaptable unity, they have to see people in environments beyond the organization. Supporting people in their home and community environments makes them feel as if they really belong to the organization. A person will allow the ethos of one environment to affect other environments to the extent that each environment supports the others. Hence, if an organization supports the home environment (instead of separating itself from it), stakeholders will allow the feeling of home (with its loyalty and closeness) to pervade the organization. The same holds true for the community. If the organization supports a stakeholder's community life, stakeholders will allow the community ethos (with its sense of common cause) to pervade the workplace. Leadership's acknowledgment of these other environments, therefore, is not a one-way street. It is repaid almost immediately by the ethos of loyalty, friendship, common cause, and idealism that come from these environments. It is the positive side to the principle of karma: what goes around comes around. Indeed, it does, for that is the essential dynamic of the interpersonal dimension.

7. A view of the whole person. The person is an indivisible whole. This last characteristic is meant simply to be a synthesis of the previous six characteristics. If we attend to the irreducible, intriguing goodness of the human being with whom we are in contact, all six characteristics will begin to manifest themselves in their relation to one another. We won't need a list to remember what to look for, for we will become habituated to allowing these characteristics to speak for themselves.

You may want to keep this list of characteristics in hand for a couple of weeks to remember what to look for, but eventually the characteristics will begin to rub off on you. When that happens, noticing them is an effortless delight. This is the nature of whole persons connecting with other whole persons.

Diversity and Unity

Diversity can build not only a healthy environment, but also a healthy economy. From a micro-economic point of view, differentiation in cultural and gender perspectives can help to eliminate blind spots and prevent a particular homogeneous group from going lock step in the wrong direction. It can provide knowledge of, and access to, an increasingly diverse marketplace. It can also enrich group actions and help teams to think "outside the box." Diversity also remedies the pettiness and "contempt of the familiar" intrinsic to homogeneous groups. If familiarity can breed contempt, then diversity ought to rectify it.

From a macro-economic point of view, diversity gives rise to stability and consistency in growth. Economic cycles are less volatile because diverse economies breed large counter cycles. The United States' economic growth is in great part attributable to its diverse work force and marketplace.

Perhaps the most important aspect of diversity is that it points to the unmistakable dignity and mystery that characterizes all of us. Diversity is easy to notice. When things are different or unfamiliar, our antennae automatically go up. We try to understand these differences, process them, learn how to work with them, integrate them into our thinking patterns, and find ways of mediating troublesome tensions. But as we perform these actions, we also seem to connect with something quite familiar: the presence, the smile, the sincerity, the idealism, the care, and the trustworthiness that characterize people at their best. When we notice differences, we're more attentive to the familiar, and the familiar is the all-too-human goodness, dignity, sincerity, friendship, and care that betokens the human spirit. If we do not obsess on the unfamiliar, it ironically becomes a vehicle for discovering the familiar—human dignity and mystery.

Although we can never divorce people from their culture, there is something in people that transcends culture, something in their common desire for unconditional Truth, Goodness, Love, Beauty, and Being, to which the differentiation of culture points. If we take note of this desire, as well as our capacity for interpersonal connection, self-communication, and self-transcendence; if we take note of our capacity for gratuitous kindness, and the incredible depth and complexity of eyes that are the windows to the heart; if we take note of the human spirit manifest in care, heroism, and self-sacrifice, then diversity does not impede unity, it enhances it. Beneath diverse expressions, cultures, mannerisms, habits, and actions lies a common human reality of stunning magnitude and immense value. If we have the right attitude when we encounter diversity, if we know what we are looking for, then diversity enhances not only the awareness of dignity, but also the experience and actualization of it. This, ironically, leads to an enhancement of unity and common cause.

If diversity is to have this unifying effect, we must be open to the mystery and dignity of others. If we are not, diversity will become an irritant, and force us to take refuge in a homogeneity that will eventually breed pettiness and contempt.

Five People Commitments

When leaders make people commitments publicly and mutually, they create an ethos, a "we," an organizational spirit, that is, *esprit de corps*.

The Five People Commitments

I commit that I will...

1) Experience connection before classifying characteristics.
2) Look at the whole person before the partial.
3) Look for intrinsic dignity in the midst of diversity.
4) Refuse to allow clichés that marginalize people to go unexamined.
5) Move from the appreciation of dignity to the actualization of unity and common cause.

1. I will experience connection before classifying characteristics. The "subject self" is really a "who" with whom one connects. This connection underlies collegiality, bondedness, and friendship. It disposes us to look for the good news in others even when we see the bad news. It allows us to seek strengths before weaknesses. It makes us pause before we criticize, undermine, or even dominate. It is the most basic level of respect.

Without this connection, respect becomes an effort, indeed, a rigorous intellectual and moral discipline. Respect may occur through rigorous discipline, but it tends to lead to respectful behaviors and expressions, and enforced external duty, instead of something elicited by the intrinsic dignity, worthiness, or likeability of others. When we connect with another's subject self, respect ceases to be a duty or a discipline. It is something natural and enjoyable. When respect is a joy rather than a duty, it opens upon ever deeper levels—levels that reveal the true strength, talents, character, and spirit of the individual. But more than this, such respect allows two or more people to draw spirit out of each other, and to elicit common cause and even heroism. Respect is the ground of all ethos, synergy, and *esprit de corps*.

Because it is preferable to see the "who" before the "what," this commitment may now be rephrased:

> We are an organization that attempts to connect ourselves with the spirit of others (manifest in a unique, connectable personal presence) before classifying the external, thingifying characteristics of others. By pursuing this connection, we hope to avoid exaggerating criticism, underrating strengths, overlooking common cause, and dismantling team unity.

2. I will look at the whole person before the partial to avoid a gigantic error of omission. People become passive aggressive, and even aggressive aggressive when they are disconnected from their families, communities, and other non-work environments. If people are seen in light of these environments, they will respond by bringing the trust and common cause intrinsic to these domains into the workplace. If leaders encourage connecting with the "who" before the "what," they may as well encourage connecting with the whole "who." This commitment may be phrased as follows:

> We remain open to non-work, personal data that enhances connectibility among people in our organization. Such non-work data may include commitments, values, family, friends, community action, social action, thinking and learning preferences, and other important intangibles. By doing this, we hope to promote the respect that naturally leads to common cause and unity.

3. I will look for intrinsic dignity in the midst of diversity. Diversity can enhance the awareness and experience of dignity, common cause, and unity. The key is not to obsess on the difference, but rather to connect with what is common to all people beneath their gender and cultural diversity (i.e., the unique spirit, desiring Truth, Love, Goodness, Beauty, and Being, and capable of gratuitous kindness, virtue, heroism, and care). This commitment could be phrased as follows:

> We pursue diversity through respect for the unique, self-communicating, self-transcendent spirit of others. In so doing, we hope to allow diversity to point to the unique dignity and mystery of individuals, and so promote common cause and unity in this profound appreciation.

4. I will refuse to allow clichés that marginalize people to go unexamined. Strategies that treat people as things or "skill sets" will, in the long term, decrease morale, increase the five debilitators, and increase critical skills turnover. In the attempt to increase short-term stockholder value, these strategies decrease long-term stakeholder benefit, decrease long-term stockholder value, and create a negative ambiance that drains enthusiasm, creativity, co-participation, and spirit. They do not treat people the way people deserve to be treated in light of their intrinsic dignity.

We can best challenge these clichés by asking pertinent and poignant questions: Will our stakeholders consider this strategy unfair, demoralizing, or debilitating? Will this strategy undermine trust? Will this strategy increase the five debilitators? Will this strategy promote a "win-lose" atmosphere? Would we leaders like to be treated like this if we were in our stakeholders' place? Do we leaders deserve to be treated like this?

When we ask these questions, we open our minds to data that might otherwise be blocked. The psyche tends to react to data that is clear and short-term, because our emotions are stimulated by such data. For example, a clear and impending fear not only focuses the mind on solutions, but also excludes other "irrelevant" (less clear, more long-term) data. The psyche will frequently block this data unless we ask a question that directly counteracts its tendency. These questions are designed to allow long-term, "people" data to interpose itself into thinking processes dominated by short-term "product" and "process" goals. We might, therefore, phrase this group commitment as follows:

> We challenge all clichés leading to the marginalization and thingification of others. We pursue this objective by asking relevant questions, seeking long-term "people ori-

ented" solutions, and showing proper appreciation for the intrinsic dignity and diversity of our stakeholders.

5. I will move from the appreciation of dignity, to the actualization of unity and common cause. When there is mutual appreciation of human dignity, trust and trustworthiness are achievable. Stakeholders are less worried about getting everything they want than about being treated fairly and with personal dignity. If these two conditions are met, an organization can enhance trust by reiterating the commitment: "I will trust you until you give me ample reason to do otherwise, and I will 'cut you plenty of slack' because I realize that, like me, you are not perfect. I expect that you will do the same for me, because that is the way we do business."

Once this personal commitment to trust others is seen in light of the group commitments to people, leaders can make a call to common cause and unity:

> We are an organization that moves toward our goals with all due diligence, creativity, co-participation, and synergy, by profoundly respecting the intrinsic dignity of all people, and by connecting with and appreciating our stakeholders as whole human beings.

Five Questions for Fostering People Commitments

1) Am I connecting with people (empathy) before looking at skill sets and utility functions?
2) Am I looking at the whole person before aspects or parts of the person?
3) Am I aware of the intrinsic dignity of the person when I am focused on his or her difference from me?
4) Do I perpetuate or consent to clichés that marginalize people?
5) Do I bring my empathetic appreciation of people to the next level (creating common cause and redressing injustice)?

Through this commitment, the seeds of *esprit de corps* are planted. A bonding, a unity, a common fabric charged with enthusiasm begins to emerge. The whole becomes greater than the sum of its parts, resilience in hard times is quadrupled, and enthusiasm in good times is quintupled. Stakeholders willingly support leaders, and leaders trust stakeholders to move in self-efficacious ways toward their goals. The culture is charged with an energy-giving, creativity-giving spirit. People enjoy coming to work. Morale is high. Competitors wonder how we could be so successful.

If these are our commitments, nothing can stop us from achieving long-term growth and quality, not even poor market conditions; for when we are together, we can adapt, pursue new opportunities, and use our group spirit to push into domains that might otherwise daunt us. These commitments bestow benefit on all our stakeholders. They enhance mutual respect which, in turn, emancipates us to actualize what we might otherwise think to be impossible.

Section 4

Ethical Commitments

We now proceed to the third set of commitments engendering spirit, trust, and common cause: ethical commitments. Like the people commitments in the previous section, ethical commitments must be embraced by both the individual and the group. When embraced by the group, they give rise to an ethos of integrity, nobility, trustworthiness, and therefore, trust.

Ethical commitments are not only essential for trust, but also for spirit. When a group lives beneath its ethical standards, when it feels ignoble rather than noble, untrustworthy rather than trustworthy, it sows the seeds of it own enervation and undoing. Though the group can experience the pleasure of winning, it cannot concomitantly experience the pleasure of nobility and fair play. Internal loyalty, the noble purpose of the vision, and the group's passion for common cause wane. Disharmonious notes of radical autonomy and base purpose arise. Loyalties have to be bought and paid for, and suspicion rules the roost.

The way out is not merely ethical commitments, but principle-based ethical commitments that call forth the highest standards, loyalty, and nobility from both individuals and the group. Through noble purpose, spirit abounds.

13 The Ethical Leader

Good ethics is good business. It not only keeps the organization out of lawsuits while enhancing its reputation, it also infuses increased spirit and synergy, peace of mind and trustworthiness. Poor ethics undermines the sense of trust, gives rise to fear, depletes energy, and creates malaise.

My intent in this chapter is to help you move toward principle-based ethics. Why principle-based? Because the alternatives do not work. The organizational world is changing so rapidly that ethical reflection is at best a permanent "gray area." Even though a company has ethical standards, many leaders have no idea how to implement them. Moreover, the noble goals of tolerance and diversity seem to be at odds with specific ethical standards. Leaders labor under the belief that to promote the noble causes of diversity and tolerance, they have to move toward the lowest common denominator of prescribed standards or principles. Leaders feel guilty about mentioning ethical standards because it seems as if they are seizing the moral high ground. They don't want to "lay a trip" on anyone. They are not priests or ministers, so they may as well let the "ethics thing" find its own level.

This unintended ethical fog has opened the door for unmitigated rationalization. The human capacity for rationalization is virtually infinite—give us five minutes, and we can rationalize any action in any situation. If we have no standards, no "uncrossable lines," we are likely to go anywhere that is not clearly illegal. This propensity has led to the bizarre phenomenon of lawyers acting as agents of ethics. Law was never intended to be the foundation of conscience.

The law's function is to protect the rights of citizens. It is minimalistic by nature. When we make this minimalistic agency the ground of ethics and conscience, we make ethics equally minimalistic.

We now face a peculiar cultural situation: Ethics seems to be in a perpetual state of ambiguity; lawyers cannot add clarity to this ambiguity without moving beyond their minimalistic function; and rationalization has become one of the primary goals of ethical reflection. As a result, we see several severe consequences: a rapid increase in lawsuits and transactional costs (monitoring, protection, insurance, legal remedies); employees attempting to get a "fair deal" from companies by stealing, absenteeism, and misuse of property; a rapid decrease in trust; a rapid increase in the five debilitators (fear, anger, suspicion, passive aggression, and compulsive ego); and a loss of the sense of integrity.

Integrity is an internal disposition that associates our identity with moral rectitude. We do not simply think that our morals are important to live with ourselves or to sleep at night, we believe that our morals are partially constitutive of our very selves. The identification of self with morals is so deep that we don't have to think about whether we are going to act according to our principles, we simply do. No psychic energy is wasted on internally debating whether a principle applies in this situation; we simply do the "right thing."

This internal disposition is progressively being replaced by an external constraint system. Instead of saying, "This action is a violation of principle," we now ask, "Please contact our lawyer to see if we have a legitimate exception to our possible violation of the latest interpretation of this statute." Using such "moral" logic, we dissociate our identity from our moral convictions. Our employees will see this, take a cue from it, and follow suit. So will our children.

The only way of reversing this disturbing trend is to return to principle-based ethics. Without principles, the process of unmitigated rationalization will worsen, because the current ambiguity amidst rapid change, complexity, and misinterpreted tolerance cannot provide internal constraints and parameters. From ambiguity comes ambiguity.

Without principles, we are reduced to emotions, intuitions, or a harms-benefits calculus, but all of these lack "backbone." Emotions can change, intuitions can be rationalized, a harms-benefits calculus can favor one group or another. To move beyond the subjectivity and ambiguity of these three arbitrary approaches to ethics, we need to set up quasi-inviolable principles upon which the community agrees.

By "quasi-inviolable" I mean "a moral objective that will not be forsaken unless it causes us to violate a higher or equal principle." This requires not only that an organization know its principles, but also rank them. Thus, principles concerning the life and safety of stakeholders might take precedence over principles concerning cheating, lying, or stealing. Even though it may seem distasteful to compromise such principles, a vague ranking will help to avoid the Kantian dilemma of the madman asking if you have his sword. If you do, shouldn't you be permitted to indicate the contrary? Such exceptions to principles, however, are quite rare. Therefore, principles should be viewed as inviolable unless their commission will automatically violate a higher, or perhaps equal principle.

When principles are inviolable, they should be viewed as the source of not only individual nobility, but collective nobility. They are not only integral to my personal identity, but to our collective identity. They are what we stand for. They describe our inner being and further describe what is likely to emerge from our individual and collective actions. When we collectively adhere to these principles, our essence takes on an inestimably positive quality that gives rise to the feeling of nobility.

Without this nobility, loyalty is blind. I can say, "I am loyal to this leader because he is the leader." But this is not loyalty. This is nothing more than fear, convention, and self-interest, as Machiavelli asserted long ago. The true feeling of loyalty (related to the spirit of chivalry) is rooted not in the position of the leader, but in the nobility of the leader.

The same holds true for groups. One might say, "I am loyal to this group because it is my group." This is not loyalty, but only fear, convention, and self-interest. True loyalty, the loyalty that would sacrifice for the group because of a belief in its intrinsic goodness, is based on nobility, that is, on the presence of principles that, when commonly held, imbue the group with a goodness worth sacrificing for.

Principles, then, not only stem the tide of rationalization, they ground true nobility, loyalty, and sacrifice by fostering intrinsic goodness in both individuals and the group. Without them, we cannot help but lapse into cynicism, for pure pragmatism is powerless to incite a recognition of intrinsic goodness, and therefore powerless to excite the human spirit. The importance of principles to organizations in the third millennium cannot be underestimated.

Introducing Principle-Based Ethics

The introduction of principle-based ethics into today's ambiguous organizational environment is by no means impossible; but it does require a concerted effort grounded in two essential action steps: 1) education in principle-based ethics, and 2) ethical systems and processes giving rise to ethical communities.

I. Education in Principle-Based Ethics

Ignorance of the following four points about principle-based ethics constitutes the most serious leadership omission in today's organizations: 1) the organizational bias against ethics, 2) the criteria for ethics, 3) the support for principle-based ethics, and 4) essential principles and questions for ethical reflection.

1. The Organizational Bias Against Ethics. Most ethics professors have, no doubt, met an alumnus 10 years after graduation. The professor may recall that the student was top in the class, had a great sense of how to resolve ethical issues, and could write brilliant case analyses. He turns to the alumnus and asks, "Did you find the course in ethics helpful?" To which the alumnus responds, "I wasn't able to use the material when I entered the real world."

Techniques for resolving cases and information about codes of conduct are not enough. If leaders want their organizations to be ethical, they need to provide an atmosphere and education that promotes a desire among people to practice what they learn. Without this desire, codes, techniques, and case studies become mere matters of abstract interest and even hassles to contend with.

Since the expression "real world" has vitiated more ethical sensitivity and codes of conduct than perhaps anything else, I must ask, 'What is the "real world'?" When I ask people this question, I only get vague answers like, "You know, the world out there, the world of competitive edge." But this vague notion is not the real world—it is a world filled with imprecision and bogeymen. Unless we replace it with the world of precise data in which rational people can act for a common good and trust one another in that endeavor, we will allow our fears to negate our best ethical intentions. In the real world, trust and the "win-win" ethic can substantially enhance competitiveness.

The "real world" bogeyman creates a vague fear of the unknown. We are not really certain about what we are scared of, but we know that the real world is hostile and, therefore, we must be prepared to cut corners. This vague fear and the preparation for cutting corners opens the door to unnecessary problems. These problems can be easily avoided if people support one another in discounting fears of the unknown or fears of the undefined "real world." If we could, as part of our vision statement, agree that we will allow no undefined fear into our culture, we would immediately resolve many of our major ethical difficulties.

Now, you may think that enhanced ethics means higher costs. But enhanced ethics leads to an enhanced sense of trust and "win-win" which, in turn, translates into enhanced quality, team spirit, and performance. Your investment in ethics will be returned twenty-fold in the long term.

While ethics is not quantitative or a hard parameter, it is not just fluff. Good ethics, like any other aspect of management, takes creativity, attentiveness, courage, and discipline. If you want to call it fluff, you must add that this fluff has the power to undermine or optimize all other functions.

2. The Criteria for Ethics. When we try to categorize the criteria people use to reckon an action right or wrong, one of two emerge as dominant: A) utilitarianism/consequentialism, or B) deontology.

A) ***Utilitarianism/Consequentialism.*** Social utilitarians are concerned with weighing harms and benefits. Their general principle might be phrased: "If the consequences of a particular action produce more harm than benefit, that action should be avoided." Some are open to a more radical phrasing: "If an action produces more benefit than harm, it should be considered." Some utilitarians worry about the drawback of the second phrasing, namely, how much harm is permissible relative to the good a particular action could produce? This group tends to err on the side of avoiding harm. Hence, they would prefer not to do a significant good if significant harms could result. Most utilitarians would agree that one is ethically bound to avoid great harms and, when possible, to do the lesser of two harms.

Consequentialists do not believe that particular actions are *intrinsically* or objectively evil. They do not believe, for example, that stealing or killing is *intrinsically* wrong. It is wrong only if the consequences are shown to be more harmful than not stealing in a particular situation. If it could be shown that stealing is less harmful than not stealing, then stealing could be considered ethical. Some utilitarians would say that if there were a benefit to stealing, with virtually no harm to any party, stealing could also be permitted.

Furthermore, utilitarians do not believe that actions are intrinsically or objectively good. Hence, they would not say that justice, truth, or love are good in themselves, and should be pursued; they would say, one ought to take a look at the consequences of trying to be just, to see whether more benefit or harm will come from it. If justice were harmful for many people, it might be thought to be unworthy of pursuit.

Therefore, consequentialists are very conscious of the harm and benefit of a particular action, and the number of people harmed or benefited. One such consequentialist phrased his primary ethical principle this way, "The greatest amount of neighbor welfare for the greatest number of people."[1]

Many utilitarians think that there can be ethical rules, but they do not believe that these rules indicate objective goodness or evil. They are merely abstractions about what is likely to cause harm or benefit in most situations. For example, the rule "thou shalt not steal" is generally valid, not because stealing is intrinsically wrong, but because most of the time, stealing will cause more harm than good. So also, the rule "pursue justice" is generally valid, for, most of the time, justice will cause more benefits than harms. Since these rules have only inductive validity (i.e., they are abstractions from an assessment of harms or benefits in several situations), they must constantly be checked to see whether, in a new situation, they are still applicable. Thus, even though stealing will generally result in more harm than benefit, we ought to check whether this is true in a new situation. The same would hold true for the pursuit of justice.

The utilitarian principle of assessing harms is extraordinarily important. After all, perhaps the oldest and greatest ethical principle is, "Do no harm." However, this principle alone may not be enough, for it allows for tremendous ambiguity in two areas of ethics.

The first may be considered from the vantage point of an old maxim: "The end does not justify the means." This means that one should not use an unjust means to get to a just end, or use an evil means to get to a good end. Though one might say one could do an evil action to prevent a greater evil, one cannot do evil to promote good that does not prevent a greater evil.

The second problem concerns utilitarians' reliance on quantity in ethical judgments. This is problematic because it can allow quantity to outweigh gravity. For example, we might think it is ethical to cause a grave harm to one person to prevent a minor harm to 10 people. Is quantity more important than gravity? Are some quantities more important than some differentiations in gravity? There is obviously a lot of room here for ambiguity and subjective interpretation that could be harmful, even immensely harmful, to a minority.

These two problems could be combined by purporting that it is ethically justifiable to cause grave harm to a minority to promote great good for a much larger majority. A host of social revolutions have used this very logic to justify killing large numbers of a particular minority to achieve "great social good" for a majority.

Although we can see the benefit of utilitarian ethics from the vantage point of its concern to minimize harm and maximize good, we must be leery of the possible prejudice and harm that might be done for the supposed greater benefit for a greater number. And, we must acknowledge the ambiguity surrounding the assessment of harm when objective rules or criteria are not used. In contemporary culture, such criteria are frequently ignored.

B) ***Deontology.*** Deontological ethics is on the opposite side of the spectrum from utilitarian or consequentialistic ethics. The word *deontology* has the Greek stem "deon" which means "duty." According to its adherents, this duty is to promote an intrinsic or objective good, and to avoid an intrinsic or objective evil. Some actions (e.g., *just* actions) are seen to be good in themselves without recourse to any harms or benefits that might follow from their consequences. Hence, deontologists would say that we ought to pursue justice even if some harmful or non-beneficial consequences could follow from it. Similarly, some actions (e.g., killing) are seen to be evil in themselves without reference to any benefit or harm that could come from their consequences. Hence, it is bad to steal even if one should see some benefits coming from it. Deontologists believe that the good or bad qualities of a given action are inherent in the action. They, therefore, exist in the action as performed. Goodness exists in the act of justice, and evil exists in the act of stealing. They are not a matter of subjective reflection. Deontologists do not reason that stealing may or may not be wrong depending on the consequences. Instead, they say, "Stealing is wrong. The very act of stealing produces evil, irrespective of its consequences. Therefore, it should be avoided." Thus, they view rules as if they designated uncompromisable duties, whereas utilitarians see them as generalizations indicating the likelihood of a harmful consequence.

Where do deontologists get their knowledge of the intrinsic good or evil quality of particular actions? From three general sources: 1) conscience, 2) cultural and parental formation, and 3) religion. Many deontologists believe in the validity of all three sources.

"Conscience" here means "a sensitivity to the intrinsically good or evil quality of a particular action through a felt awareness of nobility or guilt, respectively." A feeling of nobility, or being at home with oneself and the moral universe, points to the goodness of a particular action. A feeling of guilt, or alienation from the moral universe, points to evil in a particular action.

Deontologists hold that individuals can have these feelings of nobility or guilt in both specific situations and reflection about general principles. For them, one can sense moral alienation or guilt when actually stealing, thinking about a particular act of stealing, or thinking about stealing in general. So also one can feel noble and at home in the moral universe when being just, thinking about a particular just act, or thinking about justice in general. This is important to note, because conscience is not reducible to situational emotivism. Situational emotivism would say, "I shot Joe, and I feel bad about it. Therefore, I did something wrong." This kind of moral judgment is open to considerable ambiguity, for I could feel bad about shooting Joe because, upon reflection, I realize that he owed me a great deal of money for which I am not likely to now be compensated. Situations are filled with a panoply of feelings, making it extraordinarily difficult to isolate specifically moral feelings (conscience).

Emotivists could hold the opposite position, "I feel quite good about shooting Joe. I guess it was okay to have shot him." The good feeling may not be associated with one's conscience at all, but rather, arise out of the fact that one is glad to see the early demise of an irritating person. It is therefore safer to consult one's conscience before moving into a particular situation. If I can say that the thought of lying makes me feel alienated, or the thought of justice makes me feel noble, then it is probably safe to say that this will be my authentic moral awareness in any given situation.

Most deontologists will agree on the intrinsic good or bad quality of general actions (e.g., murder is wrong, stealing is wrong, lying is wrong, justice is good, truth is good, etc.), but there is a great deal of controversy surrounding the degree to which conscience is innate or learned. Those who believe that conscience is predominately innate hold that people know the intrinsic goodness or evil of a wide range of actions without having to learn them from family and culture. Others hold that the innate dimension of conscience is vague and general, and that our sense of the moral qualities of actions is, therefore, learned. This second view holds that conscience must be informed or trained. Such training, of course, is open to the possibility of cultural relativism (e.g., one culture may teach a child that bribery is wrong, and another that bribery is a perfectly acceptable, and even necessary, way of doing business). But such radical cultural differentiation in the dictates of conscience are quite rare.

Though most cultures and religions agree on the general dictates of conscience (e.g., that truth, love, and justice are intrinsically good, while murder, stealing, lying, and cheating are intrinsically bad), they can vary significantly on specific acts within these general dictates. Hence, one might conclude that conscience is both innate and informed. It is innate with respect to general dictates, but needs to be informed with respect to specific ones.

This can also be seen in the way that different individuals or cultures rank the relative goodness or evil of particular actions. Some individuals can hold that stealing is worse than lying. Some cultures might hold that heresy (which undermines the salvation of people and the common good) is worse than torture. Therefore, it is very difficult to use conscience (the intuitive sense of good or evil) alone as a source for norms in a pluralistic setting. It will have to be supplemented by some commonly accepted principles (e.g., harms analysis, rights analysis, or some other accepted criterion). For example, I cannot tell a person from another culture, solely on the basis of my conscience, that he cannot give a gift to a good customer. I would have to find some other objective criterion to demonstrate this to him; such as, "Gifts create an unequal playing field that tends toward monopoly, which, in turn, undermines competitiveness."

A second source of deontological awareness is religion. Most religions believe that God provides both private (internal) and public (external) revelations about what is good and evil. God reveals through inner awareness, Scriptures, and prophetic and messianic figures, which actions lead to life and which ones lead to death. Faith or trust in God's revelation, carries with it a responsibility to the intrinsic, objective goodness or evil of particular actions. Though most religions agree about which particular actions are good or bad, they rank them differently. Some religions would rank love as the primary virtue toward which all actions and all other virtues must aim, while others would say the same of justice. Still others, the same of truth. Likewise, some religions would view theological heresy as more evil than ostracization or even physical deprivation, since heresy is thought to threaten the salvation of a person, and physical deprivation is only harmful to the body. In any case, we cannot impose norms from our religion onto another person without supplementing it with an objective criterion or demonstration (e.g., harms analysis, rights analysis, etc.).

3. Support for Principle-Based Ethics. Deontologists have no problem with principle-based ethics. They not only adhere to principles, but see exceptions to their principles leading to actions that will bring evil into the world. They view these principles as moral obligations, and associate their integrity and their identity with them.

Although utilitarians do not believe in the intrinsic good or evil of actions, they can have a commitment to principles, because they see good and evil as generalizations of their harms-benefits calculus.

Utilitarians need not become deontologists to be principle-based. They need not believe that stealing is intrinsically, objectively, and universally wrong because acts of stealing bring evil into the world by their very commission. Utilitarians only need quasi-principles to be true to their primary principle of avoiding or minimizing harmful situations. Quasi-principles should not be violated unless they lead to the violation of a higher or equal principle.

My case has three points:

A) ***Generic principles within a utilitarian framework do more good than harm.*** Situation ethics allows our virtually infinite capacity for rationalization to go unchecked. As we assess the harms and benefits within a complex business situation, we can tilt the criteria for measuring harm toward the quantitative (the number of people harmed) or the qualitative (the gravity of the harm). Given the wide range of possible interpretation of harms within specific situations, anyone can, with very little effort, make any action "good" or "evil." Without a specific law, statute, or court precedent to function as an "uncrossable line," most people will settle for the most convenient resolution to their ethical query. This "most convenient solution," however, frequently leads to unseen long-term harms to others. By foreclosing rationalization, principles can open people's eyes to the possibility of these long-term harms. This would promote the utilitarian's long-term goal of minimizing harm and optimizing good.

B) ***Generic principles represent common expectations within the organizational world.*** Most of us have an expectation about "honesty in business." We expect that people will not cheat, steal, or lie. If these expectations are not met, we feel a need to redress the "dishonest" situation by legal means, cessation of further contact, public revelation of the injustice, or, at the very least, an apology followed by compensation for damages.

Violation of "common expectations for honesty" not only cause harm, they undermine the ambiance of business. They tend to blindside victims and cause them to react punitively and protectionistically. The result is devastating not only to the victim, but also to the perpetrator and the marketplace.

For deontologists, principles not only give interior guidance to individuals, but also give an ethical standard to the community. Utilitarians are not enamored of this property of "guidance and giving standards," but they must admit that, at the very least, principles reflect the community's expectation for honest conduct. If this aspect of principles is given credence by utilitarians, it will decrease the number and severity of harms in organizations.

C) ***Principles help to form ethical communities.*** Common commitments form the basis of community. If utilitarians commit to certain principles of conduct, they will enter into community among themselves and among deontologists. Of course, their reasons for committing to these principles are quite different from deontologists. Nevertheless, their commitments lead to common cause, synergy, and *esprit de corps* which will, in turn, decrease debilitators while increasing actualized opportunities, creativity, and productivity.

If valid, these three points provide a utilitarian case for replacing situationist utilitarianism with principle-based utilitarianism. Principle-based utilitarianism is more likely to decrease harm and increase benefit in most situations. No ethical group should find principles to be objectionable. Indeed, they should find them consistent with their objectives.

4. Essential Principles and Questions for Reflection. Principles can be viewed either negatively (i.e., as "inviolable unless they lead to the violation of a higher or equal principle"), or positively (i.e., as "foundational attitudes for ethical conduct"). Negatively formed principles correspond to the *Silver Rule* (Do not do unto others as you would not have them do unto you."), while positively formed principles correspond to the *Golden Rule* ("Do unto others as you would have them do unto you.").

Notice that the Silver Rule can be restated in utilitarian language as "avoid harming others, but if harm is unavoidable, minimize it." The Golden Rule may also be restated in utilitarian language as "optimize the other's benefit." The Silver Rule is more fundamental than the Golden Rule, for if I want to optimize your benefit (the Golden Rule) I will avoid harming you (the Silver Rule). It might be inconsistent for me to say, "I want to optimize your benefit, but I will first have to severely harm you." The Golden Rule goes far beyond the Silver Rule and is, therefore, much more extensive than the Silver Rule.

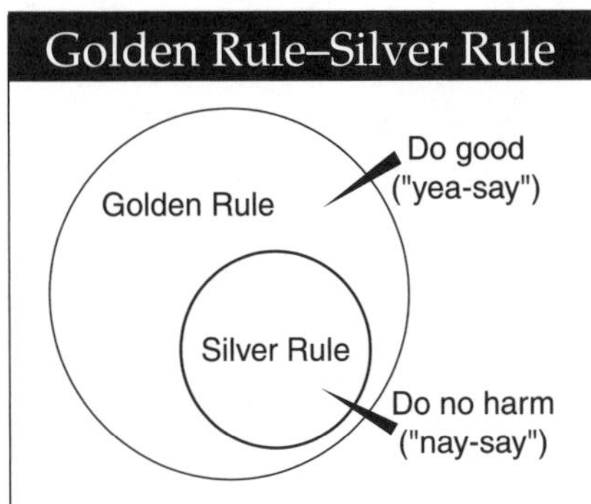

If taken seriously, these two principles of ethics can be effective in stopping rationalization. They can also provide a foundation for building trust, common cause, and *esprit de corps*. To be more effective, they need to be specified further.

THE SILVER RULE

How can the Silver Rule be further specified in principles that would be acceptable to both utilitarians and deontologists? The principles would have to fall within the range of common expectations for honesty in business. If they do fall within this range, they will avoid harm to individuals, organizations, and the marketplace.

Six such principles are widely acknowledged to fall within the range of common expectation for honest conduct:

1) Avoid jeopardizing the life or safety of others.
2) Avoid infringing upon another person's custody over his own person or actions unless he is threatening others.
3) Avoid stealing.
4) Avoid cheating.
5) Avoid exploiting the vulnerable and the helpless.

6) Avoid breaking your word (either by lying, or by breaking a promise or a trust).

The activities prohibited in these principles will, in most cases, cause harm to individuals, organizations, and markets. Even though a utilitarian will not agree that such activities are intrinsically evil, she will likely admit that their propensity to cause harm makes them prohibitable in *principle*.

If a principle is commonly accepted, people expect it to be adhered to, and hence they base their decisions on it. One cannot violate these principles and say, "Well, I didn't think that harm would come from it," because if other parties have based their decisions on them, abrogation is likely to lead to misleading information, bad decisions, and harmful consequences. Since a principle is commonly accepted, it really must be adhered to, irrespective of the consequences. This is why commonly accepted principles are binding under both deontological and utilitarian criteria. This also explains why legislation and legal precedents frequently follow upon the nuancing of these six principles. Most laws and court decisions concern these six principles. Several divisions of the government are devoted to enforcing the nuances of safety, autonomy, theft, cheating, exploitation, and dishonesty. Notice that harm does not have to be shown for legal action to be taken—all that is required is a simple violation of the principle.

Ordinarily, businesses do not need laws to determine general norms in these areas. Most people have a sixth sense about when they are straying into gray areas. We have a whole vocabulary to express our awareness: "This is not above board," "We are straying into some bad territory here," "This doesn't look good," "I don't feel comfortable with this." When people use such expressions, they normally do not believe that they are speaking only for themselves. They are appealing to what they believe other people should or could recognize to be of ethical import. They expect that their listeners can tap into the community conscience and apprehend a dimension of one of the six principles.

Tensions, of course, arise when our sense of these principles is inconvenient or unprofitable. This gives rise to a process of reflection where people consider whether a particular action is a violation of expectations. Sometimes there is no clear precedent either from legislation, the courts, company history, or case studies to shed light on whether a particular action constitutes a clear violation of the principles. Hence, people must formulate rationales and justifications for why a particular action both is and is not such a violation. Since most of the time excellent rationales and justifications can be drawn up for both positions, decision makers must break through the ambiguity by cultivating a two-fold mindset.

First, decision makers must agree to place their common desire for integrity and honesty above their common desire for convenience and unmitigated profit (i.e., profit going beyond what is needed for survival, competitiveness, or optimal, honest return on investment). If decision makers commonly agree to place integrity and honesty above convenience and unmitigated profit, they generally make wise decisions to which future generations will continuously turn.

This precedent-setting quality constitutes the second part of our mindset, namely, if we want to know whether we are placing integrity above convenience, we need only ask one question: "Do we want this decision to stand as a precedent for future generations?" If the answer is "Yes (we want this to be a precedent and to be known by colleagues and future generations)," then it is probably a "good" decision. If, on the other hand, people are saying, "Let's just keep this to ourselves," or "Let's prepare a rationale just in case someone questions us," we can assume that even though we may be able to defend ourselves, we are establishing a precedent that will, in the long run, undermine our integrity.

How can we make this mindset a reality? Obviously, it is impossible to know how each of these six principles will apply in every business situation. Each situation has unique players and characteristics, is concerned with a unique combination of the principles, and may well have implicit dilemmas where one principle will have to be valued above another. For this reason, most ethics courses are taught through the "case method." I strongly advocate that six questions be added to the decision-making process.

Why turn these principles into questions? Because of how decisions are frequently made. Most decisions arise out of a reflection on how to achieve particular goals. These goals arise out of an assessment of opportunities, resources, and problems. They are oriented toward venturing into new domains and improving old ones. Much goal setting is based on hunches. Looking at our history, our awareness of what our people are capable of, and our awareness of our resources, we have a sense of what we could achieve and what we could hope for, if we stretched ourselves.

These hunches give rise to a plan for getting to the goal. Every set of goals includes a subconscious (hunch-filled) plan for achieving it. This plan can be within a "collective subconscious" (a set of beliefs within a community or group of leaders) or within a single leader's subconscious. Whatever the case, this subconscious plan can become "a box" in which the individual leader or group constrains its thought, or a starting point for reflection that admits of data outside "the box."

The primary way of assuring that this subconscious plan does not become a box, but rather a launching pad for inclusive, creative thought, is to ask key questions at the time leaders develop goals.

The following questions have a direct impact on the ethical dimension of strategic planning:

1) Could our strategic plan jeopardize the life or safety of others? If so, how can we minimize this risk?
2) Could our strategic plan infringe on people's right to custody over their own person or actions? If so, how can we curb this propensity?
3) With respect to stealing, could our strategic plan inadvertently lead to taking our stakeholders' fair share? If so, how do we prevent this?
4) With respect to cheating, could our strategic plan lead to unfair play or unfair advantage? If so, how do we prevent this from happening?
5) Could our strategic plan lead to exploitation of the vulnerable or helpless? If so, how can we curb it?
6) Could our strategic plan lead to a violation of our word, or to outright lying or deception? If so, how can we remain truthful while being appropriately discreet?

Once these questions become "second nature" for leadership, they will introduce the six principles into every aspect of strategic planning, thus transforming the level of honesty and integrity. All other principles, commitments, and processes build on these six basic specifications of the Silver Rule. If an organization has not invested in educating its people in these six questions, its other investments in ethics (e.g., ethical consultants, processes, boards, etc.) will bear little fruit. If, however, the stakeholders "buy into" these six questions, leaders can expect a rapid increase in trust, willingness to change, common cause, and *esprit de corps*. They can also expect to find a rapid decrease in the five debilitators, turnover, and opportunity costs.

In my consultations with three organizations, I was told that it would be easier for stakeholders to make the six principles second nature if I cut the number of question areas in half. I believe the following three question areas do this:

1) ***Minimize harm.*** Could our plan cause harm? Is this harm inevitable? If so, how do we minimize it?
2) ***Keep promises***. What promises have we made in word? What promises are we making by our body language, suggestions, voice inflections? If we do not perform, would the other party think we broke our word?
3) ***Be fair***. What does the other person mean by "unfair?" Would our actions make others feel mistreated?

These three questions encompass all six specifications of the Silver Rule. They avoid rationalization by seeking definition from the other party's perspective (e.g., "Would the other party think we were breaking our word?" "What does the other party mean by unfair?"). If we could empathize with others and be true to this feeling of empathy, we could reduce the Silver Rule to these three questions, making the ethical reflection process lean, clean, and effective.

Though ethical education must include a discussion of the principles and questions specifying the Silver Rule, it need not stop there. It can venture into the areas of the Golden Rule, virtue ethics, and servant leadership, which go far beyond the minimum.

THE GOLDEN RULE

Though organizations have an ethical obligation to pursue the Silver Rule, they need not pursue the Golden Rule. Nevertheless, the degree to which they do pursue the Golden Rule will affect the levels of trust, common cause, and *esprit de corps* within them. Recall that the Golden Rule ("Do unto others as you would have them do unto you") seeks to optimize the benefit of stakeholders. It goes beyond avoiding unfair treatment of stakeholders (the Silver Rule) to pursuing all stakeholder goods that are commensurate with the common good. The Golden Rule is the stakeholder philosophy brought to full life. It might be stated as follows:

> Any stakeholder good that does not undermine the common good of the organization ought to be pursued, for it will not only optimize contribution to the stakeholder, but also cultivate benevolence, trust, openness, common cause, and *esprit de corps*.

The Golden Rule is grounded in a belief in the fundamental trustworthiness of people. If you treat people well, they will treat you well. At the very least, they won't stab you in the back. Though this is generally valid, there are rare exceptions to the rule that can be quite shocking and hurtful. If the Golden Rule is going to work, we cannot let these exceptions color our view of human dignity. A person who betrayed a trust is simply a *person* who betrayed a trust. This person's conduct should not be thought to be indicative of the rest of humanity, but rather, a rare exception. We may have to protect ourselves against this person in the future, but we should not give such a person the power to change our outlook on human dignity.

How can the Golden Rule be specified in principles and questions that will allow it to influence our strategic planning and decision making? By making use of the five personal commitments given in Chapter 11. These commitments reflect the contributory identity and the stakeholder philosophy at their best:

1) How can our strategic plan and decision making optimally contribute to our common cause and to individual stakeholders in a rational, balanced way?
2) What is the good news in our stakeholders? What do they bring in thought, depth, skills, energy, teamwork, and spirit?
3) What are the intangible qualities of the intrinsic dignity of the persons with whom we relate?
4) How do we pursue the "win-win" in every interaction with our stakeholders, especially in times of tension or disagreement?
5) How do we prepare others to receive our trust, and prepare ourselves to receive others' trust, so as to operate through collegial relationships rather than "protection, power, and political" relationships?

These five questions refocus the entire ethos and inner dynamic of the organization. If people are patient with one another, challenge one another to grow, and do not exaggerate the offensiveness of mistakes, this mentality can open up communication, creativity, and team spirit. The effects of this can transform an organization from one dominated by internal focus, turf battles, and politics, to one obsessed with new opportunities, quality improvement, and the spirit of adventure. All that is required is to give ourselves over to trust, and to allow the mentality of stakeholder benefit and the vision of human dignity to override the compulsions of ego and the suspicion engendered by past hurt. If we can do this as a community, if we can call one another to it, if we can make this Golden Rule the force of our bonding, then our natural talents and skills will be brought to fruition in creative ways.

The more we can make the Golden Rule a group effort, the greater will be our chances of success. We draw strength from one another. We will make sacrifices for others that we would not make for ourselves. We are motivated to trust by our common cause, and motivated to our common cause by our trust. If we attempt the noble cause of the Golden Rule by ourselves, we will lose all of this. If we endeavor it together and refuse to hear the chiding of the cynical few, we will take our combined patience, strength, forgiveness, and vision to a new level.

Golden Rule Ethics and Community Involvement

When an organization commits itself to Golden Rule ethics, its relationship with the community takes on greater significance. The community becomes a stakeholder much like employees, managers, customers, and suppliers. If the organization has the resources to assist the community without jeopardizing its competitive position, it will, no doubt, want to do so. It would not be surprising if the community repaid that organization with tremendous loyalty, ease of access, city and state cooperation, customers, and various kinds of goodwill. Golden Rule organizations do not seek these rewards, but nevertheless they come.

Organizations committed to Golden Rule ethics must frequently justify community involvement to certain stakeholders who need to assess feasibility and return on investment. For example, suppose that the management of a large supermarket chain wants to contribute to local food banks food reaching its expiration date. Giving this food to a needy organization would be far better than throwing it away, but the managers know that they must come up with a financing plan to subsidize the extraction, packaging, and transportation of these perishables to the needy organization. To facilitate this, they allow their customers the option of rounding their bill up to the nearest dollar or five dollars. This sum will be transferred to a fund to defray the cost of packaging and transporting the excess food. They look over the numbers and see that they are very close to breaking even, but know that some stakeholders will be skeptical about the plan because, "These sorts of activities have little direct effect on our profit margin, are always more trouble than they're worth, and will always cost more than anyone initially believes." What can management do to get these stakeholders involved in the process?

Assuming that most people would be at least open to a possibility of community benefit, the proponents will have to give them ample "ammunition" to protect against some vociferous nay-sayers. The following four-point plan can be of immense help:

1) Show the affordability of the plan using valuations that do not understate expenses or overstate revenue. The revenues should be restricted to those that can be generated by the plan alone (e.g., "rounding up to the nearest dollar"). This will prove to stakeholders that the plan is self-sufficient, and that all foreseeable expenses can be recuperated within a reasonable time.
2) Construct a marketing survey that shows any increases in patronage and customer loyalty, resulting from the implementation of the plan. New patronage should be considered a revenue beyond that generated from "rounding up to the nearest dollar."
3) Survey employees to determine whether such activity increases morale, trust, enthusiasm, and loyalty.
4) Devise a feedback loop that will measure the results of these steps as the plan is implemented.

Typically, such plans not only generate revenues, but tremendous employee and community goodwill which translate into higher morale, trust, enhanced team behavior, creativity, customer loyalty, and market share. The more these plans work, the more the culture will move to a Golden Rule position.

Community contribution plans can be accomplished in many other ways—by preserving the branch of a bank or a store in a neighborhood that is under duress, for example. If leaders ask all stakeholders to help preserve that branch, they might create immense goodwill, patronage, and gratitude. All that is required to make a feasible plan is a commitment from various stakeholders according to the parameters of their means, time, and desire. Hence, leaders may want to ask their customers to solicit new customers for the bank, or ask their stockholders to accept not a loss, but a lower return on investment. They might ask their employees to contribute some service time on a voluntary basis. They might ask the city or state government for some assistance with property or income tax rebates. Where there is a will and a common cause among diverse stakeholders, there is generally a way. If proponents can convince other stakeholders that such activity is not endangering, but rather enhancing the competitive advantage of the company, then it will become a reality. This new reality will foster community goodwill, employee morale, city and state cooperation, team synergy, and customer loyalty—not a bad return on investment for a little creativity applied to company resources.

Golden Rule thinking helps to uncover overlapping stakeholder interests. Inasmuch as it seeks the good of all stakeholders and applies its creativity to maximize not only the "win-win," but the absolute benefit to all stakeholders, it gives rise to a legacy that is broad, deep, and enduring in its scope. It not only develops strong, systemic unity, but also fosters stakeholder loyalty and credibility that goes far beyond its conceivable intent.

Virtue Ethics

Certain questions help an organization to integrate ethical thinking into its decision-making process. The more leaders embrace virtue, the more easily these questions will be transformed into ethical conduct and stakeholder benefit.

Virtue is a good habit, and a habit is an attitude that has become "second nature." This second nature is formed by choice, repetition, positive reinforcement, and the reconstruction of our self-image.

Plato talked about four cardinal virtues: wisdom, courage, self-control/perseverance, and justice. Others added generosity, magnanimity, and humility. Christianity has focused on love and forgiveness. All of these virtues are related to inspired leadership, and some of them are explicit, others only implicit in the principles and questions discussed above.

The virtue of justice is explicit in all the principles and questions concerned with fairness and unfairness. The virtues of generosity, magnanimity, and love are explicit in the five personal commitments integral to the Golden Rule. The virtue of wisdom is concerned with understanding why we want the goals we want. This virtue is explicit in the four levels of happiness. Although I have mentioned the virtues of courage, self-discipline/perseverence, humility, and forgiveness, they are worth mentioning here in light of their capacity to actualize the Silver and Golden Rules, and to bring peace of mind and good business judgment.

Courage. Courage is necessary for the pursuit of the Silver and Golden Rules. If we bend to peer pressure, fear of retaliation or embarrassment, fear of being the scapegoat, or fear of loss of esteem, we will likely compromise the principles of the Silver Rule at least twice per week. There comes a point at which our principles must be able to stand firm even against challenges to our interests and position. Courage is a willingness to sacrifice Level 1 and 2 concerns to maintain or pursue Level 3 or 4 concerns.

Though the stoics viewed courage as fearlessness or an ability to overcome fear by passion, courage might best be seen as peace of mind arising out of internal conviction in the nobility of our cause and principles. If we truly believe that our cause and principles make life worth living, then we can peacefully let go of the Level 1 or 2 concerns that stand in the way of actualizing this true meaning. It will not be easy to do this, but peace can be present in the midst of doing what is difficult.

We must not confuse courage with bravado or "macho." Courage is directed toward a higher purpose or end. It seeks contribution, the common good, and, in family life, love. Bravado makes "fearlessness" an end in itself. It therefore may not promote a good end. It might be a game of defying death for no reason other than "it gives me a rush." This should not be confused with the virtue of courage which imparts peace (not a rush) amidst the determined pursuit of correct principles and the common good.

How can we cultivate courage? By sheer conviction about our ideals and principles.

Self-discipline and perseverance. Self-discipline and perseverance are as important as courage to the actualization of both the Silver and Golden Rules. If we cannot say "no" to base pleasures, then we can always be seduced by them to give up our principles and ideals. If base pleasures take on the status of "irresistibility" or "never say no to an opportunity," then they will simply dominate our principles and ideals. Once this occurs, we will be willing to sacrifice higher ends for lower satisfactions, which are more tangible, intensive, and immediately gratifying. This gives rise to the person who "has principles" but simply cannot act according to them if a countervailing opportunity should arise at the same time.

The stoics viewed self-discipline as an exercise of mind over matter. Later philosophers viewed it as "will power." In either case, it was viewed as mental strength overcoming bodily passion.

I prefer to look at self-discipline as interior conviction about principles and ideals imparting peace to say "no" to passions that would interfere with the actualization of those principles and ideals. If, for example, my ideal were to love my spouse, then my belief and conviction in the goodness of this ideal would impart peace about saying "no" to passions that would undermine it.

Passionate negations of passion rarely work. If I shout "I will not have a drink because it is destroying me," I will probably have a drink within five minutes. My passionate refusal will likely feed my passionate desire. Peace is a much better antidote to destructive passion, for it vitiates unfulfilled desire instead of feeding it. This peace has two sources: interior conviction about the nobility of our principles and ideals, and faith and prayer. In both cases, self-discipline ceases to be a passionate denial of passion, and becomes a vehicle and a result of the purpose that makes life worth living, and leadership worth pursuing.

Humility. From the time of Socrates, humility has emerged as one of the most important virtues. In my view, it is *the* most important means of achieving higher viewpoints, and is therefore an absolute prerequisite to inspired leadership. Many philosophers have viewed humility as detachment from the world. Though this is partially true, it cannot be construed as "not caring about the world." Judeo-Christian philosophers have frequently viewed it as "being *in* the world without being *of* the world," that is, caring about what happens to the world, without living for worldly reward. In my view, humility is the ability to pursue higher goals while being detached from conflicting lower-level rewards. Humility is having our priorities in the right place not merely in thought, but also in action.

Our desire for possessions and pleasure (Level 1) and ego-satisfactions and comparative advantages (Level 2) can become dominant even after we decide to live for higher rewards. Hence, even if we are trying to contribute as much as possible to our families, organizations, and communities, we can still be possessed by ego-compulsion, ego-rage, hypersensitivity, self-pity, contempt, jealousy, suspicion, and even depressive and manic states.

These negative emotional states can seriously side track our leadership and seriously undermine our higher desires and choices. How can these negative emotions be gradually tempered so that our decisions to live for higher goals can be naturally actualized? First, we must recognize that we cannot fight pride with passion. If I shout, "I won't submit to this ego-rage!" I will simply feed it. If I direct all my "will-power" to overcoming my hypersensitivity, and shout at myself, "I will not be hypersensitive in this matter!" I will likely be sensitive to the point of being raw. Passionate negations of passion generally don't work. Peace is the key to virtue.

How is this peace acquired? I recommend two ways: first, faith and prayer, and second, an interior conviction about the nobility of our higher principles and ideals. If I truly believe in the nobility of these principles and ideals, if they are not for show, but are really the way I center my identity and my very self, then they provide the peace necessary to vitiate even the most intense hyper-sensitivity and ego-rage. This belief cuts through the passion and asserts its truth about priorities and people, about mountains being made out of molehills, about how unimportant my ego-turf really is. Armed with this humility, leaders will not only be ethical, they will inspire others with their peace, and transform their organizations into communities of trust.

Forgiveness. Forgiveness is perhaps the most difficult of all virtues because it seeks to temper vengeance, and vengeance always seems justifiable. If someone intentionally treats me unfairly, I have a justifiable claim against that person. This justifiable claim may need to be redressed in the future. But we sometimes go one step further than redressing justifiable claims. We feel intense hurt or betrayal at the others' intentional unfair treatment. This hurt causes us to seek equal, if not greater hurt for the other party. At this point, we move from redressing a justifiable claim to vengeance. But violence begets violence, and vengeance begets vengeance. Each party desires to hurt the other party a little bit more for the previous hurt caused them, until a relatively small hurt has escalated into a major incident.

Needless to say, vengeance not only undermines family life, it can undermine organizational life and turn relatively peaceful environments into armed political camps.

If such escalations are to be avoided, stakeholders will want to detach from the ego-rage associated with intentional unfair treatment. This is the only way to objectively redress justifiable claims without damaging the environment. Forgiveness, then, is a subset of humility. It is detachment from the hurt caused by intentional unfairness. Stoics might view this virtue in a very pragmatic way, "Punishing that person is not worth jeopardizing the organization," or "That person is not worth getting upset over."

The Judeo-Christian tradition goes beyond such pragmatism. It seeks to maintain respect for the dignity of the injuring party while letting go of the hurt of intentional injury. This noble endeavor considerably complicates the emotional aspects of forgiveness, for the forgiving party must now be so detached from ego-injury that she can still care about a person who does not seem to care about her. This view of forgiveness, then, is not merely detachment or letting go, it is prioritizing our care for the other above the other's care for us. It is therefore an act of selfless love.

The ancient Greeks had four words for love:[2]

1) *Storge* is the affection we feel for others toward whom we are naturally attracted.
2) *Philia* is friendship going beyond affection. It is grounded in mutual concern and commitment. The more mutual concern there is, the deeper the friendship and the longer the commitment is likely to be. Friendships grow as care is extended, accepted, and reciprocally given back. So long as the reciprocity is maintained, friendships continue and grow.
3) *Eros* is romantic love. It is motivated by feelings of intimacy and care for the other in ways that lead to an exclusive mutual commitment.
4) *Agape* is care for another motivated solely by an awareness of the intrinsic dignity of that other. It need not be supported by feelings of affection (*storge*), or by the promise of reciprocity (*philia*), or by feelings of intimacy or romance (*eros*). *Agape* arises out of a call to serve the

> intrinsically dignified other. The emotions accompanying the other three kinds of love may complement *agape*, but *agape* does not need them. This purest form of love must be motivated out of a deep, transparent vision of the intrinsic dignity of the other, or by faith and prayer.

Forgiveness is essential to leadership even if it is viewed from a pragmatic point of view. It is most effective, however, when it arises out of selfless love (*agape*), because *agape* allows the leader to redress the injustice while still caring for the perpetrator. This care will be recognized not only by the perpetrator, but by other concerned stakeholders. When they see injustice redressed in a non-vengeful way (even if it should mean termination of employment), they will invest considerable trust in the leader who displays this care. Selfless leaders do not overlook unfairness, pamper employees, act wimpish, or avoid conflict; they redress problems and unfairness with a vision of respect for the intrinsic dignity of the other. *Agape* can sometimes affect the way leaders deal with problems, but it always affects their tone of voice, mannerisms, and openness. These gestures may seem intangible, but every involved stakeholder notices them, and that makes all the difference. *Agape* is worth pursuing in and of itself. It is also one of the most effective leadership tools imaginable.

Perhaps the best way of inculcating these virtues in our lives is to put them into practice, for habits arise out of practice as much as practice arises out of habits. The best way of putting these virtues into practice, in turn, is to formulate them as questions that can be interwoven into our decision-making and strategic planning processes:

1) Do I have the peace (from conviction about my ideals and principles, or from faith and prayer) to be courageous in practicing my principles?
2) Do I have the peace to be self-disciplined (detached from passion) in practicing my principles?
3) Do I have the peace to be humble (detachment from ego-rewards, self-pity, and ego-rage) in practicing my principles?

4) Do I have the peace to forgive (let go of the hurt in intentional unfairness) in practicing my principles? Can I do this out of *agape* beyond pragmatism?

These questions are meant not only to induce the four virtues necessary for the Silver and Golden Rules but also to engender the four steps underlying the practice of ethics:

1) to engender conviction in higher principles and ideals, and in faith and prayer which are necessary for . . .
2) peace which tempers the compulsive and destructive passions surrounding compulsive, comparative, and competitive desires, which is necessary for . . .
3) the courage, self-discipline, humility, and forgiveness necessary for . . .
4) the practice of the Silver Rule and the Golden Rule.

The practice of virtue will not only affect organizational leadership, but also family life, community life, and even cultural and societal life.

I have noted that there are two steps in strengthening organizational ethics: 1) education, and 2) systems and processes. The first part of this chapter, a crash course in fundamental ethics, shows how ethics elevates not only human conduct, but also human character, happiness, freedom, and relationships. It seeks to answer the question, "Why be ethical?"

I now turn our attention to three practical areas of ethical education: 1) ethical dilemmas, 2) eight specializations of organizational ethics, and 3) ethical precendents.

1. Ethical Dilemmas

Dilemmas occur when principles come into conflict with each other. For example, I might try to maintain principle X by doing action Y. But in doing this I must violate principle Z. Action Y, therefore, will cause me to violate principle Z, while not doing action Y will cause me to violate principle X. This forces me to rank my principles and judge the severity of harms on both sides of the dilemma.

Ethical precedents can be extraordinarily helpful in resolving dilemmas. But before asking and answering the important question, "What have other organizations with similar principles done in similar situations?" it could be useful for leaders to respond to the dilemma on its own. This would give a deeper understanding and appreciation of ethical precedents, while helping leaders to see differences between their organizations and others. This, in turn, could strengthen an organization's ethical resolve.

My intent is not to give a definitive method for solving ethical dilemmas, but rather to draw upon the principles to construct a list of practical steps for solving them. Though it is virtually impossible to achieve perfect clarity about any one of these steps, leaving one of them out can lead to significant ethical problems.

Whenever they are confronted by a dilemma, leaders should try to achieve as much clarity as possible in the following four question areas:

1) What principles might be violated on each side of the dilemma?
2) How do we rank these principles?
3) What are the levels of harm done on each side of the dilemma?
4) What are the quantities of harm done on each side of the dilemma?

If leaders do not consider these four steps, they will likely make ethical decisions on the basis of emotion or intuition. By using information about principles, harms, and their ranking with emotion and intuition, leaders alleviate two potential problems: errors of omission and deciding according to the strength of the emotion instead of the merits of the case. Fear, anger, suspicion, and other emotions can be so powerful that they skew decision making toward relief from the negative emotion instead of the maintenance of principle. Leaders can gain perspective merely by asking the four questions in conjunction with colleagues or mentors.

The ordering of the steps helps us to know which principles are being violated before assessing the quantity of harm. If we reverse the order, we are likely to make ethical decisions merely on the basis of "counting the cost." This could cause us to violate high-ranking principles that may affect only a few people (e.g., the life of those in our employ), to prevent a large financial loss (e.g., $10 million). Counting the cost before we assesses the principles could easily skew decision making toward the best short-term economic solution. Such short-term economic solutions can undermine our integrity, the welfare of our stakeholders, and our trustworthiness. It is a short leap from stakeholder dissatisfaction and untrustworthiness to negative economic consequences.

In dealing with cases involving conflicting principles, I suggest you use the following chart designed to elicit the information needed to solve an ethical dilemma. The top left quadrant of the chart indicates the principles that would be violated if a person or organization were to engage in action "A" (e.g., a newspaper reporter does not reveal his source about a killer. Revealing the source could prevent additional killings). The top right quadrant indicates the same for action "B" (e.g., the reporter breaches promised confidentiality and reveals his source to prevent additional harm). In both quadrants you ought to state the principles breached (e.g., avoiding jeopardy to life and safety in action A, and keeping promises in action B). After listing the principles, you ought to rank them (i.e., is "avoiding jeopardy to life and safety" more important than "keeping one's word?"). Most people would rank the preservation of life or safety as a higher principle than promise-keeping. Indeed, they would likely rank this as the highest principle of all.

After you rank the principles, you can then assess the harms. In the example used above, the harm in action A is clear—people are likely to die. The harm with respect to action B is less clear, but we might make a case that if the press should violate confidentiality this time, then people will think that the press will reveal their sources in less threatening situations, which could eventually undermine the effectiveness of the press in protecting public safety. But the press could explain that they revealed their source only because of the threat to human life. This could enhance their credibility. Arguing harms and benefits can go back and forth almost indefinitely. Therefore, if this dilemma is to be resolved, it will have to be done on the basis of principle.

Remember: Principles are absolute unless their actualization leads to a violation of a higher principle. In this case, the press can say that they hold their promise of confidentiality to be an absolute principle unless it violates a higher principle.[3]

If we were to use this table to organize our thoughts, it might look like this:

Not Reveal Source	
Principles Violated	Rank
1. Avoiding jeopardy to life and safety	Highest
2. No complicity with death of innocent	Highest
Harms Caused	
Harm #1: Potential Death Severity: Life Probability: >50% Amount of Harm: N/A	

Reveal Source	
Principles Violated	Rank
1. Keep promises	<Highest
2. Maintain promised confidentiality	<Highest
Harms Caused	
Harm #1: Threatens future damage to reputation of press; jeopardizes openness and effectiveness in obtaining information Severity: Liberty Probability: >50% Amount of Harm: N/A	

In reality, we can't assess the harm here, because the units are different. To accurately assess the harm, the units must be the same. The left-hand side is measuring number of people killed, whereas the right-hand side is measuring damage to the reputation of the press.

2. Eight Specializations of Organizational Ethics

The resolution of business dilemmas requires providing special information to designated individuals who might then be placed on an ethics committee. There are eight specializations within business ethics:

1) Employee job security
2) Employee rights, safety, and working conditions
3) Discrimination and affirmative action
4) Advertising and marketing
5) Customer safety and product liability
6) Generic financial and accounting issues
7) Computing, information technology, and the web
8) Public safety and environmental concerns

There are thousands of published case studies and historical precedents pertaining to each of these eight areas.[4] However, you need only study the generally accepted practices in each of these areas, and such practices can be covered in a one-day seminar or in one of many principle-based texts.[5]

3. ETHICAL PRECENDENTS

The most important factor for instilling ethics after principles and virtues is experience. Like any other discipline, it helps to know how other ethical people or groups resolved ethical problems in times past. No two ethical situations are identical, but precedents are useful.

To avoid reinventing the ethics wheel, we must ask, "How have others tried to solve this ethical problem before us?" We must limit ourselves to ethical precedents that conform to our principles. We should discover the whos, whats, and whys of these ethical precedents using the following: 1) outside ethics consultants, 2) internal ethics officers, and 3) journals, books, and case studies in organizational ethics. There must also be a person (ethics officer) or group (ethics committee) who is responsible for gathering precedential data and interpreting it for decision makers. The task of such persons is to supply data on ethical precedents that can be given to decision makers who have embraced a common set of principles. As these decision makers move to consensus, they will integrate their ethical proclivities into their decisions and strategic plans.

Outside Ethics Consultants

Organizations can contract with a variety of business ethics consultants. They may be contacted through the following sources:

- Local universities (philosophy department, school of business, or special chairs in business ethics);
- National universities specializing in business ethics (e.g., Bentley College, DePaul University, University of British Columbia, University of North Carolina at Chapel Hill, Rutgers University, and University of St. Thomas. All of these universities have Web sites that can be easily accessed);
- National business and international business ethics consultants (e.g., Council for Ethics in Economics in Columbus, OH; London Research, Ltd; The Business Integrity Group, Inc. in Philadelphia; Ethics Resource Center, Inc. in Washington , D.C.; KPMG Ethics & Integrity

Services; and Professional Ethics, Inc. in Littleton, CO. These well known centers, and many smaller ones may be accessed through websites. An index may be found at the DePaul University website—www.depaul.edu/ethics/consultants.html); and

• Professional boards (e.g., the Board of Accountancy and the American Bar Association) which frequently have professional ethics divisions and will make referrals to ethics consultants if they are unable to answer specific questions.

Internal Ethics Officers

Many universities prepare Master's level students for applied business ethics consultancy. These individuals should intern with experienced ethics consultants before they take on positions of responsibility. These people have access to various business ethics sources (including library sources, annual conferences, and contacts within the profession). Hence, they can rapidly and completely answer the question, "How have others with similar principles attempted to solve this ethical problem before us?" Larger companies should consider hiring one or two of these individuals to provide data in complex ethical situations.

Though many businesses turn to attorneys for ethical advice, they are not professionally prepared to do this. Their job is to indicate when a law may be violated, but not to ask the questions concerned with the Silver and Golden Rule, or to research and apply ethical precedents. If a company's attorney is willing to educate himself in these ethical areas, then a company may consider that person as an ethics officer. However, the role of attorney is different than the role of ethicist. If an attorney feels conflict, he is likely to favor the legal domain. I recommend that companies invest in a professionally trained ethics officer.

If an organization does invest in an ethics officer, all levels of management should have access to her. She should feel sufficiently free to offer objective data and opinions to the board of directors, and should file a report of ethical trends every two years. Attorneys should also have access to this person, and she might chair an ethical strategy committee with members from the executive management, and the legal, accounting, and human resources divisions.

In my view, an ethics officer should not be merely a "research analyst" who checks ethical precedents. He must also be an educator who imparts and specifies the principles and questions concerned with the Silver Rule, the Golden Rule, and virtue ethics. Unwillingness to provide this education may indicate a reductionistic mentality (i.e., ethics equals following precedents). This mentality frequently correlates with individuals who have little knowledge or regard for principles. This lack of principle leaves an organization and its stakeholders wide open to rationalization. The ethical ethos that ensues moves from: "what is the right thing to do?" or "what corresponds to our principles?" to: "how do we justify what we have done?" or "what excuse do we have for our actions?" Such an ethics officer can lead a company into ethical decline instead of ethical efficacy.

Journals, Books, and Case Studies

Several journals catalogue and analyze ethical precedents in specific areas. These journals can provide ready reference to an ethics committee that does not have access to an outside ethics consultant or an internal ethics officer. Several of these journals can be accessed through the World Wide Web. These journals are thoroughly indexed and can be searched with the software provided by Microsoft or Netscape. The following list is divided into four parts:

1) General journals of business ethics with websites:
   International Journal of Value-Based Management: www.firstsearch.oclc.org
   Business Ethics Quarterly: www.umi.com/proquest
   *Journal of Business Ethics:*www.firstsearch.oclc.org
   Accounting Education: www.firstsearch.oclc.org
   Business Ethics: A European Review: www.firstsearch.oclc.org
   Business Ethics Magazine: www.condor.depaul.edu/ethics/bizethics.html
   Online Journal of Ethics: www.stthom.edu/cbes/oje.html
2) General journals of business ethics without websites:
   Issues in Business Ethics. (Boston: Kluwer Academic)
   Business Ethics Quarterly. (Bowling Green, OH: The Society for Business Ethics)

Business and Professional Ethics Journal. (Troy, N.Y.: Human Dimensions Center)
Business Ethics Resource. (Brookline, MA: Revehen Consultants)
Business Ethics. (Madison, WI: Mavis Publications)

3) Journals of business ethics with specific foci:
CIC brief. (New York, N.Y.: Corporate Information Center)
Annual Editions: Business Ethics. (Guilford, CT: Dushkin)
Ethics. (Chicago, Ill.: University of Chicago Press)
Business and Society Review. (Boston, MA: Blackwell Publishers)
AICPA Professional Standards. (Chicago, Ill.: Published for the American Institute of Certified Public Accountants by Commerce Clearing House)
Teaching Business Ethics. (Boston, MA: Kluwer Academic Publishers)

4) Religiously oriented journals of business ethics:
Good Business. (Lee's Summit, MO: The Unity School of Christianity)
Service in Life and Work. (London: Rotary International)
Christian Business. (Kansas City, MO: The Unity School of Christianity)
Woodstock Business Conference Report. (James L. Nolan, Woodstock Business Conference, Woodstock Theological Center, Georgetown University, Washington, D.C. 20057-1137)

II. Ethical Systems and Processes

If the Silver Rule and the Golden Rule are in the hearts of most stakeholders, the forthcoming systems and processes will take on a vital role in the ethos of the organization. If they are not, these processes will make very little difference in the level of ethics, trust, common cause, and *esprit de corps*.

A proper ethical default process has three steps: create an education and communication conduit, set up an ethics committee, and action by decision makers.

Step 1. Create an education and communication conduit. Education on principle-based ethics is the most important step in creating an ethics default process. If employees and managers are not aware of what the organization's principles are, and therefore do not know what questions to ask in decision-making processes, all the ethics committees, consultants, and resources in the world will amount to nothing. Potential ethical problems must be surfaced before they can be analyzed, and the process of surfacing problems requires principles and questions. I recommend that appointed facilitators instruct all stakeholder groups about the previously mentioned ethical principles and questions.

Three points are important here:

a) Executive management and the directors must indicate the importance of ethics and integrity by helping to pay for the course and time required to take instruction in ethics. When the organization invests in the ethics education of employees, it sends an immediate positive signal.

b) The best facilitators of ethics education are managers who show authentic enthusiasm. "Less than enthusiastic" facilitators will communicate the message that "ethics is just another hassle that executive management and the directors are imposing on us. If we jump through this hoop a few times, this new fad will pass us by."

c) If an organization is going to invest in "Silver Rule ethics education," it may as well invest in "Golden Rule ethics education," because the four levels of happiness and the five commitments will help stakeholders to understand, affirm, and live ethical principles and virtues. Living one's ethical commitments requires understanding and freedom, and this requires education about purpose in life, the comparison game, and the five commitments.

Step 2. Set up an ethics committee. Just as ethics education is vital to making routine ethical decisions, so also an ethics committee is vital for facilitating big decisions. If a potential "big problem" arises, executive management will want to have the best research and advice available to it. Without an ethics committee charged with researching and analyzing particular questions, busy directors and executives may content themselves with legal advice, or gloss over potentially serious problems. An ethics committee can provide a fully analyzed recommendation to the CFO, CEO, or board of directors.

Who should be on an ethics committee? Concerned, educated individuals from each major stakeholder group. At least one accountant, one attorney, and one personnel expert should be present on the committee because ethics decisions frequently involve specific knowledge in these areas. Experience dictates that ethics committees should not exceed 10 people. Committees should have enough people to do adequate research in specialized areas, and to spread the workload of analyzing and reporting.

The organization may want to bring in a university or national consultant for a day to familiarize committee members with the resources available to it. Some committee members will have sufficient interest to search the Web and even libraries on their own, but a one-day "crash course" can bring the whole committee up to speed very effectively.

The committee should have access to the World Wide Web, as well as certain "hard copy" resources. A consultant can easily advise an organization about the four or five most useful resources for their specific needs. Once the committee members are thoroughly acquainted with how to search these Web or hard copy resources, they can begin to research the all-important question: What have other organizations with similar principles done in this problematic situation?

Sometimes committee members will not find a precedent or case that responds to their ethical questions either because the situation is too complex, or because a precedent does not fit the particulars of their situation. At this point it might be best to consult an ethicist at a university, or to make an inquiry at one of the above interactive websites. These two sources can access many precedents and cases not reported in mainline resources. Several interactive websites provide these resources free of charge.

A succinct summary statement of the committee's deliberations should be written for the primary decision makers. This summary not only helps leaders to make a decision, but provides an historical account of their justification.

This report should include a summary of ethical precedents set by companies with similar principles, a summary of how principle-based ethicists solved similar hypothetical case studies, an analysis of how these precedents or solutions correspond to the organization's stated principles, and an analysis of how one or two proposed solutions would affect the company's "bottom line" and long-term opportunity costs.

Ethics committees not only research past precedents and cases, but also serve as the ethics conduit from employees, managers, and other stakeholders to the primary decision makers. To achieve this end, committees should meet at least once per month. These meetings should be well publicized so that stakeholders can get regular responses to questions and concerns. The committee may want to convene with a majority quorum to handle immediate, important concerns.

Larger organizations may want to hire an ethics officer to handle the day-to-day questions of stakeholders. In complex cases, an ethics committee should complement the work of the ethics officer. The ethics officer would ordinarily convene the committee and do the basic research for the committee beforehand.

Step 3. Action by decision makers. Ethics committees' reports are effective only to the extent that primary decision makers value them. The way of guaranteeing that primary decision makers will value ethics is to make them accountable to long-term opportunity cost assessment. If decision makers are using an opportunity cost method for assessing past and future performance, the ethics committee report should be integrated into their deliberations. Decision makers should be sensitive to the following opportunity costs surrounding ethics:

- legal ramifications,
- loss of customers or market share,
- inability to acquire new customers or market share,
- negative effects on long-term vendor relationships,
- effects on "just in time" inventory,
- negative effects on morale,
- the five debilitators of culture,
- employee turnover,
- increase in process flow times,
- decrease in four quality objectives (product design, improvement of product defects, decreased waste, and improvement of processes),
- increase in transactional costs, and
- adverse publicity within the community.

Executives who soberly assess these opportunity costs take their ethics committees' reports very seriously. Ethics education and committees may cost some time and resources; they may even lead to some costly, short-term consequences, but in the long term good ethics not only decreases opportunity costs, but produces dynamic spirit that can be leveraged into adaptability, creativity, and increased market share. Good ethics, in the long term, is good business.

Asking ethical questions is the quickest way of bringing ethical principles, education, and reflection into the decision-making process because these questions give rise to day-to-day judgments, become the basis for inquiries that go to ethics officers and committees, and open up mental space for ethical data in the decision-making process. They should be put on a laminated card and given to all employees. The following format might be useful for this purpose:

Most Fundamental Questions

1) ***Minimize harm.*** Could our plan cause harm? Is it inevitable? If so, how do we minimize it?

2) ***Keep promises.*** What promises have we explicitly made? What promises are we implicitly making by our body language, suggestions, voice inflections, etc.? If we did not perform, would the other party think we broke our word?

3) ***Be fair.*** What does the other person mean by "unfair?" Would our actions make others feel as if they had really been mistreated?

Essential Questions for Bringing the Silver Rule into the Workplace (Minimalistic Ethics)

1) Could our strategic plan jeopardize the life or safety of others? If so, how can we reasonably and responsibly minimize this risk?

2) Could our strategic plan infringe on people's right to custody over their own person or actions? If so, how can we curb this propensity?

3) With respect to stealing, could our strategic plan inadvertently lead to taking our stakeholders' fair share? If so, how do we prevent this?

4) With respect to cheating, could our strategic plan lead to unfair play or unfair advantage (which violates the common expectation of fair play)? If so, how do we prevent this from happening?

5) Could our strategic plan lead to exploitation of the vulnerable or helpless? If so, how can we curb it?

6) Could our strategic plan lead to a violation of our word, or to outright lying or deception? If so, how can we remain truthful while being appropriately discreet?

Essential Questions for Bringing the Golden Rule into the Workplace (Maximalistic Ethics)

1) How can our strategic plan and decision making optimally contribute to our common cause and to individual stakeholders in a rational, balanced way?
2) What is the good news in our stakeholders? What do they bring in thought, depth, skills, energy, teamwork, and spirit?
3) What are the intangible qualities constitutive of the intrinsic dignity and mystery of the person or persons with whom we relate?
4) How do we pursue the "win-win" in every interaction with our stakeholders, especially in times of tension or disagreement?

Essential Questions for Bringing Virtue Ethics into the Workplace

1) Do I have the requisite peace (from interior conviction about my ideals and principles, or from faith and prayer) to be courageous in practicing my principles?
2) Do I have the requisite peace to be self-disciplined (detached from passion) in practicing my principles?
3) Do I have the requisite peace to incorporate humility (detachment from ego-rewards, self-pity, and ego-rage) into the practice of my principles?
4) Do I have the requisite peace to incorporate forgiveness (let go of hurt in intentional unfairness) into the practice of my principles?

If an organization has invested in ethics education sufficient for an understanding and openness to these questions, it is more than two-thirds of the way to an ethical culture. The remaining one-third is practical: 1) appointing an ethics committee, 2) making ethical resources available to this committee, and 3) preparing executive leadership and the board of directors to integrate ethical decisions into their long-term plans through an assessment of opportunity costs. If these plans are carried out, ethics will be second nature within an organization, and so will the spirit, creativity, drive, and adaptability that will follow.

Section 5

Leadership Commitments

Considerations of the heart on the part of leaders are vital to culture and efficacy. This is apparent in everything from morale, to opportunity costs, to quality objectives, and to the ability to change. The heart of inspired leadership is built upon personal commitments, people commitments, and ethical commitments. If these commitments are "bought into" by most stakeholders, leaders may now make their own "commitments of the heart" toward an optimally creative, self-evolving, self-efficacious culture of inspiration. The next four chapters focus on these leadership commitments.

14 Leadership for a New Environment

The first step to creating a people strategy is to recognize that today's environment is radically different from the one of 20 years ago. In the *Introduction*, I review eight steps to describe the movement from the organization as hard structures to the organization as creative, malleable structures grounded in the spirit of people. This evolution leads not only to better quality and workplace environment, but also to an increase in wealth and welfare in the world.

In this chapter I consider the elements to which leadership must adapt to remain competitive and viable, how to adapt to this changed environment, how to overcome the generation gap, the need for cross-functional teaming, and the goal and trend of contemporary leadership.

This transition in leadership style is based on contributive principles that not only produce an increase in happiness, meaning, creativity, unity, peace, and trust, but also open upon the spirit and teamwork so necessary to adapt to increased complexity and change.

The Changed Environment

A cursory review of leadership over the last 20 years shows that leaders must adapt to several major changes in the environment resulting from the increased need for faster change, specialization of labor, self-efficacy, synergy, education, and changed expectations of stakeholders.

These changes may be grouped into 10 areas: 1) increased competitive compulsions; 2) increased education of stakeholders; 3) increased desire on the part of stakeholders to participate, create, and contribute; 4) increased desire for continuing training, education, self-development, and self-efficacy; 5) increased capacity for technical competence, particularly in data accessing, data processing, and communications; 6) increased sensitivity to dignity, rights, independence, and self-motivation; 7) increased psychological awareness (of feelings, personality, and psychological games); 8) changed expectations for work environment; 9) increased mobility and willingness to move if work becomes difficult to live with; and 10) increased desire for participation in community.

Some of these changes are deleterious to the highly adaptable, specialized organization, for they bring about fear, blame, resentment, anger, compulsion, suspicion, and passive aggression. Others directly contribute to teamwork and adaptability.

I would wager that there is substantial evidence of these 10 environmental changes manifest in the evolution of the vision, mission, and core-competency statements formulated by your organization over the last 20 years. Note changes in language, assumptions about people, goals, and ideals. Now, ask, "What will the next 20 years be like?" Do you see inevitable enhancements of these environmental changes?

Proper Adaptation to the Changed Environment

Since we can't turn the clock back, leaders must adapt to the environment to benefit both the stakeholders and the organization. Proper adaptation will lead to the synergistic teaming needed for creativity and quality. Improper adaptation will either stall the process of achieved creativity, specialization, and growth, or bring it to an end.

Proper adaptation means: overcoming competitive compulsions, and optimizing teamwork, synergy, adaptability, specialization, and creativity.

Increasing education has the good effect of increasing capacity for self-efficacy and change, technological awareness, creativity, and interpersonal relationships. However, there is a bad effect of causing people to center on achievement and winning to the exclusion of contribution and common cause. The blessing of self-motivation, adaptability, creativity, and technological competence brings with it a curse of compulsive fear, blame, resentment, suspicion, and aggression—unless we are aware of the dangers of competitive compulsions and their remedies. If these dangers and remedies are taken seriously, leading to new habits of mind, then education can free the human spirit to progress confidently beyond the limits with which it is faced.

Overcoming the Generation Gap

Positive changes are being brought into the workplace by a new generation of leaders and workers. We cannot afford to allow these new leaders and workers to leave in discouragement—not simply because critical skills turnover is a waste of time and money, but also because this new generation embraces a vision that will become the lifeblood of a self-motivated, highly adaptable, highly specialized organization. The group that entered organizational life 20 to 40 years ago may feel a bit bewildered by these 10 environmental changes. The group that has entered in the last 10 years understands them all too well. This generation gap need not be a curse. It could be a blessing if the strengths of both groups are allowed to interact.

The strength of the older generation is clearly experience (about people, customers, systems, processes, etc.), and the strength of the younger generation (with two or more years of college education) is their awareness of, and belief in, the goodness of the 10 new environmental factors. If both groups proactively listen to one another, adaptation to the new work environment will be relatively easy. However, if both groups do not proactively listen to each other, change will become turgid, in fits and starts, and adaptation will be slow and painful. In this scenario, both groups will falsely believe that they know the whole truth. This will lead to skirmishes, end runs, and frustration with an increase in fear, blame, resentment, passive aggression, and suspicion.

The older group will, at first, win most of the battles, bringing adaptation to a virtual standstill. This will force some younger employees to leave their organizations—or to remain in frustration and resentment, causing a negative ethos that is counterproductive to quality, creativity, teaming, self-motivation, openness to change, and specialization. In short, the older generation's victory will be merely pyrrhic; but in the long run it will have disastrous effects.

The younger generation might be similarly cautioned. The belief in the goodness of the environmental changes produced by education may give rise to ideals that can never be met. This could lead to an increase in frustration, resentment, and passive aggression far beyond what is warranted. When our expectations are not met, we tend to make mountains out of molehills. Failure to achieve a particular good is not nearly as painful as not getting what we expect. Dashed expectations, more than the actual failure, produce pain, anger, frustration, fear, blame, and suspicion.

Secondly, the experience of the older generation is extraordinarily important, for it allows them to think with nuance and to assess character and personality with depth, while allowing change to occur through a steady path rather than violent pendulum swings. If younger workers want change to move from the status of ideal to reality, they will have to pay attention to the experience and nuance of the older generation. The astute and the observant in the older generation are a gold mine of subtlety and depth without which the greatest ideals cannot be actualized. The "too much too soon" of idealists is the undoing of the very principles they want to actualize.

Those working for young companies and new industries may think they have avoided the problems of the generation gap because most of their work force is under 50 years of age. The 10 environmental changes mentioned above are likely to be prevalent in that ambiance, guaranteeing that there will be a high degree of technical competence, flexibility, and camaraderie. These elements can stave off the effects of competitive compulsions, but eventually fear, blame, resentment, and suspicion will find their way into the most successful of ventures, indeed, through the very success of those ventures. These organizations are left with the challenge of protecting themselves from these problems by recognizing them and setting up processes to overcome them. In my opinion, these processes are best initiated by embracing the forthcoming leadership principles.

The Need for Cross-Functionality and Generalists

Greater specialization is required not only to accommodate the complexity of products and processes, but also to accommodate efficiency and openness to change. However, greater specialization must also be accompanied by cross-functionality. If our specialists do not have an ability to communicate with other specialists, complex projects cannot be brought to fruition. Ironically, then, greater specialization requires greater generalization. We need general specialists.

Ideally the team leader would be the generalist who orchestrates all the ways the various specialists interact with each other—fitting together all the diverse puzzle pieces in a particular project or process, being the conduit for all autonomous working agents. Let the specialists be specialists, and let the leaders be generalists. Unfortunately, this ideal is not even remotely possible once a team includes more than about 20 specialists, let alone 5,000 specialists, or even 20,000 specialists. The only way to bring the puzzle pieces together, to bring the work of specialists into a self-catalyzing synthesis, is to help specialists accommodate themselves to the work of other specialists. This is what is referred to as "cross-functional teaming."

Cross-functional teaming is tricky business for, on the one hand, a leader does not want to overburden specialists with information that is not directly pertinent to either their specialty or to cross-functional teaming. Yet, on the other hand, a leader does not want to underestimate the knowledge required for self-catalyzing synthetic activity, for this will put the burden squarely and unfairly on her shoulders. How much cross-functional knowledge and accommodation are required to effect this self-catalyzing synthesis without overburdening specialists—without cluttering their minds?

The answer will lie in the exigencies of particular situations. However, a few generalizations can be made:

1) Cross-functional knowledge helps specialists to design and produce within their specialty. If I know how my colleagues use my output, I can tailor my output for them. Hence, any cross-functional knowledge that helps a specialist tailor output to other specialists is useful. In the short run, it could be viewed as "one more hassle," but, in the long run, it will help facilitate outputs within a given specialization.

2) Cross-functional relationships within teams also help specialists to tailor their outputs toward goals. Cross-functional relationships are a particularly difficult challenge for leaders because specialists would prefer to work with their own kind. They may even have a sense of pride or camaraderie arising out of their particular specialty. Mini-rivalries can easily develop: "My specialty is better than yours," "We are more important," "Our skill requires far more creativity, intellectual ability, agility, and overall competence than your skills," etc. The familiar refrain will be, "I don't see why I have to communicate with that group. Is this really necessary?" If a leader believes that a relationship is required to obtain important cross-functional knowledge and future self-induced synthesis among specializations, he must reply, "Yes."

Leaders need not be apodictic about requests for cross-functional relationships. They should tell their people why they are asking this of them, namely, to gain necessary cross-functional knowledge, to tailor outcomes to those of other specialists, and to achieve self-catalyzing processes and outcomes. If a specialist believes that certain cross-functional knowledge is unnecessary to tailor outcomes to these self-catalyzing processes, leaders will have to judge whether such remarks are true on their face value, or are simply resistance to the additional hassles involved in cross-functionality. Such judgments will depend on the personalities involved, the exigencies of the situation, and the leader's ability to see when and where connections are necessary.

Since some cross-functionality will be essential, leaders need to foster cross-functional relationships through the commitments and principles of inspired leadership.

The Goal and Trend of Contemporary Leadership

The contemporary work environment is truly diverse. The changed environment, the generation gap, and increased specialization of labor have produced a wide range of workers to which contemporary leadership must adapt.

We could look at this range from the vantage point of high oversight and supervision to low oversight and supervision.

High oversight workers tend to expect leadership to tell them what to do. Many have been implicitly told that their function is to be "non-thinking implementers." They have adapted themselves to this expectation and are less affected by environmental changes. They have very little desire to co-participate, offer ideas, or take initiative. For them, responsibility is generally someone else's business. They have little desire for additional training and education, little capacity and desire to move, adapt, or take risks, and will tend to drift if not rigorously supervised. For this group, leaders will have to spend most of their time on oversight and supervision.

The group at the other end of the spectrum (low oversight and supervision) is comprised by the top 20 percent of critical skills personnel. They have a high desire to contribute and create, though this desire can manifest itself in being more of a "superstar" than a "team player." They desire both training and education, are extraordinarily adaptable to changes, feel themselves to be both competent and esteemable, and are seeking greater status and responsibility to use their talents and training. They are sensitive to non-recognition, implicit insults, and lack of gratitude. They would rather accept responsibility than be supervised. They react adversely to too much supervision. Inspired leadership brings the best out in this group. Uninspired leadership will produce high turnover, the five debilitators, and low morale in this group. Since these people hold the future of the organization in their hands, mismanaging them will darken prospects.

How can leaders adapt to this new reality? For the low to medium oversight groups (approximately 60 percent of the organization), leaders must use leadership principles. Using fear, force, and bribe on this group will cause low morale, high turnover, low adaptability, and, as a result, low quality, production, and customer satisfaction.

For the high to medium-high oversight groups (approximately 40 percent of an organization), leaders will have to use high supervision techniques (including fear, force, and bribe). However, at least 20 to 30 percent of this group can be called to lower oversight and supervision by using higher level principles, resulting in an increase of morale, creativity, adaptability, efficacy, quality, and productivity.

Inspired leaders bring about a much brighter future by educating people about the levels of happiness, asking people to enter into "win-win"/high trust relationships, implementing the 12 principles of leadership (outlined in the next chapter), and starting a mentor program to develop high initiative.

15 The Principles of Inspired Leadership

What kind of leader can best adapt to our changing environment? Inspired leaders who spend their time, energy, and creativity on cultivating teamwork, encouraging new ideas, and helping people to become enthusiastic, spirited, and open to change. Inspired leaders facilitate the growth of spirited "thinking implementers" and pave the way for high performance teams. The style of an inspired leader is a combination of "win-win" and "soft-bargaining." Leaders use these tools to engender a sense of both friendship and common cause. Friendship (in the sense of "liking," of enjoying another person, of spirited collegiality) is very desirable for teamwork, creativity, and self-efficacy.

Inspired leaders not only have responsibility for budgets, quality, and oversight, but also the cohesive, creative, synergistic operation of people. Therefore, they spend part of their time decreasing the five debilitators, increasing trust, educating, training, and advising people, and encouraging and rewarding creativity, self-motivation, and teamwork. They distinguish between low oversight and high oversight people. They know when to get out of the way, when to call people to greater accountability, and how to adapt their leadership style to the needs and capabilities of others. When inspired leaders have done their job, the need for oversight will decrease, leading to greater synergy and collective serendipity. Such leaders turn dying companies around, pave the way for new levels of achievement, quality, and performance, and allow companies to adapt to rough marketplace conditions, changing technologies, and increased complexity. These leaders are the guiding lights for the 21st century.

Inspired leaders replace oversight with inspiration to the greatest extent possible. The mentality of oversight encourages extrinsic motivation (fear, force, and bribe). Inspired motivation encourages intrinsic motivation by fostering enthusiasm, creativity, individual initiative, and teamwork. For approximately 60 percent of the workforce, high oversight is a waste of a leader's time. It promotes non-thinking implementers, the five debilitators, and an inability to change. It is also a "turn off" for those who have a desire to participate and create, and, therefore leads to high turnover among the top critical skills personnel.

At times, oversight is necessary, as some people cannot function without oversight. They are not content to do a good job, to receive praise or promotion, or even to do what they're paid for. But since these people represent only about 20 to 40 percent of the working population, we need not apply a model intended for this group to the other 60 to 80 percent. Leaders must cultivate two styles: an inspired, proactive, and team-building style for the 60 to 80 percent, and a fear-based, oversight style for the other 20 to 40 percent.

Leaders can't afford to have only one style. Although the culture encourages narrow self-definitions, we are capable of multi-faceted behavior. For example, I may be tempted to say, "I am an ENTJ" (a particular personality type within the Myres-Briggs personality inventory). But when I use this designation, I imply that I cannot act like an INFP when I want to. I might even try to make myself into an "archetypal ENTJ," forcing myself to have only ENTJ responses. I have discovered my identity not in my ideals, commitments, aspirations, loves, and contributions, but in a personality type! This personality can become the fixed pillar of my identity, and I cannot see myself acting in any other way.

Although all of us have certain propensities, those propensities are not us. We don't have to be this way. We need not make ourselves archetypally narrow. We don't have to associate our identity with our personality type. Leaders must be acutely aware of this, for if they believe they are a particular kind of leader (rather than having a propensity toward a particular leadership style) they won't meet both the inspirational and oversight needs of their organizations.

Developing Inspired Leaders

Once leaders accept that they are capable of multi-faceted styles of leadership, they should become well-versed in three primary skill areas of inspired leadership.

1. Vision for the Common Good

Interestingly, the principles of inspired leadership connect felicitously with traditional philosophers' views of good leadership. As can be seen in Plato, Aristotle, Aquinas, Montesquieu, Locke, Rousseau, Confucius, Lao Tzu, Ben Sirach, Emerson, Thoreau, de Tocqueville, Dewey, and thousands of other philosophers, what defines a good leader is his or her vision of the common good. So long as a leader 1) yearns for the good of a community (more than self-interest and special interest), 2) has a vision of what that common good would look like, 3) has the prudence to actualize that vision through diverse groups, and 4) has the courage to achieve it with justice, that leader will improve the environment over which he or she has been given authority. Greater or lesser success will be determined by external environmental factors, but the fact of success or improvement will be virtually unquestionable.

If, however, a leader should lack one of these virtues, the probability of success or improvement will be diminished. If a leader concerns himself with self-interest or special interest more than the common good, he will create a state of inequity that would mean creating a "win-lose" situation devolving into a "lose-lose." "Yearning for the common good" means letting contributive attitudes remove the compulsions of an exclusively competitive identity. If a leader has no specific vision of the common good, but only ideals and good feelings, he will actualize nothing, for an ideal, desire, and passion must be translated into real world constituents. If a leader lacks "prudence" or "wisdom," he can't facilitate his vision within a diverse populace, for he can speak only to himself and others like him. If a leader does not seek and support talents and strengths other than his own, the organization will decrease in specialization, self-motivation, and adaptability. Finally, if a leader does not act with courage and justice, then he will create inequity as well as injustice.

Certain dimensions of leadership are perennial (i.e., the common good, prudence, courage, and justice). They may need to be redefined to reflect environmental changes, but they reveal the deepest yearnings of the human spirit.

2. *Dealing with Negative Feedback*

Few leaders can make these principles realities by shear force of personal conviction and commitment. Because they are besieged by a myriad of short-term pressures and problems, most leaders need a feedback adviser to help them stay focused, to make suggestions for progress, and to pursue common cause.

A feedback adviser is a peer who is respected and trusted, but whose status is not threatening. The relationship between a leader and a feedback adviser must be such that data can be accepted without defensiveness. The feedback adviser must have some acquaintance with the leader's team, group, or organization so that he can be in tune to the "people atmosphere" in that work area and give a leader appropriate feedback. Leaders should meet with feedback advisers at least once every two weeks, if only for 15 minutes, to determine whether their perception of reality resembles the "people atmosphere" in their work area. If the perceptions should differ, they can be brought into line through honest dialogue.

A good adviser not only gives honest feedback, but also knows when and how to give suggestions and guidance. He provides camaraderie so that leaders do not think they are trying to pursue these higher viewpoints and commitments by themselves. These relationships can be reciprocal, though they do not have to be. Just as leaders have consultants about product design, processes, and administration, so also they might have advisers about the "people atmosphere." If the people atmosphere is to be improved, leaders will first have to look at attitudes, then they can reflect on commitments, structures, and skills. If they attempt to introduce skills to remedy a morale or team problem (without addressing commitments that touch the hearts of people), they are likely to be viewed with suspicion: "What does management have up its sleeve today? How are they going to benefit from this?" The only way of getting around this suspicion is to cultivate trust, and the only way to cultivate trust is for leaders and people to pursue together attitudes that will decrease the five debilitators and cultivate genuine common cause. If leaders do not have feedback advisers in the people area, I strongly advise that they obtain feedback regularly from some other source who offers regular guidance on attitude development.

Once leaders obtain feedback, they should reflect on it and act upon it. If the feedback is somewhat negative, leaders must expect feelings of either hurt or anger. If these feelings are allowed to arouse ego-defensiveness, they will push a leader toward harmful compulsions. Therefore, leaders need to calm down before formulating a strategy to act on the feedback. Peace of mind, which may come days after hearing criticism, can transform initial defensiveness into a proactive strategy for positive change.

Leaders are likely to experience a three-fold reaction when receiving negative feedback.

Shock or surprise. If I am convinced I am doing a good job, negative feedback will undermine my positive self image. Although this negative feedback is only a partial aspect of my identity (probably less than five percent of my attitudinal makeup) I will view it as if it is a critique of my whole person. Instead of thinking that Joe is critiquing my impatience in a particular situation, I believe that he is critiquing me and my self worth in all situations. This unjustified, negative generalization frequently occurs in people who are new at soliciting feedback, because bad news has far more force than good news. It provokes fear, undermines identity, and calls for an almost immediate defensive reaction. Today we tend to associate the significance of a statement with the power of the emotions elicited by it. If a critical statement provokes powerful feelings, I am likely to apply it to the whole of me and the world. Conversely, if a positive feeling from a compliment is less powerful, it will be seen to have less importance, and therefore to apply to less of me and the world. Although this dictum is frequently false, it feels true. Therefore, most people will credit criticisms with an exaggerated applicability and find them quite devastating. The only way they can react to this is with defensiveness, for their psyche cannot absorb the blow of thinking that they are essentially negative or worthless. This defensiveness provokes a second reaction.

Self-pity or blame. To defend ourselves from a perceived assault, we may move to an equal and opposite exaggerated reaction—excuse and blame. If we cannot excuse ourselves, we will either blame inwardly (self-pity) or outwardly (foisting responsibility on another party). Inward blamers do not want to hurt anyone else, so they typically say, "This criticism is really a reflection on my whole being, clearly substantiating the opinion that I am neither needed nor worth much to anyone." If this myth is believed, it can lead to growing isolation. The self-pitier's friends do not understand why the self-pitier is saying these things. They think he is fishing for a compliment. After a while, when they are annoyed, they tend to withdraw, confirming the self-pitier's assessment that he is neither needed nor worth much. If this cycle continues, it can lead to depression and even self-destruction.

My advice at this juncture is to refuse to believe the myth. Stop the self-pity in its tracks and resume your normal relationships with colleagues and friends.

Externalizers defend themselves against psychic assault by blaming outwardly: "This problem situation is not my fault. It was brought on by my boss, my colleagues, troublesome employees, my teachers, my parents, or the social conditions of the world." The difficulty with blaming outwardly is that the blamed party feels that she is being treated unjustly and generally reacts to the blamer with silent resentment, passive aggression, and even aggressive aggression. This confirms the blamer's belief that other people are at fault for what is happening to him. If the cycle continues, a leader could undermine significant relationships and the morale of the entire team or organization. Just as the self-pitier is bathed in isolation and depression, so the blamer is bathed in isolation and anger. Interestingly, the more we blame, the angrier we get. We convince ourselves that the other party really meant to hurt us and to undermine our life. Once we attribute these false intentions to others, we become swept up in defensiveness, anger, and indignation.

Again, my advice to blamers is to challenge the myth when it appears. The criticism that elicited all this does not have to be blamed on someone; it simply needs to be dealt with. Your whole past life has not been lived in aberration; merely one aspect of your leadership style or relationships needs improvement.

Resignation or isolation. If we stew and brew about these exaggerated emotions for weeks, we will eventually give up on either ourselves (self-pity) or others (external blame). In either case, the result is increased isolation, increased resistance to criticism, and decline in morale. The consequences are so disastrous, I believe leaders should not ask for feedback until they are ready to deal with criticism in a balanced, proactive, positive way.

How can we as leaders handle negative feedback well? First, we must return to our attitudes about purpose and happiness in life. If we are truly convinced that contribution is the essential meaning of life, then comparative advantage will seem far less important. This makes the blow to the psyche far less significant, thereby stemming the negative emotive tide. Recall that high achievers who constantly up the stakes on themselves have exceptionally high ego-sensitivity. The slightest criticism can frequently induce rage toward ourselves and others. If we are to avoid this ego-sensitivity, we must earnestly call to mind our contributive identity. This identity tones down the sting of criticism while manifesting positive effects. This can produce the detachment necessary to reflect and act on the criticism constructively.

This detachment does not come from contempt or sour grapes ("What do they know, anyway?"). We can always distinguish between positive detachment and negative detachment by attending to the degree of "coolness" we display toward the sources of criticism. Negative detachment leads right back into the cycles of self-pity and blame.

Second, if positive detachment is achieved, we should move to reflection. Helpful reflection can only occur when we are no longer susceptible to the exaggerated mood swings arising out of defensiveness. At this point, we can look at the criticism analytically as a problem to be solved. Successful reflection depends on consulting others who have been through the same problem. We can be sure that no matter what the criticism may be, thousands of other people have to deal with similar criticisms. Hence, there are likely to be books, consultants, and institutes devoted to overcoming such difficulties. We must remember that we are not alone, but indeed, in elegant company.

Some people have good common sense. They need neither books nor expert consultants, but just some time to think about helpful strategies and solutions. Other people see how others have done it in the workplace: "Mary used to have a tendency similar to mine; I'll watch what she does." If you have faith, you may want to use prayer to bring about the peace and detachment leading to self-transformation. Whatever way you choose to reflect on the problem (books, consultants, strategic planning, good examples, prayer) you will probably require at least one week to develop a strategy to move beyond the problem.

The third step is to set realistic goals for dealing with the criticism. We must select only one or two realistic goals to deal with negative feedback. Any more than this will likely be forgotten when we next experience "mind clutter." These goals should also be shared with our feedback adviser who can help us to get a true sense of progress and to be accountable to our goals.

If we follow these three steps, negative criticism will lead to growth and impart wisdom about how to give feedback (both positive and negative) to others. Eventually, we will cultivate a habit of listening to, and acting on, criticism without undue ego-involvement. Such a habit will not only produce remarkable advances in our relationships with others, but also unparalleled openness to change and creativity.

In organizations, leaders who act upon negative feedback cultivate trust, openness to change, and ability to take risk on the part of their people. People either see or find out that a leader has changed as a direct result of feedback. As a consequence, they are less prone to fear, suspicion, and anger. They accord the leader greater credibility which paves the way for enhanced spirit.

3. Soft-Bargaining

"Soft bargaining" is concerned with helping stakeholders to achieve a "win-win" when their interests diverge. Since hard-bargaining frequently leads to "win-lose" and "lose-lose" "solutions," it should be the method of last resort. To explain how soft-bargaining works, I will discuss forming a soft-bargaining team and using a soft-bargaining process.

Forming a soft-bargaining team. Suppose that our organization has two stakeholder groups, employees and managers, whose interests diverge. Suppose further that these diverse interests are beginning to make the two stakeholders defensive, and that ego-compulsion, anger, fear, passive aggression, and suspicion are growing. At the first available opportunity, the affected stakeholders should appoint members to a soft-bargaining team. The purpose of this team is to construct an initial proposal that can act as a starting point in the process of achieving a "win-win" agreement.

Who should be on this team? Leaders from both sides who have made the five personal commitments and the five people commitments and are actually walking their talk. These individuals will have the interior freedom to proactively listen and to seek common cause and the "win-win." In addition to providing us with a higher sense of purpose in life, greater happiness, better relationships, a better sense of opportunity, and better team behavior, the contributive attitude provides yet another benefit: a greater interior freedom to enter into principled negotiation resulting in a "win-win." The contributive attitude allows leaders to listen, negotiate, and strive for the long-term common good of the whole organization, thus decreasing fear, resentment, passive aggression, compulsive ego, and suspicion. It allows leaders to listen without filtering data through a defensive screen. Leaders can recognize good ideas, places of connection, mutual opportunity, and even look out for one another's long-term concerns. The need to win at all costs (even against our own stakeholders) is also diminished, meaning that we do not have to play out the internal competition game until it results in one stakeholder winning at another stakeholder's expense. The more deeply we appropriate the contributive attitude, the more we are freed from all the games that destroy our organizations (the blame game, the defense game, the internal competition game, which all derive from the comparison game).

Soft-bargaining team members must also have transpositional empathy—the capacity to understand and sympathize with concerns outside of their area of interest. Some people have to be encouraged to pursue mindsets other than their own. They love their specialization and tend to think other specializations are inferior or a waste of time. Others are intrigued by knowledge outside their specialization and need very little encouragement to become cross-functional. I believe that this second group must constitute soft-bargaining teams. Notice that those who lack transpositional empathy are not necessarily compulsive, but their interests do not extend beyond a particular domain, and so it is extraordinarily difficult for them to empathize with people in other domains. Despite their good intentions, they do not seek a "win-win" because they do not have sufficient interest to empathize with another group's concerns.

If we were to set out a number line from 1 to 10, where 1 represents a leader from stakeholder group A (employees) with virtually no transpositional empathy, and 10 represents a leader from stakeholder group B (management) with virtually no transpositional empathy, a soft-bargaining team would ideally consist of 4s and 6s.

All leaders do not have to have a high degree of transpositional empathy, but all leaders should be aware of whether or not they possess this quality. If they do not, it would be best for the common good to appoint other leaders who have this quality to the soft-bargaining team.

It will take courage on the part of both stakeholder groups to implement this soft-bargaining method, because a group of hard-bargainers will likely resist this effort with great energy. They will first try to strike fear into the hearts of both stakeholder groups by telling them that "without down-in-the-trenches, hard-bargaining techniques, our side will come out the losers." If this tactic does not work, they will relate in lucid detail the entire history of bad relations with stakeholder group B. Even though that history may stretch back to the 1930s, stakeholders will believe that the harms done 70 years ago were done to them! And if that doesn't work, they can at least make recourse to suspicion: "We can't trust those guys too much." This at least leaves the door open to "I told you so," if something goes wrong.

The tactics of the hard-bargaining faction include fear, anger/resentment, and suspicion. These debilitators, though absolutely destructive to team behavior and common cause, seem legitimate because "history tells us...." No doubt we can learn much from history, but we are not victims of it—we fashion it according to our principles and our ideals. The moment we feel victimized by history, we are doomed to relive it. Therefore, leaders need to respond to the tactics of hard-bargainers incisively.

With respect to the fear tactic (we will be losers unless we engage in hard-bargaining), Leaders should respond that no soft-bargaining agreement will go into effect without support from at least two-thirds of the membership of both stakeholder groups. In other words, the soft-bargaining team has no power in itself. Its role is to facilitate the process of an agreement by formulating the first drafts of such agreements, seeking feedback from stakeholder groups, and helping to reach consensus. If two-thirds of one of the stakeholder groups rejects such an agreement, consensus will not be reached and the agreement will not go into effect. The stakeholder leadership and membership have complete veto power over any agreement.

With respect to the anger/resentment tactic (the history of bad relations with the other stakeholder group), leaders ought to indicate that we are not victims of our history. Environments, attitudes, culture, and leadership can change. We are not doomed to repeat the mistakes of the past. We need not open up old wounds if we don't want to. Why assume that the negative dimension of history must prevail?

Again, leaders may want to pull out the vision, mission, and core-competency statements from the last 20 years. Note the evolution toward a people-centered organization. This should be evidence enough for any hard-bargainer that we need not repeat the mistakes of the past. We are progressing toward a "win-win," team-oriented, adaptable organization. Leaders cannot afford to let hard bargainers control the telling of the history of an organization. They must also tell their own story based on the evidence contained within their own archives and living memory.

With respect to the tactic of suspicion (calling lack of trust "properly prudential"), we will always encounter people from whom we must protect ourselves. More often than not, they are compulsive rather than malicious but, unfortunately, the negative results are the same. Leaders cannot afford to be naive with respect to this group of individuals. They must take steps to protect the best interests of their stakeholders. However, in the case of soft-bargaining, there is no need to treat an opposing stakeholder with suspicion, because no decision made by the soft-bargaining team can become policy until consensus is reached among two-thirds of the leadership and membership. Premature suspicion makes for bad agreements and bad relationships, and, consequently, for bad history and bad blood. The real prudential course of action is to withhold suspicion until there is reason to believe that the party in question is not trustworthy, not bargaining in good faith, or claims to be something that she is not. Why call a person a liar before she has lied, a thief before he has stolen? Prudence dictates that we assume the best until someone has manifested the worst.

A fourth tactic that sometimes arises is blame (blaming all troubles on the other stakeholder group). Leaders must again take responsibility for telling the story of the organization. A "history" that is oriented toward blame is nothing more than a propaganda instrument. It is not meant to be a way of guiding us to better conduct, it is meant to increase factionalism by appealing to emotions.

The old philosophical cliché—"There are far more errors of omission than commission"—applies especially to the historical enterprise, for historians do not have to lie to manipulate, they only need to leave out information that could lead a listener to another conclusion. Aside from preparing a nation for war, propaganda has little value to individuals, organizations, cultures, and societies. Leaders might agree ahead of time that the objective of telling history is to learn from the mistakes of the past, and this can only happen when errors of omission are kept to a minimum. We need to see what happened, not what we want to believe happened. When blaming and finger pointing come up, it should be a neon sign proclaiming that we are moving from history to propaganda and, therefore, from open communication to closed communication, from a horizon of the "win-win" to the propagation of the "win-lose." Again, unless a group is preparing for war, factionalism has a negative value.

Soft-bargaining is the only way of cultivating long-term, productive relationships with our stakeholders. Leaders must try to find creative, ingenious, discreet, and prudential ways of cutting through the myths of hard-bargainers. Perhaps the best way to begin this enterprise is to remember that many hard-bargainers are not malicious. They do what they do and say what they say out of feelings of loyalty, generosity, and concern for the welfare of the group. Hence, many hard-bargainers are not compulsives. They may well be persons who have simply emphasized the negative dimensions of organizational and cultural history.

Confronting the myths and tactics of hard-bargainers requires extraordinary respect. If a hard-bargainer is a Level 3 person, she will be inclined to move from propaganda back to history. Even though her sense of loyalty may cause her to be suspicious or even cynical, she will have an inclination to look for contribution and the good news, and to pursue the "win-win" in trust. When relating to such a person, it is best to appeal to the higher viewpoints and commitments. If a person is a hard-bargainer out of competitive compulsion, it would probably be best to confront more directly the hard bargaining tactics. In either case, respect, dignity, and proactive listening is the best way to courageously pursue the "win-win" through soft-bargaining.

The Process of Soft-Bargaining. Once both stakeholder groups have appointed an appropriate number of participants with a high degree of internal freedom and transpositional empathy to the soft-bargaining team, the team can begin forging a "win-win" agreement. There are four steps in forging such an agreement.

Step One. Team members must meet their confreres and determine whether or not a member of the team should be replaced. If a compulsive person with low transpositional empathy should be mistakenly placed on a soft-bargaining team, he will create so much defensiveness that the work of the team will take three times longer than needed. Sometimes a compulsive person can sabotage the team's efforts completely. Obviously, it is an extraordinarily touchy matter to replace a person who has been appointed to a team, but there is really no other way out if this team is the only vehicle through which a "win-win" agreement can be achieved. Hence, the leaders of both stakeholder groups must make their selection of team members very carefully.

Step Two. Once the team is content with the membership of both sides, they can go about their business of listening to one another's fears and hopes. Both sides might prepare, in writing, a brief synopsis of the fears and pressures with which they are concerned, and the hopes and aspirations they have for a successful agreement. These documents might be exchanged before a meeting to draft an agreement. It takes time to proactively listen to another viewpoint. Therefore, if each group is allowed to reflect on the other group's fears and hopes for three or four days, they can think about where the avenues of opportunity, the open windows, and the possible connections and compromise might occur.

Step Three. After the period of reflection, both groups come to the table with some ideas about how to fashion a "win-win" agreement. It would probably be a good idea to review the five commitments with one another before discussing specific proposals. Once this is done, both groups can share ideas about where they think compromise can best occur. The group must strive to arrive at an agreement because if it cannot, the recourse will likely be hard-bargaining and long-term losses. When an agreement is reached, it should be written in language that allows for adjustment and flexibility by the leadership and membership of both sides.

Step Four. The initial proposal should then be presented to both sides, along with a history about how and why the proposal was formed. Suggestions should be solicited from the leadership and membership of both sides, and these should be taken back to the soft-bargaining team. Suggestions that can be accommodated should be. Inevitably, many suggestions can not be accommodated, and these must be taken back to the leadership and membership of both groups.

The process of going back and forth between the team and the leadership and membership might be called "consensus building." We should never stop communicating and bargaining until a final agreement has been reached. If communication stops, then soft-bargaining will stop. And if soft-bargaining stops, the probable result will be hard-bargaining with all its negative consequences. Continuous communication not only keeps the feedback loops open, it also helps leadership and membership to understand the position of the other stakeholder group. When people who lack transpositional empathy hear a position presented from different angles four or five times, they begin to understand and accommodate what they may have formerly misunderstood. Mutual understanding, however, requires that the leadership and membership on both sides keep their frustration level low. Patience fosters understanding. Look at how General George Marshall convinced the allies of the efficacy of the Marshall plan—a remarkable "win-win" agreement that occurred in the midst of considerable hard feelings.

The tactics of soft-bargaining—how each party should present its interests to the other party—are outlined succinctly in a curriculum from Harvard University.[1] These tactics provide a protocol for both the soft-bargaining team and the leadership of both stakeholder groups.

Soft-bargaining is useful to maintain a long-term "win-win" atmosphere. It helps to bind stakeholders together when their interests diverge, and it can heal ruptures in stakeholder relationships that arise out of past difficulties. Therefore, it leads directly to a decrease in the five debilitators and an increase in morale, team function, and spirit.

The 12 Principles of Inspired Leadership

The 12 principles of inspired leadership may appear daunting to leaders who came into the workplace 15 to 20 years ago, who are all too familiar with "high maintenance" personnel, and who view the hard tasks of day-to-day operations as more important than the long-term striving to move an organization toward a people-oriented environment. Still, I invite you to take them seriously because they can help you use the strengths of people in the new environment to create adaptability, self-motivation, specialization, and creativity; overcome the generation gap by allowing both older and younger employees to use their strengths for optimal benefit; help resolve existing problems produced by this changed environment; and build a people system that will allow for higher rates of adaptation and self-motivation in the future.

The following 12 principles represent a summary of the ideals of inspired leaders. They show at once how to bring ourselves and our organizations into today's fast-changing, specialized, autonomous work environment. Proper adaptation to environmental changes can be best expedited by appropriating these principles. Principles 1, 2, and 3 concern attitudes; principles 4, 5, and 6 concern the regular treatment of stakeholders; principles 7 and 8 concern reward structures; principles 9, 10, and 11 concern teaming; and principle 12 concerns the wisdom to know when oversight is appropriate.

Principle 1: To strive to live according to the six higher viewpoints. What we as leaders believe and live personally fashions our style of leadership. What is going on in our personal life affects our work life, and what's going on in our work life affects our personal life. Adopting the six higher viewpoints can remove the compulsions from our leadership.

We can't achieve instantaneous and perfect appropriation of the higher viewpoints; however, striving for these attitudes will show our colleagues and coworkers that we are serious and authentic about pursuing them. Perhaps more importantly, the appropriation of these higher viewpoints will facilitate the living of the five commitments and the precepts of organizational vision. They will, therefore, decrease compulsion and increase adaptation to environmental changes.

Principle 2: To walk the talk of the five personal commitments. The five personal commitments issue directly from the six higher viewpoints. Hence, if a leader is striving for higher viewpoints, the commitments will become integral to her life.

These commitments must become integral to a leader's style and to the environment in which she operates. To do this, leaders must not only inspire their people to live according to these five commitments, but also help to create an environment where these attitudes can be improved. Leaders should publicly demonstrate, in small and large ways, these five commitments—particularly the commitment to pursue a "win-win" for all stakeholders, and should seek regular guidance (at least 15 minutes every two weeks) from a trusted feedback adviser to obtain another viewpoint on the people atmosphere within their team, to set goals for attitude development, and to find ways of inspiring people to imitate these goals.

Principle 3: To embrace the vision of people and ethics that manifest the ideal organization. Embracing a principle-centered vision helps leaders move to a higher perspective on people and ethics. These principles constitute ideals for stakeholders in contemporary organizations. By taking them seriously, a leader can decrease compulsions and enhance the workplace environment (e.g., by increasing education, the desire to participate and create, sensitivity to the dignity, rights, and autonomy of others, self-motivation and self-efficacy, and capacity for technical competence). This vision statement will also enable leaders to minimize the negative effects of mixed blessings in the changed work environment (e.g., hyper-independence and autonomy, hypersensitivity to guidance, unrealistic expectations for success, and a belief that dreams alone—without work and education—will be sufficient to advance).

Sometimes pushing these negative buttons is unavoidable, if not necessary; however pushing them without cause only leads to consternation, frustration, resentment, and the familiar refrain, "That's not fair!" Hypersensitivity in the workplace is a product of a changed culture and a changed work environment. The commitments, questions, and principles are designed to move around these hot buttons while playing to the strengths and good will of people.

Principle 4: To seek and support the talent and the "good news" of stakeholders. The more we support, praise, and thank others for the good work that they do, the more they will feel appreciated and needed. The more they feel appreciated and needed, the more they will derive purpose and energy from their work and their relationship to the organization. The more they derive purpose and energy, the more creative, proactive, cooperative, and happy they will be. This will bring about an adaptable, self-motivated, synergistic environment.

Principle 5: To listen proactively, making stakeholders' concerns your concerns. If employees are observant and cooperative, they will likely see at least 60 percent more than any leader can see because they are closer to the point of origin of data (e.g., customers, the production line, technical support teams, vendors, etc.). If a leader proactively listens to his employees, his decisions will be better informed and more effective. If he reacts to the employees defensively, he will receive little data and hear even less. In place of defensiveness, he would be attentive to all suggestions of stakeholders, act upon usable data and give credit to the stakeholder who offered it, listen most carefully to stakeholders who indicate that something is not going right, and seek a way of redressing this negative feedback if it is found to be accurate.

When a subordinate or team member approaches a leader with a problem, the leader's first reaction might be, "I don't have time to deal with this right now," or "This will be a real hassle. I'm going to stave it off as long as possible." Escape can sometimes bring relief, but it generally undermines creativity, quality, and synergy. Most people are not incessant complainers. They generally point to real problems that will only get worse in the future. Leaders need not face these problems alone, for the people who point them out normally have several thoughts about alleviating them. If a leader brings these suggestions back to the environment where the problem is occurring, gives credit to the co-worker who gave them, and (if possible) forms a consensus around her suggestions, problems will be averted, the person who made the suggestions will feel encouraged to do more, and the leader will build credibility and trust within the team.

Since the rewards of listening are so great, leaders will want to schedule particular times for feedback.

Principle 6: To increase trust in the environment through empowerment and education. The more a leader expresses trust for stakeholders, the more the stakeholders feel at least partially accountable to that trust. Leaders still need to check financial records, production, and quality (especially in organizations where people's lives could be jeopardized by a mistake), but they should keep checks to a minimum and trust to a maximum.

We might apply the following rule of thumb: first, analyze safety parameters; second, assess the time period in which unsupervised problems could become critical; and third, assess how much oversight is required for particular persons and groups. We can then estimate the checking that needs to be done. If we discover that more oversight is required, then we can ease it back in. If people are using our trust well, we might reduce the oversight.

Empowerment has gone through a series of peaks and troughs. It was thought to be the "cure-all" for business because it was oriented toward self-motivation, self-efficacy, self-accountability, openness to change, and openness to reasonable risk. It seemed to be the foundation of "thinking implementers." Unfortunately, the first attempts to empower people fell on hard times because individuals were empowered but not groups and teams, people were not prepared to be self-accountable and became fearful of failure and blame, and a compulsive atmosphere confirmed people's suspicions that they were risking too much by accepting this so-called power. They viewed empowerment as a Trojan horse. It seemed beautiful on the outside, but an enemy was within. It seemed to encourage autonomous action and increased education and creativity, but in the end, would foist additional risk and uncompensated responsibility on those who accepted it. Most people returned the horse to the Greeks.

I hesitate to use the word "empowerment" in expressing this principle because it carries so much negative baggage. However, the concept is still relevant. All we need to do is change how we achieve it. As noted, people are more desirous than ever to participate, create, and enter into significant teaming relationships. They want to accomplish something. They want to know how these accomplishments contribute to the company, to the industry, and to the community. They enjoy using their talents, energy, and intellect for worthwhile projects. They want to be needed and to be of value.

Leaders can help to overcome compulsive suspicion, blame, resentment, fear, and ego in the workplace by keeping people focused on contribution and commitment.

As an attitude of trust begins to emerge, empowerment becomes a real possibility. In fact, it may become the very agency through which many of these problems are alleviated.

To produce an environment of empowerment and trust, leaders must also prepare their people to succeed at taking additional responsibility. They need to offer training and education to encourage interior freedom, generativity, and proactive habits. Training builds additional skills and competencies, and humanistic education leads toward enhanced self-efficacy, self-motivation, generative behavior, teamsmanship, and creativity. Such focused education can lead directly to thinking implementers.

Finally, empowerment must occur within a team. Some leaders can accept responsibility for a project by themselves. They are the Harry Truman types who can really say and mean "The buck stops here," or "If you can't stand the heat, get out of the kitchen." But most people (including many leaders) do not like standing alone with the entire organization resting on their shoulders. Most people would prefer to be empowered in teams, to have self-accountability within collective accountability. This means that they must have an awareness of how their part links up with other parts, to see where there is overlapping, the points at which they can share data with and receive data from others, and the points at which collective creativity and synergy can occur. This requires enabling specialists to be generalists and enabling meaningful cross-functionality to occur within teams.

Recall the fundamental rule of leadership: "To replace oversight with inspiration wherever possible." This means estimating the minimum amount of oversight and adjusting upward or downward from there in real situations. Empowerment cannot occur without trust. If certain conditions are not met, individuals will not be adequately prepared to take on additional responsibility and accountability. In addition to trust and individual empowerment, leaders need to help people get a sense of the cross-functional picture and assist them in working in a cross-functional environment.

Principle 7: To find better ways of rewarding stakeholders who practice the five personal commitments, people commitments, and ethical commitments. Contributive attitudes pave the way for trust. Trust paves the way for empowerment through teams. Reward structures reinforce and make systemic these enhancements of the people system. A leader's objective is not merely to enhance trust, empowerment, thinking implementers, self-motivation, teamwork, creativity, and synergy; it is also to make these features a recurrent and enduring part of a team or organization. Hence, a leader must not only pave the way for change, she must create a scheme of recurrence, a system.

Schemes of recurrence connected with people are intimately concerned with reward structures. If reward structures reflect what is asked for, it will become a systematic reality. If they do not, requests will fall on deaf ears. This is not because stakeholders are greedy and self-seeking, but rather because they make a very simple judgment: "If this is really important to leadership, they will reward us for it. If this is just trendy, or a new experiment, they won't. We know what's really important by how much leadership invests in the request."

Moving from a competitive culture to a contributive culture does not mean abandoning rewards such as money, promotion, and prestige. Such rewards are connected with workers' self-esteem. Corporate culture for years has reinforced the opinion that greater pay and greater promotion represent greater worth. To the degree that people care about the worth that others assign to them, and to the degree that such rewards signify worth, people will care about them. Also, such rewards affect domestic tranquillity. To the degree that these rewards are necessary for one's children's education, or to the degree that a person is concerned with a spouse's level of promotion, people will care about these rewards. Leaders must use such rewards to reinforce desired behaviors, particularly new desired behaviors.

Leaders must also infuse Level 3 rewards into the culture. These rewards are concerned with thanking co-workers and telling them about the contributions they make and how much they are needed. They promote increased training and humanistic education. They lead directly to a decrease in oversight (an increase in trust). They provide additional avenues for participation, creativity, and synchronicity. They lead to enjoyable work, which gives rise to a high-energy, synergistic, participative, co-creative atmosphere that many workers will consider of equal (if not greater) importance than money and ego-gratification. Leaders need to think about how to produce these rewards, for they will decrease critical skills turnover, increase team synergy, and reinforce the contributive behaviors anticipated by the higher viewpoints and commitments.

What should be rewarded? In addition to some traditional objectives (performance, quality, and cost-containment), certain team building objectives must also be rewarded. Of particular importance would be: acting upon the five commitments, bringing a "win-win" attitude into one's team or organization, bringing creative ideas to the team, seeking and taking justifiable risks in cooperation with leadership, taking steps to help others in their work performance, taking steps to pursue cross-functional knowledge and relationships, taking steps to ease tension within the work environment, and actively supporting and encouraging others to support the team and its objectives.

Organizations can benefit tremendously by allowing people to help others grow in competence. Sometimes this may take only 10 minutes (e.g., turning to a co-worker and saying, "You might try it this way...."). It might come in the form of a course where a qualified person might give instruction to a group, or where co-workers help train and educate others for the long-term common good. This atmosphere of the "learning organization" not only increases competency, but builds group ethos and bonds of camaraderie.

Principle 8: To initiate 10 percent team rewards (rewards given to the team leader who, in turn, distributes it to the players). If an organization is to show that it values teams, then it must not only reward individuals for team behavior, but also reward teams for high performance. If a team is rewarded as a whole for high performance, people will work for team objectives to receive those rewards and, furthermore, be convinced that leadership really does care about high performance teaming. Many books are devoted to creative schemes for team rewards.[2] My purpose here is not to delineate them, but merely to encourage their use.

Principle 9: To use "soft-bargaining" techniques to solve problems and facilitate consensus in large teams. Soft-bargaining is essential to cultivating a "win-win" atmosphere which, in turn, is integral to high performance teaming. Soft-bargaining techniques can be used in a variety of circumstances such as bringing together stakeholders with opposed interests, and healing past troubled relationships. They can also be used to maintain team unity when different subgroups within the team are at odds with one another. If the team has less than 20 members, it is not necessary to create a soft-bargaining committee. The team leader may, therefore, apply consensus-building techniques directly to the problem.

Principle 10: To use co-designed and co-owned experiments to improve quality, processes, structures, and relationships. A co-designed experiment is a way of using these leadership principles to bring about improvements in processes, structures, product development, relationships, waste control, and product design (in short, quality). This experimental approach not only produces quality improvement, but helps stakeholders to adapt to change, to be open to risk, to increase trust, and to take ownership of their work and team tasks. It is the essential underpinning of a flexible people system that can endure for decades.

Principle 11: To cultivate inspired leadership and facilitate team objectives, team unity, and team empowerment. Inspired leaders spend their time, energy, and creativity not only on budget, administration, and oversight, but also on cultivating teamwork, encouraging new ideas, helping people to become enthusiastic and spirited, helping them to be open to change and to take reasonable risks, facilitating the growth of thinking implementers, promoting "soft-bargaining," promoting personal, people, and ethical commitments, promoting friendship and collegiality, cultivating a cohesive, creative, synergistic operation of people, and knowing how to let collective serendipity happen.

Inspired leaders develop these qualities in their leadership style. If leaders truly value these qualities and experience their efficacy in the workplace, they will make them "second nature."

Principle 12: To cultivate the wisdom to know when oversight is required and to facilitate appropriate feedback-adviser relationships. Perhaps the most difficult task of inspired leadership is judging how much oversight is needed for particular groups and individuals. The new environmental factors almost certainly assure different levels of desire for participation, creativity, and contribution within teams. Leaders can accommodate this wide range of capacity for empowerment by leaning toward minimum oversight. As the new generation begins to move into the workplace, the desire for participation and creativity will increase. Hence, leadership should err on the side of minimum oversight rather than maximum oversight.

Minimum oversight must be judged according to three parameters: 1) safety, 2) the time period in which unsupervised problems could become critical; and 3) the oversight expected by the majority of the group. If the safety of people is at stake, then managers cannot err on the side of minimum oversight. Oversight must be judged in accordance with what is necessary to be certain about safety. If safety is not a factor, the time devoted to oversight should be judged minimalistically. Leaders should not deviate from this standard unless they discover that their people are not yet capable of self-motivation. Oversight should be timed to coincide with the points at which problems could occur.

If workers are capable of functioning adequately with minimum oversight, leadership must thank them for it; and support, reward, and reinforce them in it. If leaders do not thank, reward, and support this behavior, workers will think that self-accountability is foolish, for every time they are self-accountable leadership's expectations go up without any concomitant increase in credit and reward. If minimal oversight is going to work, leaders must be sensitive to, and deeply aware of, how much more they rely on their people.

The oversight required directly depends on the oversight expected. If workers expect considerable oversight, leaders must give it to them. That is why leaders need to wean their people off of a high supervisory expectation. Such expectations have two disadvantages. First, leaders have to spend time supervising instead of educating and inspiring their people toward self-motivation. Self-motivation has a huge future dividend, while supervision has benefit only in the present. Secondly, any work group will be composed of those who need much oversight and those who need little. It is fatal to err in favor of those who need much oversight, for we will wipe out the self-motivation of those who need little. They will see their initiative and creativity falling on deaf ears, and most of the leader's time and attention being spent on those requiring high maintenance. This will lead to discouragement and even cynicism on the part of those who are most empowered.

The better route is to err on the side of those who need minimum supervision by helping those who need much to expect less by educating and training, thanking and rewarding, and treating setbacks as educational experiences rather than as shameful failures. The last quality is extremely important and requires further explanation.

I am reminded of a large organization that hired a young vice-president right out of a Ph.D. program at a prestigious American university. This young vice-president took several reasonable risks to help enhance product development and market share. Some of these risky endeavors fell on hard times, and he lost X million dollars. Thinking that he would surely be fired, he went back to his office to pack up his personal items. The president of the company got wind of what he was doing and went to meet him, asking, "Where are you going?" The young man responded, "Well, I lost X million dollars so I figured I would be fired." To which the president responded, "Oh, no. I'm not firing you. I just invested X million dollars in your education, and I'll be darned if you're going to take it to the competition." The president's attitude was sound, for he realized that setback is education, not an occasion for blame. With a modicum of creativity, that education can be transformed into highly innovative product designs, processes, and market strategies. I might add that the company benefited from the decisions of the young vice-president for years to come.

As with the personal, people, and ethical commitments, I suggest integrating these principles (stated below in question form) into your decision-making processes and daily reflections.

Essential Questions for Bringing Leadership Principles into the Workplace

Questions concerning fundamental attitudes:

1) Am I trying to appropriate "the five commitments for increasing trust" into my personal life?
2) As a leader, am I walking the talk of "the five personal commitments for increasing trust?"
3) As a leader, am I walking the talk of the people commitments and ethical commitments?

Questions concerning regular treatment of people:

4) Am I seeking and supporting the talent and the "good news" of stakeholders?
5) Am I proactively listening to stakeholders, and making their concerns my concerns?
6) Am I increasing trust within the organizational environment by empowering and educating stakeholders?

Essential Questions for Bringing Leadership Principles into the Workplace (continued)

Questions concerning reward structures:

7) Am I finding Level 2 and Level 3 ways of rewarding stakeholders who are practicing the "win-win" principle and ethics?

8) Am I trying to initiate team rewards (rewards given to the team who, in turn, distributes them to the players)?

Questions concerning teams:

9) Am I using "soft bargaining" techniques to solve problems and facilitate consensus in teams?

10) Am I using the techniques of co-participation and co-ownership to facilitate teamwork?

11) Am I cultivating inspired leadership and facilitating team objectives, team unity, and team empowerment?

Wisdom:

12) Am I cultivating the wisdom to know when oversight is required? When it is required, am I facilitating appropriate relationships?

16 Self-Motivation, Creativity, and Care

Leading by higher principles decreases the five debilitators while increasing trust, common cause, spirit, team performance, openness to change, openness to cross-functionality, and ability to take reasonable risks. It also has a profound effect on self-motivation and creativity.

Self-Motivation

The following chart indicates the long-term effects of external motivation—fear, force, and bribe—and inspirational self-motivation.

Level 2	Level 3
Force/Fear/Bribe	*Inspirational*
Short Term ↓ Passive Aggression ↓ Negative Ethos ↓ Negative Supervisor Structures ↓ Aggressive Aggression	Long Term ↓ Inspirational & Empowering ↓ Trust and Open Communication ↓ Leaders spend time on "Win-Win" & Teams instead of Oversight ↓ Synergistic Teaming

EXTERNAL MOTIVATION

External motivation—fear, force, and bribe—conforms itself to the following five-step progression:

First, external motivation is short-term. The energy used and the atmosphere created by this motivation is essentially negative and has negative consequences on turnover of critical skills personnel and morale. With respect to turnover, fear, force, and bribe will discourage people who have opportunities to work in more positive, participative environments. People with these opportunities are generally highly self-motivated, creative, and quality driven. These people generally view the atmosphere in which they work to be of high priority in job selection. They will even sacrifice up to a 15 percent drop in salary to work in such an environment. Needless to say, turnover among this group not only costs the organization time and money for retraining, it creates a "brain drain." The long-term consequences for future adaptability, risk taking, creativity, and quality are, as a result, substantially diminished.

With respect to morale: fear, force, and bribe create long-term passive aggression. These motivations can have a substantial short-term effect, even help people who are not particularly self-motivated to change their attitudes; but in general, negative motivations tend to kill proactive behavior because this might jeopardize employment. Hence, people tend to develop two personalities: one for the boss (a forced, but nevertheless pleasant, smile) and one for their co-workers (essentially negative and gloomy). This bifurcation of personality generally takes the form of passive aggression. Though people are pleasant, they are always a bit on edge and resentful about having to do things for an unappreciative or even compulsive boss. As a result, they fight themselves to participate in the boss' project. They don't feel excited or positively engaged in being part of the leader's project. Despite their affected pleasant disposition, it takes them longer to do tasks. They seem to be easily exhausted, and they begin to play little control games with the manager.

Passive aggression is a substantial but needless waste of time, money, creativity, and resources. Inasmuch as people have to use twice as much energy to do the same work, they begin to slow down. Standards are lowered, expectations dropped, and, even then, people still feel overworked. The games are costly, too. Employees take a certain delight in watching the boss squirm when his timetables cannot be met and pressures mount. The best part is, they cannot be held accountable for it. Whatever they are doing is excusable. They may say, "I have so many other tasks from so many other managers," or "I haven't been trained to do that," "It's not in my job description," or they may make little mistakes that get lost in the shuffle, but affect quality.

This leads to the third stage: negative ethos. Passive aggression has an odd way of becoming collective. When particular employees practice it for six months or more, they tend to make the negative aspects of their employment the focal point of their work lives. This not only leads to an atmosphere of complaint, discouragement, and cynicism, it also increases the passive aggressive behavior in the workplace. This negative atmosphere will manifest itself in increased flowtimes, lower performance, and decreased quality which will, in turn, alarm leadership.

This leads to leadership's enhancement of fear and force through increased supervision. Most leaders will not recognize passive aggression to be the true reason behind decreased performance and quality. They will normally blame these problems on laziness, incompetence, and the bad will of workers. Belief in these negative motives will enflame a leader's compulsive ego. He will not want to let these "so and so's" get away with this, and will have to push back. But pushing begets pushing; negativity begets negativity; and vengeance begets vengeance.

The negative supervision creates an atmosphere ripe with the anticipation of collective aggressive aggression. All that's needed now is one little manifestation of insensitivity to trigger collective aggressive aggression. This could manifest itself as a group's refusal to engage in a process or to act like a team, increased antagonistic union activity, or even a strike. In any case, such aggressive actions take years to heal. The increased suspicion and resentment enhances and perpetuates passive aggression on unprecedented levels.

So, fear, force, and bribe is not an altogether intelligent long-term strategy for retaining critical skills personnel, enhancing morale, and alleviating passive aggressive and aggressive aggressive environments.

INSPIRATIONAL MOTIVATION

We see opposite consequences arising from inspirational motivation. Inasmuch as inspirational motivation enhances participation, creativity, and teamwork, it must also provide a desirable atmosphere for self-motivated, high quality, critical skills personnel. Such an organization will not only attract a future generation of leaders, it will help those who formerly required more oversight to become more self-motivated and independent. In addition, it will enhance morale, opening the way for better teaming.

Inspirational motivation tends to be more long-term than fear and force. Instead of creating passive aggression, it actually frees workers to offer goodwill toward leadership. Indeed, their sense of empowerment and respect—and possibly even collegiality with leaders—motivates them to do the best possible job, to go the extra mile, to offer their creativity, and even to inspire others around them. This tends to enhance energy within the workplace. Even though people are doing far more, pursuing quality far more conscientiously, and even making innovations, they feel less burdened and tired. They look forward to coming to work and even feel a sense of excitement and accomplishment about what they do. As long as management recognizes this, thanks them, rewards them, and empowers them, they will continue to progress. Passive aggression will be replaced with enhanced goodwill, self-motivation, and synergy.

Just when fear and force are transforming passive aggression into negative ethos, inspirational leadership is transforming goodwill and synergy into a positive ethos. When individuals feel an enhanced sense of energy, they not only manifest their goodwill toward leadership, they manifest it toward one another. This gives rise to both open communication and an openness to teaming. It creates collective spirit, friendship, and spirited collegiality within the workplace. These friendships not only decrease the fears underlying suspicion but also increase the desire to trust. Friendship and trust continue to open the way to communication, synergy, and collective spirit.

Leaders can now afford to move from supervisory/oversight roles to more inspirational roles. Just when fear and force are leading to increased negative supervision, inspirational motivation is opening the way to a decreased need for supervision and oversight. Ironically, inspirational leadership feeds itself. It gives rise to the very collective spirit that allows leaders to transfer their time from oversight functions that pay dividends only in the present; to the education, empowerment, and team-building that give rise to dividends far into the future.

The empowerment of individuals through inspiration, spirited collegiality, and teams allows both leaders and team members to pursue quality objectives through co-designed experiments. When successful, these experimental projects build trust, team spirit, openness to risk and change, and creativity, while they improve quality in the areas of product design, elimination of product defects, elimination of waste, and improvement of processes. In short, when fear and force are a hair trigger away from aggressive aggression, inspirational leadership is overcoming opportunity cost and creating quality improvement through a people system that will last long into the future.

The consequences of inspirational leadership are too significant to be overlooked. The difference between the extrinsic and inspirational models of leadership spells the difference between a downward and an upward spiral; between suspicion and trust; closed communication and open communication; resistance to change and openness to change; bad morale and good morale; negative ethos and positive ethos; unsuccessful teams and high performance teams; investing only in the present and investing in the future.

Creativity

Insight occurs when one grasps a connection among diverse realities. It is not simply an experience or observation, it is an awareness of relationships. These relationships could be temporal, geographical, cause and effect, numeric, attitudinal, ethical, or interpersonal. Some natural connections already exist, and are there to be discovered. Other connections await a creative mind to invent them (e.g., a process, a system, or a culture). Whether we are discovering connections or inventing them, we must have the capacity to see them.

Seeing connections may be provoked by necessity (in times of famine or war), by love of a discipline (the discovery of a new mathematical method), love of humanity or desire to contribute (the creation of the Peace Corps) or some combination of love and necessity. Necessity and love provoke questions. Questions are a state of conscious desire, a mental openness that can recognize the rightness or wrongness of a connection when it comes. Even though it has not yet grasped the connection, the questioning consciousness has a pre-awareness of the conditions that must be met to have a right, good, and correct answer.

Seeing a new connection can be impeded by too much dependence on past ways of thinking, by pressure (provoking fear), or by overplanning or premature planning. These conditions cause blind spots that inhibit new perspectives by forcing old perspectives into one's process of inquiry. In the creative enterprise, it is important to test the adequacy of old ways of thinking and to acknowledge that an older way of thinking may not any longer do the job. It is not so much that the older way of thinking is wrong, but that it is missing something that has become crucial to overcoming the more complex questions and problems of the present day.

Why are there so many more errors of omission? Because omissions do not become obvious until our questions and problems outstretch the complexity of the previous system of answers and connections. Necessity gives rise to more complex problems which, in turn, reveal omissions which, in turn, compel us to overcome these omissions through new connections (insights).

Once we know that something is missing (but not what is missing) we need to move outside the realm of conventional thought and achieve a higher viewpoint. We must stand outside the problem and look at it from new and different perspectives, being open to clues arising out of this serendipitous enterprise. Insight has a way of creeping in. As we play with the problem by looking at it in various ways, seeking new perspectives, trying to release ourselves from conventional connections by hovering above the data and looking at newer ways in which it might be connected; we begin to get an inkling of a solution, the beginning of excitement, a sense that we caught a glimpse of something, but were not yet able to fix on it.

This reveals two dimensions within the human psyche: 1) a conventional dimension that patterns itself according to old routines and familiar methods, and 2) a serendipitous dimension that has little concern for old methods and connections and is open to new ways of looking at things—to surprise, to clues, to analogies and associations. In this second dimension, routine is boring and invention is adventure. The conventional function enjoys reaching the goal while the serendipitous function prefers exploring. It appreciates the new, enjoys surprise, and thinks by association and analogy, which, for the conventional mind, is bothersome, disordered, and likely to get in the way of moving routinely to the goal. The conventional function does not like surprises. The serendipitous side lives for them. In a way, the serendipitous part of the psyche is childlike. The conventional function is more serious, like a parent. If we can achieve that childlike wonder, openness, and love of associations and analogies, we will likely hit upon new connections and ways at looking at things that the conventional function would never dream of.

Serendipity works by free associations and analogies. When the psyche is confronted by a problem that old methods do not resolve, it becomes contemplative and begins to associate aspects of the problem with aspects of experience. Sometimes it gets lucky and finds a real analogy and experience that provides the answer to its question.

A classical example of this is the story of Archimedes, a physicist of ancient Greece. He was given a commission by the King of Syracuse to determine whether a crown was made of real gold. To make this determination, he had to know the precise volume of the crown. But because of the peculiar shape of the crown, he was not able to use traditional Pythagorean formulae. How could he determine the volume of the crown without reshaping it to conform to a Pythagorean sphere or cube?

At this point, Archimedes' conventional psyche had run out of possibilities, and so he wandered around the streets of Syracuse seeking an association, a clue from some part of his experience that could provide an analogous solution. He found himself at the baths of Syracuse, and upon sinking into the bath, detected the water rising. He immediately associated the displacement of the water upwards with the volume of his body, and saw the analogical implications for his problem. The displacement of the water was uniform, and therefore could be easily measured, giving the volume of the crown. He got up out of the bathtub and shouted, "Eureka! I have found it!"

This famous example shows how creativity works: 1) a part of Archimedes' experience connected with a part of his problem (a peculiarly shaped body and a peculiarly shaped crown), 2) this experience provided an analogous solution to his problem – the water rose uniformly as his non-uniform body sank into it, 3) insight: non-uniform body is to uniform water displacement as non-uniform crown is to uniform water displacement.

When did Archimedes' conventional psyche disengage? At the very moment he recognized the inadequacy of conventional method. This is not easily accomplished, for the conventional mind wants to believe that its conventional solution will work. It could, therefore, be stubborn, satisfy itself with mediocrity and second-class solutions, and ignore problems. Not wanting to reorient its world view, it holds on to the old perspective. In the case of Archimedes, it was patently obvious that the convention (Pythagoras) wasn't going to work without a uniform shape. In other cases, it is possible to continue testing inadequate hypotheses and asking wrong questions for weeks or more.

How is it that we finally stop repeating the same mistakes? It seems as if the serendipitous part of the psyche comes to an inverse insight.[1] After much frustration, the psyche realizes that it must get outside of its conventional box. It must bring something new to the inquiry, and so it begins to look around for associations and potential analogies that will help it to meet its objective.

At this point, the serendipitous mind takes over and allows itself to wonder, to place together connections in odd, new, even random ways, to embrace data in free associations in the anticipation that a new connectedness will jump right out in answer to new problems.

Serendipity works best 1) when the psyche disengages its conventional function, 2) when it feels free to take risks, 3) when it is relaxed, and 4) when it has time to allow connections and clues to naturally emerge.

How can the psyche disengage its conventional function? By being true to inverse insights. When it runs up against a brick wall and tries again and again to make the conventional mode of thinking work, but fails to do so, it must admit the unworkability of routine. The psyche will battle itself for it will become time conscious. Routine is fast. New ways of looking at things are not only slow, they could be completely unproductive—"I could be wasting my time." But the disciplined psyche knows what it has to do: disengage from the quick and easy routine and wander into a wilderness where connections and analogies, though present, may be difficult to see.

The psyche not only wants to hold onto routine, it also wants to hold onto security. When we feel insecure or there is blame or adversity in the atmosphere, we will rely on our conventional and routine ways of thinking to defend ourselves. In the past, convention has helped us to cope with adverse situations and to deal with predators. Its soothing presence helps to assuage fear and adversity. In short, if the atmosphere in which we dwell is filled with fear, blame, and suspicion, the psyche will not feel free to disengage its conventional function. It will run the conventional mode at hyperdrive to protect itself. It thinks more quickly with routines, and besides, new is dangerous.

Relaxation also seems to be integral to serendipity. Insight frequently occurs when we are taking a walk or relaxing in a comfortable spot, when we are falling asleep, daydreaming, and dreaming in our sleep. When the psyche is on a forced march, has to meet an unmovable deadline, or is overloaded with "administrivia," it will default to its conventional function. Convention will facilitate its forced march, its need to organize the myriad of administrative details, and to meet its deadlines. But when it gets a little distance, when it feels relaxed and contemplative, it can achieve a most remarkable openness.

The fourth condition of creativity concerns having adequate time to be creative. Again, if the psyche feels itself up against a hard deadline, it will default to its conventional function, for this is the only way that it can cope in a routine manner with the pressure of the deadline. Creativity, then, is best facilitated by soft or flexible deadlines and open horizons. If genuine creativity is required (if a team or organization really does want to move beyond routine functions to think outside the box), it is best to plan for additional time and even for horizons beyond that additional time.

The conditions for creativity are, in some respects, opposed to regular management functioning. This forces leadership to make hard judgments about situations that concern long-term relationships, team building, and quality improvement. These long-term judgments require teams to think outside the box, which can only occur if leadership delegates some administrative details that may impede genuine creative activity.

Leaders must not only make room for creativity in specific long-term planning situations by suspending some standard operating procedures, they must also allow for creativity in day-to-day operations by encouraging a contributive environment through the 12 principles of leadership. If we examine carefully the four conditions of creativity, we can readily see that the 12 principles of leadership allow the serendipitous function of the psyche to emerge naturally in the course of business. Conversely, compulsive environments seriously impede creativity.

The fear and force intrinsic to competitive motivation compels the psyche to engage its conventional function to the exclusion of its serendipitous one. The fear and blame in the environment leaves no room for risk-taking, relaxation, or soft deadlines. The psyche will, therefore, do anything and everything to conform to standard operating procedures, direct orders, hard deadlines, and well-known processes. It will not only confine itself to being inside "the box," but will also confine itself to the narrowest box possible. It will, therefore, plan for acceptable results instead of creative results. It will drive itself to "crank out" a plan that can be shown to a leader and then filed away for posterity.

So much of our planning and so-called creative endeavors never get used. The plan is acceptable, but not usable. The "acceptable plan" will probably cost a lot to implement and will produce very little advantage over the status quo.

The status quo, therefore, seems to be the best option for the moment, and real creativity is never endeavored. The 12 principles of leadership are geared toward inspiration and creating an environment that allows for self-motivation, self-efficacy, risk, common cause, the common good, and synergy. They open the way to the four conditions for creativity.

The 12 principles of leadership also open the way to *collective* creativity by engendering a spirited, openly communicative team environment. Collective creativity is somewhat difficult to grasp. There is, however, tremendous evidence of it in the scientific, engineering, and business communities. When a group of creative individuals comes together filled with a spirit of common cause, they seem to have an openness to one another's thought processes that goes beyond what is verbally articulated. The individuals in such groups build on one another's ideas spontaneously, have an awareness of what's coming next, and have a unified sense of which ideas are going in the right direction and which ones are not. They have a sense of how to organize, actualize, experiment with, and correct these ideas. The experience seems to be playful yet energizing, filled with abandon yet utterly productive. The presence of many interactive minds will necessarily compound the associations and the analogies that constitute creativity.

Collective creativity complements synergy, and this synergy, in turn, complements collective creativity. Most of the great advances in history have been through this collective creativity. It is vital to organizations not only because it helps to make quantum leaps, but also because it provides the continuous creative reflection that results in major long-term changes. The 12 principles of leadership foster this environment by promoting trust, common cause, spirit, and open communication in high-performance teams.

Care for Society

Society is in dire need of inspired leaders because the changes that have transformed the workplace have also transformed society. Many people are afflicting themselves and others with competitive compulsions. Traditional value systems are frequently ignored or forgotten, and yet group members desire to participate, to create, and to be self-motivated more than ever before. If leaders have successfully used the benefits of the changing environment to overcome compulsions in their own organizations, they can also help society to make the same adjustment.

Fortunately, inspirational leadership is infectious. Once leaders see its proficiency, they are likely to use it in a variety of situations in the areas of education, community service, cultural development, and economic improvement. Most leaders generally want to optimize the good they can do both inside and outside the organization. They are likely to sit on boards of trustees, service boards, advising committees, and the like. Even though it is unnecessary to convince most of these leaders of the desirability of optimizing the good for society, their efforts can be enhanced by making their operating principles explicit. These leaders can then inspire those whom they serve in the community and society to embrace the same principles. Thus, for example, it is great that leaders serve on the boards of trustees of universities and charitable organizations; it would be greater still if they could convey the six higher viewpoints, the five commitments, and the 12 principles of leadership to the other members of these boards.

The five organizational debilitators are also societal debilitators. They undermine not only the political system, but also the educational system, the administration of social services, and every other institution. The more our leaders overcome these debilitators, the better society will be. Inspired leaders will not only create better organizations, they will also extend their gifts to society, and produce increased social stability, economic stability, cultural direction, desire for education, desire for self-efficacy, and social unity.

Leaders are ideally suited for this task, for they not only have an awareness of the power of principles, they also have skills and competencies in business and technical areas. They are aware of future educational needs. They understand the competencies that will be required of the future work force and where and how they are to be used. They understand the efficient use of resources, the value of creativity, the capacity to create long-term plans, how to assure quality, and how to form and perpetuate empowering, high performance teams. Such leaders, therefore, carry with them a unique synthesis of spirit and skill, trust and competency, educational ideals and necessary training, the requirements for high culture and the needs for technical proficiency, sensitivity to creativity and to administrative efficiency. They are uniquely qualified to maximize spirit, technology, practical know-how, the "win-win," and mutual concern.

I invite all leaders to follow their natural instincts to take their spirit and skills beyond their organizations, and to join forces with other leaders to create a society with internal peace, vision, hope, and spirit. Rising to this challenge has all the earmarks of optimizing good. It is imbued with common cause, synergy, and, above all, the *esprit de corps* that gives life to us individually and collectively.

17 Co-Ownership and Team Building

How can *esprit de corps* be put into continuous practice? Perhaps the most effective way is to develop an atmosphere of co-ownership. Stakeholders who believe that they have real ownership in an organization will have a desire for the common good leading to common cause and synergy. This, in turn, will open the way for greater participation, communication, openness to change, cross-functional teaming, and creativity. To the degree that we feel like co-owners, we begin to invest more of our identity in the group. As this occurs, stakeholders become co-responsible, and therefore free to act for the good of the group. This freedom to act for the good of the group decreases defensiveness and opens the way to increased trust and a willingness to go the extra mile.

Co-ownership can occur with many different groups. Intimate co-ownership occurs within a family or among good friends. Collegial co-ownership can occur at work or in a community organization. Civil co-ownership can occur within political or cultural groups. As the individual invests himself in more groups, he becomes more and more interpersonal in his identity. He becomes free for the good of these groups, that is, the common good. This individual has created a contributive and positive social self beyond his smaller inner world. It creates more responsibilities, but they are worth it, for they all contribute to the richness of his inner world, and he gives this richness back to the outer world. His life is effective, influential, positive, and, in many ways, indispensable to the others around him.

The more an organization allows members to feel like co-owners, the more positive consequences occur. Leaders can help people make commitments and use these commitments to develop a sense of co-ownership by co-participation in decisions that affect stakeholders.

Co-participation is achieved in four stages: 1) solicitation of ideas for upcoming decisions, 2) sharing relevant information with stakeholders about decisions, 3) proactive listening, and 4) feedback and response.

I recommend using these techniques whenever you want to correct a problem or improve morale, relationships, or quality. Many excellent texts give a full description of the range of co-participation.[1] I will give only a minimalistic model and a maximalistic model and allow you to discover an appropriate middle range for yourselves.

A Minimalistic Model of Co-Participation

Minimalistic models are normally used to promote an ongoing general sense of co-participation and co-ownership. They are not designed for problem solving, improving tenuous relationships, or effecting major changes. Since this model does not require extensive time or deep soul-searching, it can be integrated into the regular routine of an organization and become a habitual promotion of co-ownership and quality improvement. It is grounded in the following four steps.

Step 1. Solicitation of ideas. Many companies have regular ways of soliciting ideas from their stakeholders.

With respect to employees, some organizations hold a monthly forum where management listens to and rewards employees for outstanding ideas in all functions—production, marketing, finance, accounting, etc. Sometimes leadership can use these sessions to gather information about how to improve cross-functional teaming. Naturally, such sessions would go beyond specific function areas. Recognition and reward systems should be devised to insure employees that they are being listened to and appreciated. At the beginning of every session, leaders should convey how ideas are being used, and express gratitude for employees' contributions.

With respect to customers, many companies hold regular listening sessions or open space sessions to solicit ideas on how to better design products or provide services. These sessions are oriented toward cultivating long-term relationships, and doing business in new ways.

Similar open space sessions can be developed with suppliers. This allows suppliers to ask questions that will better help them to serve the organization. This not only helps to develop open communication with suppliers, but also cultivates long-term relationships. To the degree that suppliers see themselves as co-participators in the business, they will actively seek satisfaction of not merely the organization, but also its customers. Customer satisfaction can be enhanced if suppliers are in direct contact with customers. If I am an airplane manufacturer, the supplier of my doors should be in direct contact with my customers, for if the customer prefers those doors to be built according to vertical specifications instead of horizontal ones it would be helpful for the supplier (the real manufacturer of the door) to know as soon as possible.

The same can be said for community relations. Again, business leaders can hold sessions with people in the community to ascertain community concerns and the places where the company and employees can help. This builds goodwill, community relations, and good customer relations.

Step 2. Sharing information. Leaders need not share sensitive information that goes beyond stakeholder interests; however, they do need to share the organization's needs. By doing this, stakeholders are not only given the essential parameters for thinking about a problem, but are also shown that they are needed. Without this sense of being needed, co-participation tends to be half-hearted, and people feel that their time and energy are not being spent well because they are not living up to their potential meaning and purpose. Hence they become listless, non-participatory, and sometimes even passive aggressive. Perhaps the most important thing for leaders to convey in an "idea sharing" session is that both the leader and the organization need stakeholders' ideas, stakeholders' willingness to help, and above all, the stakeholders themselves.

Step 3. Proactive listening. Proactive listening requires a sense of common cause, and therefore mutual concern on the part of both the speaker and listener. This allows for transpositional sympathy—the ability to put yourself into the shoes of another. This means not merely experiencing the concerns of another, but also the mental framework and perspective of the other. You do not need to know as much as the other (not even 10 percent as much) but you must sense the perspective and direction from which the other's ideas are likely to emanate.

Stakeholders know when leaders listen with proactive transpositional sympathy. When stakeholders realize that they are being genuinely listened to, they tend to be more openly communicative and more creative. They get a kind of "high" from their sense of the importance of their contribution to the common cause. This "high" engages them in both their conventional and serendipitous thinking processes. So long as leadership shows appreciation for, and the potential usefulness of, these insights, the stakeholder's contribution will be transformed into a sense of co-ownership.

The leader also benefits from proactive listening. The idea may produce production or quality improvements, or force a leader out of conventional thinking patterns. When leaders experience transpositional sympathy and hear an idea as the speaker conveys it, they are forced to think outside their particular box, compelling them to a higher viewpoint that will accommodate both their box and that of the speaker. Creativity occurs most frequently when we are thinking on the level of such a higher viewpoint because we can accommodate the best of both viewpoints. For example, if the speaker is thinking geometrically and the listener is thinking algebraically, the listener will have to move to the level of analytical geometry (the higher viewpoint) to achieve transpositional sympathy. This viewpoint is far more creative than the other two. It does not bias the listener's thinking toward either geometry or algebra, but rather allows him to use each in its own best capacity.

Step 4. Feedback and response. If these three steps are to produce co-ownership in the long term, leaders not only need to express appreciation for ideas, but also to give credit where credit is due. If an idea is implemented in any way, leaders should inform the stakeholder who suggested it either by note, phone, or public acknowledgement. If the company has a standard policy for rewarding this initiative, the reward should accompany the acknowledgement.

Minimalistic models of co-participation can also be used for building teams. Leadership can solicit ideas about how to reward and acknowledge the team, and how to produce cross-functionality. If team members provide the ideas, and if leadership supplies necessary information and proactively listens to and acknowledges these ideas, a high-performance team will emerge quickly.

There are hundreds of other areas in which these four steps of co-participation can be used. Remember that a contributive atmosphere (cultivated through commitments, vision, and leadership) will substantially enhance co-participation. The more leaders encourage co-participation, the more they encourage co-ownership with all its benefits.

Co-participation is also essential for process management.[2] One key tenet of process management is that decisions should be made by leaders who are most closely connected with the place and people most affected by the decision. This accelerates the lines of communication and ensures that leaders are intimately acquainted with the data required for good decisions. To the degree that leaders can foster co-participation, they can get even closer to the places and people most affected by the decisions. Hence, co-participation will foster better data, communication, teamwork, and decision making. Again, inasmuch as a contributive atmosphere enhances this process of co-participation, it will enhance all of the beneficial results of process management.

A Maximalistic Model: Co-Designed Experiments

This model is best used to remedy morale problems, improve relationships, change obsolete structures, and brainstorm ways to adapt to marketplace changes. To accomplish this, the model must take the four steps of co-participation to a deeper level. The maximalistic model is far more dependent on a Level 3 atmosphere. A personal belief in ideals, a personal commitment to the "win-win" and to trust, and a vision of success, people, and ethics are indispensable for producing more beneficial change, more teamwork, and more healing of relationships.

I suggest a technique called co-designed experimentation. I use the word *experiment* to designate not so much a pilot project, but a method well known to natural scientists. When a scientist designs an experiment, she would like its results to have lasting significance. Nevertheless, she is aware that there may be many false starts and that the experiment will have to be adjusted and fine-tuned before it can manifest true data about the empirical world. A pilot project is an experiment done merely to test the plausibility of a hypothesis. This kind of experiment entails more than testing a hypothesis. It intends to produce change and improve quality over the course of many years.

A co-designed experiment follows essentially the same four steps mentioned in the minimalistic model. I reclassify them slightly to accommodate the more complex exigencies of the maximalistic model.

To best explain this model, it would do well to think of a particular problem area in your own organization. Think, for example, of a structure or a process that needs to be changed. It may have been relevant a decade ago, but today most people recognize not only its obsolescence but its tendency to retard creativity or adaptability. Again, if structures or processes are not an issue, think of a relationship that may need to be healed between stakeholders or groups of stakeholders. Perhaps there is a history of mistrust, unresolved tension, bad will, or a strike. Objective observers on both sides have come to recognize that the tension is unnecessary and is being fueled by unresolved resentment, compulsive egos, violence begetting violence, and vengeance begetting vengeance. If this is not a problem in your company, you may perhaps be faced with having to adapt to new marketplace conditions and new competitors. Perhaps these new conditions and competitors are forcing you to look at your markets and marketing from a completely new perspective. To be competitive, you may be faced with positioning your products or services in a new way that may be overly challenging to people who have been accustomed to a "different way of doing things."

Let us begin with a reclassification of the four steps of co-participation. Stages 1 and 2 (the solicitation of ideas, and the sharing of relevant information) can be viewed as the Preparation Phase of the experiment. Stage 3 (proactive listening) could be considered part of the Design Phase of the experiment. In addition to proactive listening, there will also have to be formulation of an experiment. Finally, stage 4 (feedback and response) must be combined with fine-tuning and action to form the Implementation Phase.

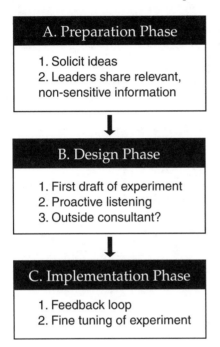

A. Preparation Phase

1. Solicit ideas
2. Leaders share relevant, non-sensitive information

B. Design Phase

1. First draft of experiment
2. Proactive listening
3. Outside consultant?

C. Implementation Phase

1. Feedback loop
2. Fine tuning of experiment

Preparation Phase. The Preparation Phase begins with the solicitation of ideas. Suppose that we need to change a process or a structure. Leaders could begin by gathering either all or a significant group of stakeholders to discuss how a particular obsolete structure can be changed. This serves two functions. First, it warns all stakeholders that a change is about to be actively considered. Secondly, it obtains relevant data from those stakeholders who are closest to the structure or the process. An announcement should be made at least five working days before the actual gathering to assure that people will think about the change and the potential opportunities and threats that might be involved in it. As the gathering begins, leaders should bring out the five commitments and assure the stakeholders of their desire to pursue the "win-win" and trustworthiness.

After reaching tacit agreement on the five commitments, leaders will want to indicate their agenda (opportunities and apprehensions) and ask others to do the same. Exposing agendas can prevent game playing that could undermine trust. Since most people know what another group's agenda is and are politically astute enough to know when a game is being played, organizations have everything to lose by keeping agendas hidden.

The actual solicitation of ideas can now proceed. Leadership may want to suggest certain ideas and ask for immediate feedback. They may also want to ask certain questions without making any suggestions at all. Obviously, the way the questions are phrased will affect not only the quality of the data, but people's reaction to them. In any case, rewards can be given for outstanding ideas contributed by both individuals and groups. It takes more time to solicit ideas from groups. This requires a workshop model with small group or team discussions with readouts. This could take two to three hours and must be very well planned.

As the solicitation of ideas is proceeding, leaders should notice where their people need additional information. If trust is to be gained, and if the ideas solicited are to be relevant, leaders must be forthcoming with this information. Where there is little endangerment of trade secrets or competitiveness, and where the need for information is acute to build trust and creativity, it is always better to err on the side of giving information rather than withholding it.

Even though prudence requires us to keep our cards close to the vest, excessive caution undermines creativity, communication, trust, and adaptability. We are not negotiating with our enemy—we are trying to improve our organization. Even though there are divergent interests, all stakeholders must be viewed as friends, for their welfare is inextricably intertwined with ours. If one or more of these experiments is successful, it will show all parties the power of sharing information and communicating openly. The benefits of sharing so exceed erring on the side of caution that most concerned parties will move toward greater openness.

There are also risks associated with not sharing information. If participants in the experiment discover that leaders did not share relevant, non-sensitive information at the time of solicitation of ideas, it will undermine co-participation and the feeling of co-ownership. Stakeholders will believe that leadership did not trust them, was playing a "power game" with them, and was wasting their time. Such belief will increase fear, resentment, and cynicism. Leaders should not embark on a process of co-participation and co-ownership until they are ready to share information. Otherwise, the outcome is likely to be more harmful than good.

Soliciting and sharing ideas can be done dialogically. An idea on the part of one party will elicit information or ideas from the other party, which will elicit further ideas from the first party, and so forth. Eventually, this joint cooperation will give rise to a set of objectives, parameters, hints, and clues on how to proceed. It now remains to generate the first draft of an actual experiment that comprises the second phase of this process, namely, the Design Phase.

Design Phase. The objective of the Design Phase is to formulate a first draft of an experiment for change. Obviously, this cannot be done by a large group. Hence, the first part of the Design Phase must be to form a committee of no more than 12 people who can accomplish this task. The committee must be made up of an equal number of members from all relevant stakeholder groups.

Committee members should be committed to contributive attitudes and leadership principles, be open to soft-bargaining, promote trust, and have transpositional sympathy.

They should be respected by their constituencies for their competence, intelligence, and nuance. Members who may be incapable of soft-bargaining, transpositional sympathy, or working together with others should be replaced.

Once the committee is constituted, the process of formulating the initial draft of the experiment can begin. First, stakeholders' ideas raised in the Preparation Phase should be ranked one to five (one representing a rather minor idea, and five an idea that cannot be ignored in the first draft of the proposal). All ideas ranked four or higher should in some way be included. Second, the concerns raised by stakeholders in the Preparation Phase should be similarly ranked. All concerns ranked four or higher should be addressed in the proposed experiment, otherwise, committee members won't be able to sell it to their constituencies.

If changing the structure gives rise to considerable factioning, leadership should consider hiring an outside consultant to facilitate the process and to obtain answers from the participants on the committee. Hence, the facilitator might want to organize some listening sessions aimed at discovering the range of opinions in a particular problem area; suggest two or three ways of reconfiguring the structure that meets all parties' needs; submit these ideas to the committee who would give feedback on the suggestions; and integrate these as much as possible into the plan and again solicit feedback until an agreeable first draft is formulated.

If the ideas do not come from the committee, then its members will not "sell" the proposed experiment to their stakeholder groups. If the committee members have a vested interest in the draft, the stakeholders will perceive it, and this will pave the way for its acceptance. Consultants must be chosen not only for their experience and problem solving ability, but also for their listening and synthetic ability.

If the committee becomes too dependent on the consultant, it may think that the five commitments and proactive listening are no longer necessary. The consultant will take care of everything. Nothing could be further from the truth. If the committee is not pursuing the "win-win" and the cultivation of trust through proactive listening, the consultant will be forced either to give up or to write his own proposal (which committee members will not want to sell to their constituencies). Proactive listening makes another's concern one's own concern, and thereby changes the way one phrases suggestions and reacts to other groups. What the consultant hears is what the committee gets. If he hears dialogue, consideration, "win-win," and trustworthiness, his draft of the experiment will reflect all of this and more. If he does not hear any of this, his draft of the experiment will likely be so legalistic that it will drain the enthusiasm out of the most ardent supporters of the experiment.

If the committee does not hire an outside consultant, the members will have to perform all of the consultant's functions on their own. This could be done by means of subcommittees dedicated to the listening sessions and the drafting of proposals. Documents written by committee are frequently drawn out and unwieldy, but if committee members are transpositionally sympathetic they may formulate an initial draft of the experiment in a reasonable time.

Once the draft is written, it must be taken by the committee members to their constituencies. After feedback is obtained, the information should be given to the consultant or subcommittees to make additions or changes to the proposed experiment. If feedback cannot be acted upon, the consultant or subcommittees must explain why. The proposed experiment may have to be submitted to constituencies several times before a draft is accepted.

Implementation Phase. Once a draft of an experimental change has been accepted by all constituencies, it must be put into practice. If changes are major, they should be phased in over time. If they are small, they can probably be done immediately. In either case, experimental structural change will run into problems. There is simply no way that the committee or a consultant can foresee all the difficulties likely to arise in changing a structure. That is why this method is called an "experiment." It anticipates the need for ongoing adjustment and fine-tuning as the hard realities of implementation become apparent.

In the Design Phase, so much attention is given to creating a "win-win" that some details of practical implementation are overlooked. This should not be viewed as negative because the Design Phase must be more concerned with the goals or objectives than the means or the "how." Becoming too concerned with the *how* in the Design Phase will make the initial draft of the experiment too cumbersome and inflexible. It will also bring the "super realists" out of the woodwork. "Super realists" are those who tell the proactive goal-seekers that their plans are unrealistic and unimplementable. They do this not to undermine progress, but "for the goal-seekers' own good." They realize that the goal-seekers have not considered every possible problem that could arise in every possible situation of implementation. Though they tend to undermine the Design Phase by putting too many "hows" before the goal, they are indispensable in the Implementation Phase because they are completely alert to all the ways in which the experiment must be fine-tuned.

The Implementation Phase begins with the reorganization of personnel and processes around the proposed experimental structure. Once these changes have been made, a feedback loop must be set up immediately to both the consultant and the committee. Problems will arise almost immediately, and the committee must determine whether these are attributable to flaws in the proposed experiment or are simply troubles to be expected in any structural change.

Consultants or change agents who have experience in these matters can make recommendations almost immediately. If the problem arises more out of the general process of change instead of a specific flaw in the experiment, the committee or consultant can recommend some strategies for coping with it. If, however, the problem arises out of a flaw in the experiment, then the committee/consultant will have to make adjustments to the experiment. These adjustments must receive the tacit approval of all constituencies before they can be implemented. The feedback mechanism may be diagramed as follows:

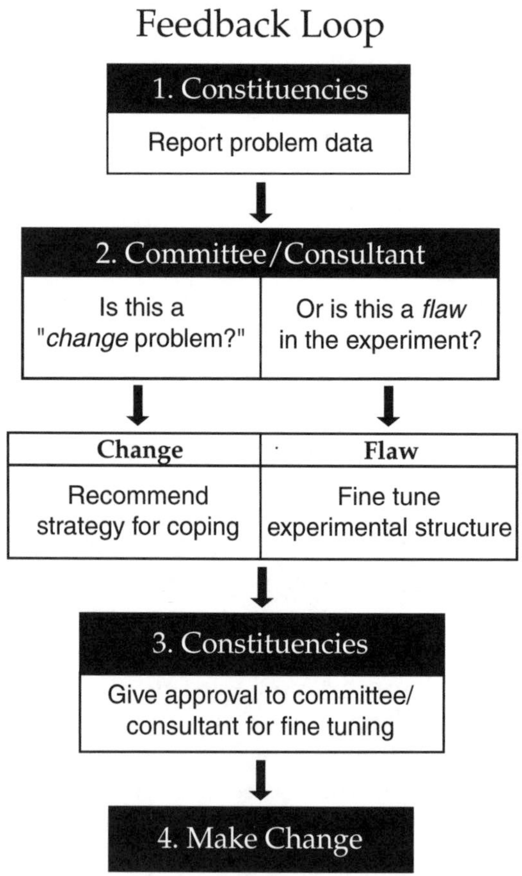

The 12 principles of leadership are of particular importance during the Implementation Phase. Leaders cannot supervise every detail of change. The success of change will depend on the absence of the five debilitators. If these debilitators are present, trust and goodwill will be low, making change difficult and short-term. If the debilitators are low, trust and goodwill will be high, allowing change to take hold and last. Since the five commitments and the 12 principles of leadership are crucial to the decrease of the five debilitators, they must be practiced throughout the experiment. Hence, leaders must concentrate on inspiring rather than on overseeing; on encouraging team behavior, common cause, and *esprit de corps* instead of inducing fear; on listening, responding, and rewarding rather than on ordering and compelling. The leader's primary responsibility is to inspire her constituencies to organize themselves as a team with long-term commitment to common cause and the common good. The more the constituencies are educated about the five commitments, the easier leaders' tasks will be. When co-designed experiments succeed, the results are fantastic for every aspect of the organization.

Co-participation leads to co-ownership, and co-ownership to adaptability, trustworthiness, teamwork, and quality. Co-designed experiments double or triple these effects because they endeavor more pronounced improvements. These improvements in structures, processes, and relationships will last much longer than those designed without co-participation, because they are planned by those who have to live and work with them. They are based on better data and fostered in an atmosphere of goodwill, feedback, and creativity by people who have a stake in their design and outcome. If these co-designed experiments are successful, and most of the time they are, they not only make significant changes and improvements, but also transform the ethos of the organization in the direction of high flexibility, self-motivation, high-morale, team orientation, and continuous quality improvement.

Successful co-designed experiments (and even minimalistic co-participation) can transform the culture. One success paves the way for even more co-participation and even bigger co-designed experiments. The trust, openness to change, cross-functional teaming, and co-creativity arising out of one experiment lays a foundation for more extensive and challenging ones. If the same techniques bring about bigger objectives within this larger group, they can again be used for even bigger challenges within still bigger groups. If trust has been built, it should be used to achieve both greater improvements and greater trust. This creates a systemic momentum not only toward a people system, but toward maximum adaptability, learning, trust, respect, and co-creativity.

To achieve these results, leaders may want to integrate the following questions into their thinking and reflection:

1) How can I better solicit ideas from various constituencies and stakeholders? How do I acknowledge, appreciate, and reward co-participators?
2) What non-sensitive information will help stimulate ideas and enthusiasm on the part of diverse constituencies and stakeholders? What means should be used to communicate them?
3) How can I better put myself into others' "shoes?" How can I better achieve transpositional sympathy and reflect diverse opinions in my decision making?
4) How can I create feedback loops to continually assess and fine-tune new processes, policies, and structures?

These questions may be combined with the commitments and questions mentioned in previous chapters to create a reflection process capable of cultivating the heart and mind of effective teams and inspired leaders. In short, they lead to *esprit de corps.*

18 Creating Esprit de Corps

Esprit de corps arises out of the hearts of leaders and their organizations. It may be hard to imagine that organizations have a heart, but when we consider that a culture can be charged with either negative or positive emotion, can drain us or energize us, and can incite disparity or common cause, we cannot deny the existence of a powerful ethos that may be likened to the hearts of individuals.

In this chapter, I indicate a way to jumpstart the process of cultivating the heart of leaders through peace, interior freedom, and education.

Spirit, Peace, and Interior Freedom

"Spirit" refers to that dimension of human beings that transcends the material world. It refers to the capacity of people to gain energy when doing something creative, the capacity for creativity, the capacity to step outside of any system or method to devise something entirely new. "Spirit" also extends to interpersonal relationships; not merely to the trust that gives rise to common cause and collegiality, but also to the domain of ethics and the desire to accord people the respect and dignity they deserve. "Spirit" also extends to the domain of the ultimate, unconditional, perfect, and infinite. Spirit is the capacity to go beyond the self, beyond known paradigms, beyond material limitations of energy, even beyond the finite, the conditioned, and the entire universe.

"Spirit" carries with it the connotation of self-movement, energy, dynamism, and vitality. Spirit is what makes us come alive, or come to be more alive. Self-transcendent activity gives greater energy and vitality. Creativity, collegiality, common cause, love, and faith turn us on, infuse us with well being, and open us to the future.

From the literature of love to the history of war, from the chronicles of scientific creativity to the domain of art and music, we may clearly perceive a common thread: where there is "going beyond," there is "inspiration." Where there is inspiration, there is inspirational leadership toward the common good. And where there is inspirational leadership toward the common good, there is ordered, synergistic, progressive, and perduring value for groups, organizations, societies, and nations. When leaders commit to principles, they allow the spirit of commitment, trust, creativity, vision, teamwork, and co-ownership to come fully alive.

Organizational spirit now plows itself back into individual spirit by giving individuals greater interior freedom. Spirit not only moves beyond, it moves within. When we achieve a higher viewpoint, have a deeper and broader appreciation for what really matters, and a more comprehensive understanding of the mystery of life, our judgment becomes more subtle, our timing more acute, and our emotions more balanced. When self-transcendence brings this depth, balance, and calm it enables us to let go of the fixed, tangible, and superficial structures upon which we formerly relied.

Without the effects of self-transcendence (creativity, common cause, etc.) we seem to rely on fixed rather than fluid structures, on solid rather than subtle structures, on static rather than dynamic ones. We tend to rely on what we can grasp, hold onto, fix our gaze on. Sometimes we think that if we let go of this crude and bulky structure, we will be swept away. But for those who have discovered the self-transcendent, inspirational, interpersonal, and creative dynamism within them, for those who have forged into the realms of contribution and cooperation even for but a short time, the illusion of these non-malleable structures, these blunt instruments of control, these merely exterior "symbols" of success become apparent. As the illusion becomes progressively apparent, we gradually immerse ourselves in contribution and common cause in all its fluidity and dynamism, and find there a solace, a happiness, indeed, a way of being that the so-called fixed, external, permanent manifestations of control can not provide. Slowly we relax our grip on what seemed so "secure," and enter into the fluid and the new in a spirit of self-transcendence and interior freedom.

We like to suppose we can "will" ourselves away from the five debilitators, but over time we begin to see that the way beyond the debilitators is through calm, balance, and subtlety made possible through the gifts of spirit. Thus, spirit brings inspiration outside the self while bringing calm into the self. It brings excitement outside while bringing insight inside. It brings energy outside through stillness inside. We can always tell when spirit is genuinely present because these seemingly opposed qualities will be simultaneously present. They are not opposed, but complementary. The stillness on the inside allows for great breadth. Our breadth of field increases when we are not focusing on a particular object. We are open to everything in the visual field, allowing the various elements of the field to speak for themselves rather than having to be selected one at a time by us.

Calm not only improves the breadth of judgment, it also improves its subtlety. The calmer we are, the more we are-open to the highest viewpoint and its relationship to all other lower viewpoints. When we are fearful or angry, we tend to focus on particular lower viewpoints. When higher viewpoints are effectively ignored, subtlety and timing become increasingly difficult because good distinctions can only be held together by a higher viewpoint embracing both sides of the distinction. In short, people who lack spirit lack good judgment, self-control, detachment, and, interior freedom.

The qualities of spirit may be diagramed as follows:

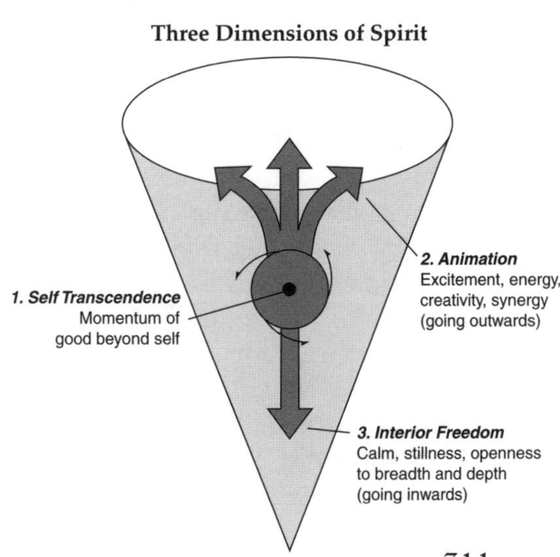
Three Dimensions of Spirit
1. Self Transcendence
Momentum of good beyond self
2. Animation
Excitement, energy, creativity, synergy (going outwards)
3. Interior Freedom
Calm, stillness, openness to breadth and depth (going inwards)

I am often told that unspirited people sometimes make highly effective leaders. I reply, "Yes, many unspirited people can be very driven leaders, but this does not mean that they produce the fruits of inspired leadership."

Inspiration proceeds from self-transcendence, a desire to do the good beyond the self, and even faith. This leads to depth and breadth, to the calm of good judgment, and the excitement, energy, and synergy of both cooperation and goal achievement. Inspiration, then, is the achievement of goals in a broad and deep context, with a spirit of subtlety and calm in mutual concern and cooperation with others.

Drivenness, in contrast, focuses on the goal in an exclusive way. The power of admiration, comparative advantage, wealth, achievement, and control produces tremendous energy and excitement. In the short run, this can appear to be similar to inspiration. The person involved can achieve remarkable short-term results. But, I would ask: "Did this person's achievement of goals lead to greater teamwork or less teamwork? ...decrease the five debilitators or enhance them? ...empower others or oppress them? ...lead to greater collective creativity or greater passivity? ...dignify and respect others or ignore or even disdain them? ...open others to change and complexity or close them? ...retain and inspire critical skills personnel or chase them away?"

Even if a business remains solvent in the midst of its leadership's drivenness, I would ask "What potential was lost through the absence of inspiration?" Entrepreneurs, whether inspired or driven, last only one generation. Their histories are frequently not as important as the legacies they leave behind. Inspired leadership leads to growth, unity, and adaptability in its second generation, while driven leadership leads to chaos, struggle for power, and ambiguous direction.

Once again, we see that the spirit of leaders gives rise to the spirit of the organization. If the spirit of leaders is self-transcendent, it will produce not only short-term excitement and growth, but long-term synergy and openness to future growth. Great leaders, whether political, organizational, military, or societal, display this quality of inspiration arising out of interior freedom.

Spirit is not only the inspiring force of individuals, it is the lifeblood of communities and organizations. It leads to the decrease of the five debilitators, an increase in trust, openness to change, cross-functional specialization of labor, the ability to take risks, creativity, self-motivated "thinking implementers," and to every other form of community spirit sparked by its contagious dynamism.

The dynamics of spirit open upon interior freedoms. When we attempt to transform our attitudes and commitments, we immediately confront limits to freedom. But the more we achieve interior calm and peace of mind and let go of ego-compulsion, the greater will be our freedom to be creative, take reasonable risks, and to communicate with, work with, and empower others. We will not be agents of the five debilitators, but rather agents of trust. We will not run from ongoing commitments, but pursue them as if our purpose in life depended on them. We will not neglect our collegial relationships and friendships, but foster them as if they were a very precious yet fragile work of art.

The dynamics of spirit are the dynamics of interior freedom, and the three dimensions of spirit are likewise the three dimensions of interior freedom.

Given the importance of this interior calm, we must avail ourselves to it as much as possible by valuing, remembering, affirming, and practicing it; holding ourselves accountable to it; and evaluating our progress in it. We might also integrate it into our prayer life (e.g., "Thy will be done") for grace can bring a peace that is beyond all understanding.

I define "interior freedom" as spirit (self-transcendent calm) oriented toward a permanent, general objective (e.g., looking for the good new in others or taking reasonable risks). It is not like pursuing a transitory goal (like finishing a budget) where we push ourselves, give extra effort, and get tough when the going gets tough. These characteristics can be added to interior freedom to achieve remarkable results, but interior freedom is not, at root, an exertion. It is a sense of purpose imbued with inner calm that receives and interprets data with such remarkable agility that it allows for almost effortless, comprehensive decision making.

This mixture of purpose and calm affords us the capacity to see comprehensively the long-term, systematic, interpersonal consequences of data. We almost effortlessly interpret this data, organize it both systematically and practically, and act upon it without interior conflict. Without this freedom, we tend to fight ourselves on all three levels—interpretation, organization, and action.

We have all had the experience of fighting ourselves in the pursuit of something we desire. "I should get these exams corrected. If I do, I will have the rest of the weekend free," and then, turning right around and reading a novel. We keep telling ourselves to stop reading that novel. The objective we seek is so easily within our reach. But, we keep reading the novel. If we had of purpose and calm, we would cease fighting ourselves about correcting the exams. Calm and purpose make expending energy desirable and interesting, rather than an obligation or constraint.

Calm and purpose help move us beyond emotional blocks and the burden of expending energy by affording us a contributory attitude. If, for example, I desire the welfare of the students and see my life's purpose as contributing to them, I will correct exams. However, if I forget my contributory purpose, I will view the exams solely as a problem, thereby causing me to look for a distraction. The least distraction will seem far more important than the exams ("Who knows what great insight could come from reading this detective novel? Besides, I've had a hard day and I need to relax; besides, all work no play makes Jack a dull boy; besides....").

A contributory purpose enhances calm while calm enhances purpose. By valuing, desiring, remembering, and acting upon both calm and purpose together, we allow each to complement the other, giving rise to an interior freedom that can overcome the most stubborn temptations, emotional blocks, and resistance to effort.

This interior freedom enables us to take reasonable risks, to organize our time effectively, and to pursue long-term goals and commitments. It engenders self-motivation and self-accountability and enhances all 12 principles of inspired leadership. It engages the serendipitous dimension of consciousness that gives rise to creativity and it provides a purity of motive to treat others with dignity and respect. It enables us to live out of the truth of ourselves. We no longer have to act out of a restless spirit, a sense of comparative inadequacy, or a desire to put others down to enhance our own image.

For the person of calm and contributive purpose, truth is more than enough.

Individual spirit and freedom give rise to organizational spirit and freedom. This occurs through the following stages. First, spirited, free individuals tend to connect with each other. They respect each other for their purpose, calm, contributory attitude, inspiration, and resolve. This respect forms the basis for common cause toward the common good. Trust and open communication soon follow. This opens the way to "having fun" or "getting high" in pursuing the common good, which gives rise to synergy and creativity. This natural connection provides the internal framework for cross-functional teaming, rapid adaptation to change, effective specialization of labor, and self-motivated and self-accountable thinking implementers.

The natural connection among individuals that forms the basis for organizational spirit can be contagious if people have sufficient education to be disposed to it. If leaders share this information with their team members, and if they create an atmosphere where setbacks are viewed as education and risks are shared, then every member can enter into a natural, free, and spirited connection with others. Organizational spirit and freedom spread naturally when people are given an adequate education and working environment.

This may seem like a long and arduous journey toward high performance teams, but it is really the only way to create them. Without this spirit and freedom, without this calm and purpose, the five debilitators will undermine team efficacy, creativity, and adaptability to change. Leaders cannot create good teams from the outside in by putting together an external structure, giving an external mandate, and by teaching communication skills, team-building skills, and conflict resolution skills. Rather, they must create teams from the inside out by first transforming personal attitudes and horizons, then fostering organizational commitment, vision, and culture, and finally engendering co-ownership. Through it all they must incite spirit and interior freedom so that a contagious natural connection can occur.

This natural, interior connection is far superior to any forced exterior connection between people. If people are concerned about one another, respect one another, and derive energy from one another in an atmosphere of calm and purpose, they will achieve synergy and enhanced creativity. As a group, they will lessen their in-fighting. The free flow of information, the atmosphere of collective serendipity, and the sense of collective purpose cannot help but move performance to a new level. No external mandate can create this internal group drive. No external structure can create this cohesive, openly communicating, synergistic unity. Indeed, without this collective spirit, external mandates and structures seem to be vapid. People look at them and say, "Yeah, yeah, another mandate. We'll do just enough to keep the external forces off our back, but nothing more."

Teams without interior freedom and spirit are likely to lead to mediocrity. However, teams built upon the natural connection arising out of freedom and spirit are likely to be extraordinarily creative and productive. They are also likely to give energy and an enhanced sense of meaning and well-being to their participants. This has effects not only within the organization, but also on the family and community lives of team members. If cross-functional teaming and rapid adaptability are the keys to future success, then spirit cannot be avoided. If we do not take a few moments of our busy days to tend to the domain of spirit, we will find ourselves mired in waste—wasted plans, wasted effort, wasted mandates, wasted flowcharts, wasted speculation, wasted bureaucracy, and wasted oversight.

At first glance, it might seem as if spirit is a waste of time because it is so intangible and so difficult to capture. Yet, not attending to spirit is the far greater waste of time, for we can create the best plans, but our people may be completely closed to change. We can create the most complex systems, but our people can resist specialization and cross-functional teaming. We can create the best reward systems, but our people can content themselves with minimum expectation. If we do not make time for that amorphous, intangible creator of unity, synergy, creativity, adaptability, and self-accountability, we will watch our concrete and tangible work be hamstrung by fear, complacency, anger, suspicion, passive aggression, blame, and ego-compulsion. A bit of the intangible liberates and enhances the tangible. If we allow ourselves to believe that long-term viability and creativity can be created with only external structure and hard metric, we will have to content ourselves with short-term viability and a legacy of fragmentation, opportunity costs, and struggle for power.

Cultivating Inspired Leadership

If leaders are to acquire contributory qualities enabling them to inspire opportunistic thinking, common cause, changeability, creativity, and teamwork, they will have to interiorize and exemplify the commitments that not only lead to inspired leadership, but also to the cultivation of peace and interior freedom. Awareness of these commitments for inspired leadership enables us to pursue the peace to interiorize these commitments. The peace and interiorization process continue to reinforce each other.

What is the most effective way of initiating this life-long process of inspired leadership? First, set aside at least 10 minutes for contemplation at the beginning of the day. Second, internalize the commitments for inspired leadership during this time of contemplation.

In my life, I follow a six-step process of contemplation and commitment. You may need to configure this process to the exigencies of your own life.

1) Center on what is really important. As you begin a daily ritual of contemplation, recognize what gives meaning and purpose to your life. You may want to write down the specifics of how you can contribute to others this day. Remember that these contributions give meaning to your life (i.e., "For these, I came!").

Consider also the goals that will give your life ultimate significance (e.g., "Love one another as I have loved you." "Love the Lord your God with all your heart, mind, and strength, and love your neighbor as yourself." "Act justly, love tenderly, and walk humbly with your God"). You may also incorporate prayer into your contemplation, for prayer can lead directly to peace and interior freedom.

Contemplation is indispensable, because it gives you distance from the compulsions of life. The minute you enter the workplace, you are likely to encounter a context for a comparison, an irritating person that rivets you to the "bad news," a manifestation of office politics that forces you to abandon common cause and protect yourself. Contemplation helps you to affirm what really matters before you are gripped by the stimulants of compulsion.

Contemplation cannot work instantly, but its effects are evident over time in your attitudes, workplace judgment, self-efficacy, and team efficacy. Peace, depth, wisdom, and contribution slowly replace sporadic hyperactivity; overreaction; narrow, short-term thinking; and "team busting" behavior. You probably won't identify when and how this change came to pass, but your friends will begin to say, "You've changed. There's something about you I didn't notice before." What they mean is, you've changed for the better, and they respect you more as a leader and a human being.

Another reason why contemplation is so important is because it is the only time you can consider your attitudes and frame of mind to be of equal importance to your goals and strategies. When you enter the workplace, the drive to achieve goals and implement strategies becomes paramount. Healthy organizations create group momentum toward their common cause. Hence, you can expect to get caught up in this very healthy and good momentum.

However, this healthy momentum should not replace the attitudes of inspired leadership (e.g., looking for the good news in others, even when you see the bad news). If you allow this competitive momentum to replace the attitude of contribution, it will make you a more driven and less inspired leader, one who will push people from the outside without inciting the drive toward common cause on the inside. Pushing will never get to a fast-changing, team-working, co-participatory, opportunity-seeking organization. It will only produce water-treading, survivalistic, protectionistic achievement of mediocre objectives. It will promote "foot dragging" instead of sprinting; passive aggression instead of spirit; mediocrity instead of quality.

To avoid being caught up in the healthy momentum of goals and strategies, leaders need a time each day when personal commitments can be viewed as equally important to goals and strategies. This "one time" is the moment of contemplation at the beginning of the day.

2) Focus on peace. After considering what is truly important, you must consider the most important quality you wish to bring to the workplace, the one quality that will affect all other qualities, principles, and commitments, the most important quality for inspired leadership, namely, peace of mind. Consider not only the importance of peace, but how you want to bring peace to the specific activities of your day. Consider how you will bring peace to a particular meeting, negotiating session, evaluation, group of employees, customers, and upon returning home, to family members, friends, and community members. Consider that this peace will make or break the effectiveness of all your actions and judgments in all contexts during the day. It is the one thing you have to remember and put into practice.

I encourage you to bring the prayer "Thy will be done" into the beginning of your day. As you move through the events on your calendar, you will want to say, "Lord, if it be Thy will, let this succeed, and create opportunity; but if not, Thy will be done." This prayer is capable of creating peace through abandonment to divine providence.

3) Focus on the commitment of the day. Peace is the most important personal quality to take into the workplace. However, peace need not be exhaustive. You may wish to concentrate on another specific quality or commitment. In previous chapters, I have suggested about 44 commitments. You may want to prioritize the commitments that seem most important to you, and bring them to your contemplation. For a specific commitment to have transformative value, it must be considered daily for at least one week.

4) Focus on the reason for the commitment. Consider why a particular commitment is so important. This may not be obvious when you are caught up in the goal-oriented concerns of the workplace. So, during the time of contemplation, consider, for example, that "this ethical principle is important because it will cultivate my ability to be contributory, which will improve my interpersonal relationships as well as my leadership credibility. This, in turn, will increase my sense of purpose, spirit, and happiness, while increasing my effectiveness both inside and outside the workplace."

5) Bring the desired commitment into the workplace. When your contemplation comes to an end, your challenge now is to take the fruit of this contemplation into the workplace.

The reason I put many of the principles and commitments of inspired leadership into question form is that questions are easier to remember, and they stimulate reflection.

6) Review the day. When you return home from work and get some time to yourself, you might sit down in a comfortable chair for five minutes and clear your mind of all the clutter of the day. When the clutter is gone, ask yourself, "How successful was I in bringing peace of mind and my specific commitments into the workplace?" The objective, here, is not to punish yourself for doing an inadequate job, but rather to simply notice when you could do better next time.

Again, I recommend that you prioritize the principles and commitments, and begin the integration process in earnest. The effects of this process on leadership ability, workplace efficacy, family life, and personal happiness, will soon become apparent. It makes little difference what personality you have, internalizing these commitments will allow an inspired, wise, and benevolent leader to emerge, leading to a better organization and a better world.

Creating Organizational Spirit

How can inspired, wise, and benevolent leaders optimally use their gifts to cultivate *esprit de corps* in an organization? I find six steps to be useful. I encourage you to tailor this information to your own needs.

STEP ONE—AN EDUCATIONAL PROGRAM

Esprit de corps requires an organization-wide education program. Education as deep and challenging as this cannot be accomplished in a single lecture. Most people need to hear the material several times and assimilate it over three to four months. It takes time to remember the various parts, and to understand how the parts fit together in a single system.

Moreover, the material must be experientially verified. To overcome the negative emotions of the comparison game, you must first recognize compulsiveness in your life and even experience its deleterious effects on family, friends, teams, and in your style of leadership. Such reflections take both time and effort. Overcoming these compulsions (through the five commitments) requires even greater effort and reflection. But there is no substitute for it. Personal change cannot happen without insight and desire, and insight and desire cannot happen without reflection and experience.

It will take time for a critical mass of people to collectively appropriate the organizational commitments. Not all people will see the information as valuable. Some will see the information as valuable to others, but not to themselves, and still others will find the information to be unnerving. They may resist it with skepticism and cynicism. You need not convince every member of the efficacy of the five commitments, but only to build a critical mass of conviction. If a few stakeholders are convinced, and if they are courageous enough to hold to their self-appropriated beliefs, they will form a dominant organizational philosophy, giving rise to irresistible momentum, which will attract many of the unconvinced. The unconvinced will eventually have to curtail cynicism and adjust their behavior patterns to get along with the critical mass. So long as the majority of leaders can support moving beyond the comparison game, and most stakeholders have sufficient education to understand why leadership is moving in this direction, a positive ethos will eventually take hold.

Reciprocity is key to the effectiveness of the five commitments. If I commit to a person who is willing to commit to me, I am far more free than if I am committed to people about whom I am uncertain. Reciprocity paves the way to freedom, to mutual accountability, and, therefore, to greater growth in commitment. The absence of reciprocity gives rise to the fears of being vulnerable and of being manipulated. Committed individuals fear that they will make these commitments and then be slighted or ridiculed.

This fear can be alleviated by starting small, and growing a critical mass of reciprocally committed individuals. If people can identify a few others (even two) who are striving toward Level 3 and can see that they intend to reciprocate the five commitments, they can immediately initiate a trust-based relationship. These small trust-based relationships can affect the culture substantially. People who might have been skeptical, but open, will begin to see how efficacious and synergistic these trust-based relationships are, and desire to be part of them. The larger this community of trust-based individuals becomes, the more outsiders will want to become part of it. Eventually, a critical mass will form.

In small companies, a critical mass can be achieved rather quickly. If most leaders become part of the trust-based community, they will accelerate its acceptance.

Larger organizations (5,000 employees or more) require more time to transform. Nevertheless, the formation of small, trust-based communities within teams, workgroups, and sections will eventually pay off. When they become large enough, they will naturally connect with other teams, work-groups, and sections.

A trust-based community need not be composed of perfect people. All that is required is conviction sufficient to induce commitment to contribution, and willingness to work in a community that will call people to accountability. This does not mean expecting perfection, but rather tolerating and challenging one another with great patience and understanding as we grow together. In this atmosphere, trust will reap its usual benefits—open communication, heightened morale and energy, cross-functional teaming, co-creativity, and self-motivated quality improvement.

STEP TWO—LEADERSHIP SUPPORT

If most leaders support Level 3 commitments, they will transform their organizations and will enjoy the fruit of rekindled trust and spirit.

I recommend that leaders be given special training in the 12 principles of inspired leadership, team-building structures and skills, and concrete structures to develop co-participation and co-ownership.

Feedback Advising. In addition to leadership education, I highly recommend a program of feedback advising, coaching, or mentoring. Touching base with peers, and obtaining careful, honest feedback is indispensable for helping leaders grow in Level 3 principles and vision. Many organizations provide excellent assistance in developing mentoring programs; however, I suggest that organizations also use the principles in this book to develop their own system.

Leadership Growth Plan. I recommend that leaders set out specific objectives for growth. These may be organized along the lines of the six viewpoints, the five commitments, or the 12 principles of leadership. Other objectives may also be integrated into a growth plan, namely, team-building, soft-bargaining, conflict resolution, facilitating change and risk, and promoting co-participation and co-ownership. A growth plan should include long-term objectives, short-term objectives, and immediate action steps. Self-assessment should be done monthly, and, if possible, feedback obtained from feedback advisers. Self-assessment of particular action steps should happen almost daily or weekly. Repetition and reflection are the parents of understanding, insight, and change.

As leaders move toward a Level 3 model, they naturally accelerate the process of forming trust-based communities. Starting small trust-based communities produces a remarkable transformation of the organization's ethos. This transformation will be greatly accelerated if a critical mass of the leadership forms its own trust-based community. This will occur because leadership can reduce the five debilitators, create an atmosphere of reasonable risk, and determine the reward structures. If these three pieces are in place, and if leaders are walking their talk, the transformation of ethos can be quick, incisive, and efficacious. Indeed, an organization of 100,000 people might change within a year. The fruit of this transformed ethos (improvements in morale, reduction of critical skills turnover, enhanced cross-functional teaming, co-creativity, synergy, adaptability, quality, and productivity) would be actualized almost immediately. This would markedly reduce opportunity cost, and improve net profit and return on investment.

Step Three—Level 3 Strategic Vision Building

The purpose of strategic vision building is to provide momentum and goals for the future. Forming trust-based communities (grounded in reciprocity of the five commitments) and implementing Level 3 leadership principles will change the organization's ethos for the short and middle term. But without a vision that presents a horizon of hope and growth, this transformation is difficult to sustain. Vision acts not only as a horizon, but as a horizon beyond the horizon. It is a call, an invitation, an objective, and a challenge. It is not immediately implementable, but then again it shouldn't be. It's supposed to have the quality of a horizon, the "not yet realized," the hope from which aspirations spring. If a vision statement is co-produced and co-owned by a critical mass of stakeholders, this horizon creates an attractive, energizing, optimistic momentum. It prevents the short and middle-term impetus from being wasted. It is the power of follow through.

Strategic visioning processes can be applied to develop products, enhance market share, improve processes, and eliminate waste. Many organizations already use these visioning processes with respect to product and process, but not with respect to people. Therefore, organizations may want to integrate several of this book's 44 commitments into their strategic visioning process. This will assure that commitments leading to spirit and trust ("people commitments") will always accompany announcements about product and process goals.

STEP FOUR—FOSTERING CO-PARTICIPATION AND CO-OWNERSHIP

I have given minimalistic and maximalistic models for fostering cross-functional teams through co-participation and co-ownership. The minimalistic model can achieve immediate improvements in team communication and performance if implemented within the context of the previous three steps.

STEP FIVE—IMPLEMENTING TEAM STRUCTURES

Once the first four steps have been initiated, organizations can move toward team structures. A circular model has the advantage of decreasing the totemism implicit in hierarchical structures, which, in turn, empowers thinking implementers while decreasing political in-fighting.

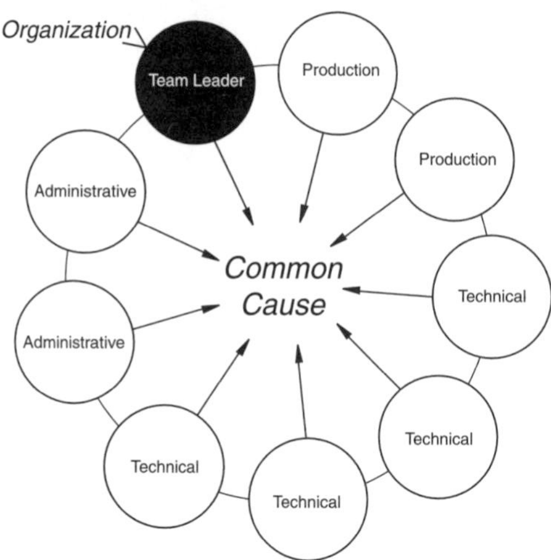

Obviously some hierarchical structures cannot be avoided, but some can be replaced by circular team structures that allow team members to exercise their expertise and leadership potential.

Whether an organization decides to move toward a circular team structure or not, promotion of team leadership and team spirit is essential. Cross-functional teaming can be promoted simply by reserving oversight to those who need it while implementing Level 3 leadership style for the organization. As leaders promote the five commitments, common cause, trust, and spirit, team building skills can be folded into the mix. Communication skills, conflict resolution skills, and other team skills will now have maximal rather than marginal impact. An organization will want to invest in these skills to the extent that cross-functional teaming is a necessity for doing business.

STEP SIX—FEEDBACK LOOPS AND MEASUREMENT OF RESULTS

A measurement system can be set into place by determining in advance which metrics would be most useful in assessing morale, performance, flow time, team activity, quality, opportunity costs, transactional costs, and turnover. These measurements can be developed internally or through outside consultants.

Measurement instruments should be used to test the effectiveness of the five steps for building organizational spirit. This should be done in two steps: 1) measurement of morale data, and 2) measurement of opportunity costs.

The resources required to implement these six steps are mostly centered on the cost of education, namely, facilitated video sessions and audio follow-up. There could be additional costs to set up mentoring programs, strategic vision building sessions, and co-participation. Additionally, an organization may also want to invest in communication skills, team skills, and quality improvement systems.

The "how to" steps in this chapter are not intended as schemes of implementation but to provide ideas for getting started on a Level 3 organization. Some steps may seem unimplementable or unintelligible, while others will seem imminently useful. Each organization should adapt them to its particular circumstances. By emphasizing the five personalistic commitments along with Level 3 approaches to people, ethics, and leadership, organizations will inevitably grow in *esprit de corps*. This will lead to an ethos of "opportunity seizing" through creativity, common cause, contributory attitudes, interior freedom, and peace.

Conclusion

In Chapter 2 I noted that *esprit de corps* is fostered by three elements: vision, rational communication, and four sets of commitments. Vision and rational communication emphasize the mind, while the four sets of commitments emphasize the heart.

Organizational vision includes long-term vision of the common good, fairness to stakeholders, and balance among stakeholders. Rational communication includes setting up vehicles of communication, giving a rational explanation of vision and goals, and reporting good and bad news. The four sets of commitments are concerned with personal commitments, people commitments, ethical commitments, and leadership commitments.

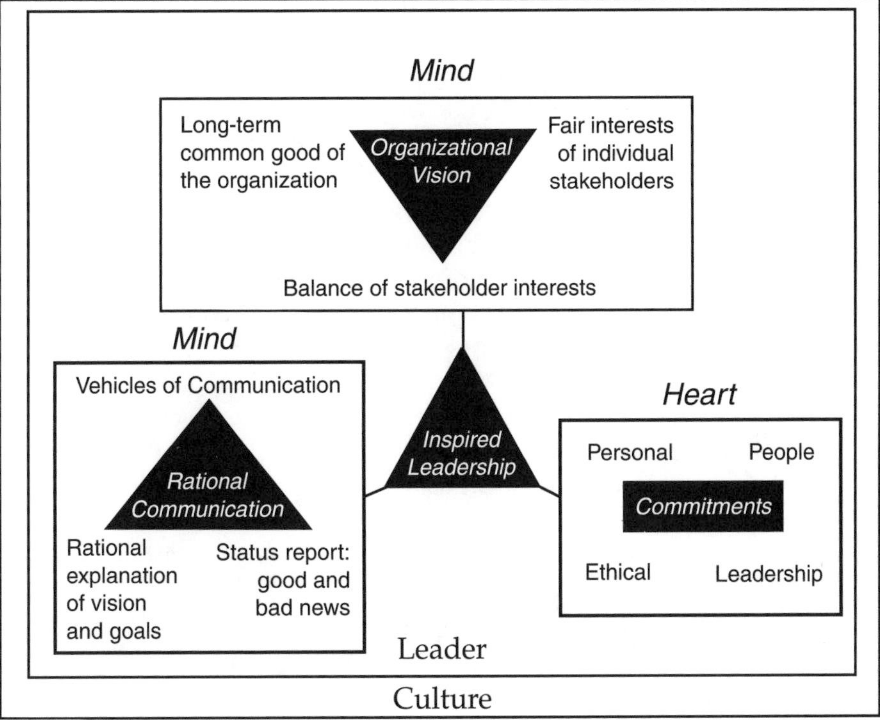

My objective is to provoke the contemplative process of developing the mind and heart of inspired leadership, and thereby to prevent you from falling prey to my oft-quoted cliché, "There are far more errors of omission than commission." I hope to prevent you from inadvertently ignoring, or even annihilating your heart. There is no short and easy path to this objective.

The achievement of this objective by both leaders and organizations requires three conditions for the education of the heart: 1) contemplation, 2) organizational commitment and reinforcement, and 3) repetition and continual feedback.

I have much to say about these three conditions for educating the heart in this book, and I encourage you to remember them, for without them, trust, peace, common cause, care, and *esprit de corps* would be substantially curtailed.

In the third millennium, organizations will have to cultivate heart and spirit. If they do not, they will simply be outpaced by organizations that possess these intangible qualities. For spirit enables us to transcend the limits of the material world; to transcend through creativity, energy, synergy, flexibility, resilience, and vision.

The necessity of spirit is not limited to organizations. It must be rekindled in families, communities, cultures, and societies. Nationalistic spirit could be negatively cultivated by making other nations enemies, but in a world that cannot afford the degradation of war, dysfunction, and disunity, in a world where each constituent part needs the other more and more, this myth can no longer afford to be perpetuated. Spirit is produced not by manufacturing enemies, but by cultivating vision, rational communication, people commitments, ethical commitments, and leadership commitments. This is the longer way to spirit—positive spirit, unifying spirit, spirit that brings peace instead of hatred, contribution instead of enmity. The longer way is the better way. We can no longer afford to take short cuts based on animosity. We must therefore embark on a long journey together.

Fired with this sense of common cause, filled with a sense of camaraderie, enlightened by co-creativity, and committed through a sense of peace, let us attend to the light beckoning ahead, so that the purpose surging within our collective nature will respond.

Appendix: From Contemplation to Inspired Leadership

The four sets of commitments advocated in this book are set out in summary form to help you with your contemplative appropriation of the qualities of inspired leadership.

The first chart indicates the six steps for contemplation.

Six Steps for Contemplation
1) Center on what is really important.
2) Focus on peace.
3) Focus on the commitment of the day.
4) Focus on the reason for the commitment.
5) Bringing the desired commitment into the workplace.
6) Review the day.

The following questions are derived from the personal commitments for increasing trust in Chapter 11.

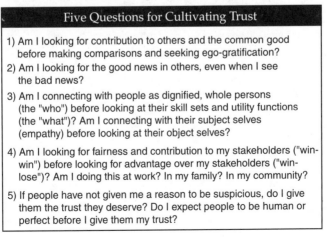

Five Questions for Cultivating Trust
1) Am I looking for contribution to others and the common good before making comparisons and seeking ego-gratification?
2) Am I looking for the good news in others, even when I see the bad news?
3) Am I connecting with people as dignified, whole persons (the "who") before looking at their skill sets and utility functions (the "what")? Am I connecting with their subject selves (empathy) before looking at their object selves?
4) Am I looking for fairness and contribution to my stakeholders ("win-win") before looking for advantage over my stakeholders ("win-lose")? Am I doing this at work? In my family? In my community?
5) If people have not given me a reason to be suspicious, do I give them the trust they deserve? Do I expect people to be human or perfect before I give them my trust?

The five people commitments from Chapter 12 assist us in deepening our relationships and friendships.

Five Questions for Fostering People Commitments

1) Am I connecting with people (empathy) before looking at skill sets and utility functions?
2) Am I looking at the whole person before aspects or parts of the person?
3) Am I aware of the intrinsic dignity of the person when I am focused on his or her difference from me?
4) Do I perpetuate or consent to clichés that marginalize people?
5) Do I bring my empathetic appreciation of people to the next level (creating common cause and redressing injustice)?

The following questions summarize the content of Chapter 13 on principle-based ethics.

Questions for Basic Ethical Commitments

1) Minimize harm. Could our plan cause harm? Is it inevitable? If so, how do we minimize it?

2) Keep promises. What promises have we explicitly made? What promises are we implicitly making by our body language, suggestions, voice inflections, etc.? If we did not perform, would the other party think we broke our word?

3) Be fair. What does the other person mean by "unfair?" Would our actions make others feel as if they had really been mistreated?

Essential Questions for Bringing the Silver Rule into the Workplace (Minimalistic Ethics)

1) Could our strategic plan jeopardize the life or safety of others? If so, how can we reasonably and responsibly minimize this risk?
2) Could our strategic plan infringe on people's right to custody over their own person or actions? If so, how can we curb this propensity?
3) With respect to stealing, could our strategic plan inadvertently lead to taking our stakeholders' fair share? If so, how do we prevent this?
4) With respect to cheating, could our strategic plan lead to unfair play or unfair advantage (which violates the common expectation of fair play)? If so, how do we prevent this from happening?
5) Could our strategic plan lead to exploitation of the vulnerable or helpless? If so, how can we curb it?
6) Could our strategic plan lead to a violation of our word, or to outright lying or deception? If so, how can we remain truthful while being appropriately discreet?

Essential Questions for Bringing the Golden Rule into the Workplace (Maximalistic Ethics)

1) How can our strategic plan and decision making optimally contribute to our common cause and to individual stakeholders in a rational, balanced way?
2) What is the good news in our stakeholders? What do they bring in thought, depth, skills, energy, teamwork, and spirit?
3) What are the intangible qualities constitutive of the intrinsic dignity and mystery of the person or persons with whom we relate?
4) How do we pursue the "win-win" in every interaction with our stakeholders, especially in times of tension or disagreement?
5) How do we prepare others to receive our trust, and prepare ourselves to receive others' trust, so as to operate as much as possible through collegial relationships rather than political, protectionistic, and power-based relationships?

Essential Questions for Bringing Virtue Ethics into the Workplace

1) Do I have the requisite peace (from interior conviction about my ideals and principles, or from faith and prayer) to be courageous in practicing my principles?
2) Do I have the requisite peace to be self-disciplined (detached from passion) in practicing my principles?
3) Do I have the requisite peace to incorporate humility (detachment from ego-rewards, self-pity, and ego-rage) into the practice of my principles?
4) Do I have the requisite peace to incorporate forgiveness (let go of hurt in intentional unfairness) into the practice of my principles?

The following questions are derived from the 12 principles of inspired leadership given in Chapter 15.

Essential Questions for Bringing Leadership Principles into the Workplace

Questions concerning fundamental attitudes:

1) Am I trying to appropriate "the five commitments for increasing trust" into my personal life?
2) As a leader, am I walking the talk of "the five personal commitments for increasing trust?"
3) As a leader, am I walking the talk of the people commitments and ethical commitments?

Questions concerning regular treatment of people:

4) Am I seeking and supporting the talent and the "good news" of stakeholders?
5) Am I proactively listening to stakeholders, and making their concerns my concerns?
6) Am I increasing trust within the organizational environment by empowering and educating stakeholders?

Essential Questions for Bringing Leadership Principles into the Workplace (continued)

Questions concerning reward structures:

7) Am I finding Level 2 and Level 3 ways of rewarding stakeholders who are practicing the "win-win" principle and ethics?

8) Am I trying to initiate team rewards (rewards given to the team who, in turn, distributes them to the players)?

Questions concerning teams:

9) Am I using "soft bargaining" techniques to solve problems and facilitate consensus in teams?

10) Am I using the techniques of co-participation and co-ownership to facilitate teamwork?

11) Am I cultivating inspired leadership and facilitating team objectives, team unity, and team empowerment?

Wisdom:

12) Am I cultivating the wisdom to know when oversight is required? When it is required, am I facilitating appropriate relationships?

The following questions are derived from Chapter 17.

Essential Questions for Bringing Co-Participation, Co-Ownership and Teamwork into the Workplace

1) How can I better solicit ideas from various constituencies and stakeholder groups? How do I acknowledge, appreciate, and reward co-participators?

2) What non-sensitive information can I share with stakeholders to stimulate ideas and enthusiasm? What means should be used to communicate this information?

3) How can I better put myself into others' "shoes?" How can I better achieve transpositional sympathy and reflect diverse opinions in my decision making?

4) How can I create feedback loops to continually assess and fine-tune new processes, policies, and structures?

Notes

Introduction

[1]The case mentioned here is a collage of well-known published case studies and personal experiences. Each aspect of the case represents a real leader in a real organization within the last 15 years. When the parts are assembled, the story refers to six different leaders, myself included, in six organizations. I have taken nothing from my consulting experience, but rather refer only to organizations whose difficulties have been made public in either case studies or the business press.

Chapter 1

[1]Isabel Briggs Myers and Peter B. Myers. *Gifts Differing*. (Palo Alto, CA: Consulting Psychologists Press, 1980). See also, David Keirsey. *Please Understand Me: Character & Temperament Types*. (Del Mar, CA: Prometheus Nemesis, 1984).

[2]This is one of the objectives of this book, which is almost absent in the literature of organizational leadership.

[3]Various aspects of opportunity costs can be measured, such as increased market share, decreased flow times, elimination of waste, and elimination of product defects.

[4]There are some glaring exceptions to this generality caused by either natural catastrophe or by a general failure to appropriately distribute goods and services to those who have just claims or are in need.

[5]See, for example, Paul Pilzer. *Unlimited Wealth: The Theory and Practice of Economic Alchemy*. (New York: Crown Publisher, 1990).

[6]*Ibid*., pp. 12-22.

[7]This insight about the future of the organization being tied to the ability to change is not new. Peter Drucker has been writing about it since 1944, but sees its increasing importance in the present time. Many books have been written about the need for adaptability and change as this became the most urgent leadership requirement in the 20th century. Peter Drucker reflects this increased urgency in his later works: *Managing in a Time of Great Change*. (NY: Truman Talley Books, 1995), and *Management Challenges for the 21st Century*. (NY: Harper Business, 1999).

See also, Douglas K. Smith. *Taking Charge of Change*. (Reading, MA: Addison-Wesley Publishing Co., 1996); Warren G. Bennis. *An Invented Life: Reflections on Leadership and Change*. (Reading, MA: Addison-Wesley Publishing Co., 1993); and Morris R. Schecktman. *Working Without a Net: How to Survive and Thrive in Today's High Risk Business World*. (Englewood Cliffs, NJ: Prentice Hall, 1994).

[8]Thomas J. Peters. *Liberation Management: Necessary Disorganization for the Nanosecond Nineties*. (NY: A.A. Knopf, 1992).

[9]See, for example, H. Skip Weitzen. *Hypergrowth: Applying the Success Formula of Today's Fasting Growing Companies*. (NY: Wiley, 1991). See also, Peter Schwartz. *The Art of the Long View*. (NY: Doubleday/ Currency, 1991).

[10]Daniel C. Morris. *Re-engineering Your Business*. (NY: McGraw-Hill, 1993).

[11]W. Edwards Deming. *Quality, Productivity, and Competitive Position*. (Cambridge, MA: MIT Press, 1982).

[12]Deming anticipated systems theory in his total control model. He summarizes this in *The New Economics: for Industry, Government, Education*. (Cambridge, MA: MIT Press, 1996), pp. 58-66.

One of the finest summaries of systems theory and its relationship to "the learning organization" may be found in Peter M. Senge. *The Fifth Discipline: The Art and Practice of the Learning Organization*. (New York: Doubleday, 1990). This volume contains an outstanding bibliography of systems theory and its relationship to other dimensions of organizational leadership.

[13]See, for example, Abbass F. Alkhafaji. *A Stakeholder Approach to Corporate Governance: Managing in a Dynamic Environment*. (New York: Quorum Books, 1989); Gavin Kelly, Dominic Kelly, and Andrew Gamble. *Stakeholder Capitalism*. (New York: St. Martin's Press, 1997); Ann Svendsen. *The Stakeholder Strategy: Profiting from Collaborative Business Relationships*. (San Francisco: Berrett-Koehler Publishers, 1998); Archie B. Carroll. *Business and Society: Ethics and Stakeholder Management*. (Cincinnati, OH: South-Western College Pub., 1996); Joseph W. Weiss. *Business Ethics: A Stakeholder and Issues Management Approach*. (Fort Worth: Dryden Press, 1998).

[14]Stephen Covey has ingeniously organized Deming's 14 points with his seven habits and stakeholder analysis in *Principle-Centered Leadership*. (New York: Simon & Schuster, 1992), pp. 224-236, and 267-277.

[15]Stephen Covey seems to have used this phrase originally in *The Seven Habits of Highly Effective People: Restoring the Character Ethic*, (New York: Simon & Schuster, 1989). See also, *Principle-Centered Leadership*, pp. 207-208.

[16]Lloyd Pressel. *The New Creators of Empowered Workers: The Supervisor's Guide to Managing*. (Bisbee, AZ: Loma Linda Publishers, 1993); Kenneth H. Blanchard. *Empowerment Takes More than a Minute*. (San Francisco: Berrett Koehler, 1996) and *The Three Keys to Empowerment: Release the Power Within People for Astonishing Results*. (Berkeley, CA: Berrett Koehler Publishers, 1999); Stephen J. Wall. *The New Strategies: Creating Leaders at All Levels*. (NY: Free Press, 1995).

[17]John Case. *Open-Book Management: The Coming Business Revolution*. (New York; Harper Business, 1995) and *The Open-Book Experience: Lessons From Over 100 Companies Who Successfully Transformed Themselves*. (Reading, MA: Addison-Wesley, 1998). See also, Jack Stack. *The Great Game of Business*. (New York: Doubleday Currency, 1992); and John P. Schuster. *The Open-Book Management Field Book*. (New York: Wiley, 1998).

[18]Susan Smith Kuczmarski. *Values-Based Leadership.* (Englewood Cliffs, NJ: Prentice Hall, 1995).

[19]Robert K. Greenleaf. *Servant Leadership: A Journey into the Nature of Legitimate Power and Greatness.* (New York: Paulist Press, 1977) and *On Becoming a Servant-Leader.* (San Francisco: Jossey-Bass Publishers, 1996). See also, *Reflections on Leadership: How Robert K. Greenleaf's Theory of Servant Leadership Influenced Today's Top Management Thinkers*, ed. by Larry Spears. (New York: J. Wiley, 1995).

[20]Glenn M. Parker. *Cross-Functional Teams: Working with Allies, Enemies, and Other Strangers.* (San Francisco, CA: Jossey-Bass, 1994).

[21]Kenneth H. Blanchard. *The One Minute Manager Builds High Performance Teams*, (New York: Morrow, 1990); James B. Miller. *The Corporate Coach.* (New York: St. Martin's Press, 1993); Daniel A. Tagliere. *How to Meet, Think, and Work to Consensus.* (Amsterdam; San Diego: Pfeiffer, 1993).

[22]Jon R. Katzenbach and Douglas K. Smith. *The Wisdom of Teams: Creating the High-Performance Organization.* (Boston, MA: Harvard Business School Press, 1993); Steven R. Rayner. *Recreating the Workplace: The Pathway to High Performance Work Systems.* (Essex Junction, VT: O. Wight Publications, 1993); Susan Albers Mohrman, *Designing Team-Based Organizations: New Forms for Knowledge Work.* (San Francisco: Jossey Bass, 1995); and Frank Ostroff. *The Horizontal Organization: What the Organization of the Future Looks Like and How it Delivers Value to Customers.* (New York: Oxford University Press, 1999).

[23]Stanley M. Herman. *A Force of Ones: Reclaiming Individual Power in a Time of Teams, Work Groups, and Other Crowds.* (San Francisco, CA: Jossey-Bass, Inc., 1994).

[24]Harvey Robbins. *Why Teams Don't Work: What Went Wrong and How to Make it Right.* (Princeton, NJ: Peterson's Guides, 1995).

CHAPTER 2

[1]Sir Arthur Eddington. *The Nature of the Physical World.* (Cambridge: Cambridge University Press, 1928), pp. 327-328.

[2]Max Weber. *Max Weber on Charisma and Institution Building: Selected Papers.* Ed. by S.N. Eisenstadt. (Chicago: University of Chicago Press, 1968); and *Max Weber on Law in Economy and Society.* Ed. by Max Rheinstein. (Cambridge: Harvard University Press, 1954).

CHAPTER 3

[1]Earl S. Landesman. *Corporate Financial Management: Strategies for Maximizing Shareholder Wealth.* (New York: John Wiley & Sons, 1997); Alfred Rappaport. *Creating Shareholder Value: The New Standard for Business Performance.* (New York: Free Press, 1986).

[2]Ronald H. Coase. *The Firm, the Market, and the Law.* (Chicago: University of Chicago Press, 1988) and "The Problem of Social Cost," 1960, reprinted in *Great American Law Reviews*, ed. by Robert C. Berring and Sally Gunderson. (Legal Classics Library, 1984.)

[3]See Peter Senge. *The Fifth Discipline: The Art and Practice of the Learning Organization.* (New York: Doubleday, 1990), pp. 174-272.

[4]See the references in notes 11, 12, and 13 in the *Introduction* to this book.

[5]John Case. *Open-Book Management: The Coming Business Revolution.* (New York: Harper Business, 1995) and *The Open-Book Experience: Lessons From Over 100 Companies Who Successfully Transformed Themselves.* (Reading, MA: Addison-Wesley,

1998). See also, Jack Stack. *The Great Game of Business*. (New York: Doubleday Currency, 1992); and John P. Schuster. *The Open-Book Management Field Book*. (New York: Wiley, 1998).

CHAPTER 4

[1]Martin Seligman. *Learned Optimism*. (New York: A.A. Knopf, 1991).

[2]Paul Pilzer. *Unlimited Wealth: The Theory and Practice of Economic Alchemy*. (New York: Crown Publisher, 1990).

[3]Ibid., note1, Chapter One.

CHAPTER 5

[1]W. Edwards Deming. *The New Economics for Industry, Government, and Education*. (Cambridge, MA: Massachusetts Institute of Technology Center for Advanced Educational Services, 1994). Pp. 92-153.

[2]In addition to over 1,000 books published in the last ten years on this subject, there are also at least16 journals devoted to it: *Asia Pacific Journal of Quality Management, Benchmarking for Quality Management and Technology: An International Journal, Business Process Management Journal, Business Process Re-engineering and Management Journal, Center for Quality Management Journal, Integrating Total Quality Management in a Library Setting, International Journal of Quality Science, Journal of Quality in Maintenance Engineering, Journal of Quality Management, Quality Assurance Journal, Quality Management Journal, Tapping the Network Journal, Total Quality and Site-Based Management Journal, Total Quality Review: The International Journal of Effective Organizations, TQM Magazine, Training for Quality.*

[3]Help may be obtained from the American Society for Quality Control, the American Society for Quality and Participation, and the American Production and Inventory Control Society (APICS).

[4]Kathleen Meyer and Laura Wattenberg. Fel-Pro, Inc. A Case Study. (Cambridge: Harvard Business School Publishing, 1994). Fel-Pro, Inc., an automotive parts manufacturer, decided to expand their benefits programs at a time when competitors were cutting back on their expenses. Fel-Pro's "daring" move led to just-in-time inventory, increased market share, and low turnover (i.e., significantly decreased opportunity costs). This case, and many other similar cases, are "must reads" for those interested in a generative mentality optimizing opportunity.

[5]Mary Scott and Howard Rothman. *Companies with a Conscience: Intimate Portraits of Twelve Firms that Make a Difference*. (Secaucus, N.J.: Carol Publishing Group, 1994).

[6]Robert Cooter and Thomas Ulen. *Law and Economics*. 2nd ed. (Reading, MA: Addison-Wesley, 1997), p. 86.

CHAPTER 6

[1]See, for example, Edith Hamilton and Huntington Cairns, ed. *The Collected Dialogues of Plato*. (Princeton, NJ: University Press, 1973): *The Republic*. Books VI and VII (pp. 720-772); *Phaedrus* (pp. 475-525); and *Symposium* (pp.526-574).

Soren Kierkegaard. *Works of Love: Some Christian Reflections in the Form of Discourses*. Trans. by Howard and Edna Hong. (New York: Harper & Row, 1962); *The Sickness Unto Death: A Christian Psychological Exposition for Upbuilding and Awakening*. Ed. and trans. by Howard and Edna Hong. (Princeton, NJ:

Princeton University Press, 1980); *The Concept of Anxiety: A Simple Psychologically Orienting Deliberation on the Dogmatic Issue of Hereditary Sin.* Ed. and trans. by Reidar Thomte. (Princeton, NJ: Princeton University Press, 1980); and *Either/Or: A Fragment of Life*. Trans. by David F. Swenson and Lillian Marvin Swenson. (Princeton, NJ: Princeton University Press, 1944).

See, for example, Richard McKeon, ed. *The Basic Works of Aristotle*. (New York: Random House, 1941): *De Anima*, Book III (pp.589-603); *Nichomachean Ethics* (complete).

Karl Jaspers. *Way to Wisdom*. Trans. by Ralph Manheim. (New Haven: Yale University Press, 1954) and *Reason and Existenz*. Trans. by William Earle. (New York: Noonday Press, 1955).

St. Augustine. *Confessions*. Trans. by F.J. Sheed. (Indianapolis: Hackett Publishing Co., 1993).

Jean-Paul Sartre. *Being and Nothingness*. (New York: Random House Co., 1994); *Nausea*. Trans. by Lloyd Alexander. (Norfolk, Conn.: New Directions Books, 1959). See also, Wilfid Desan. *The Tragic Finale: An Essay on the Philosophy of Jean-Paul Sartre*. (New York: Harper & Brothers, 1960).

Viktor Frankl. *Man's Search for Meaning: An Introduction to Logotherapy*. Trans. by Ilse Lasch. (Boston: Beacon Press, 1992); *Man's Search for Ultimate Meaning*. (New York: Insight Books, 1997); *The Doctor and the Soul: From Psychotherapy to Logotherapy*. Trans. by Richard and Clara Winston. (New York: A.A. Knopf, 1965); *Psychotherapy and Existentialism: Selected Papers on Logotherapy*. (New York: Simon and Schuster, 1967).

Abraham Maslow. *Motivation and Personality*. (New York: Harper & Row, 1970); *Toward a Psychology of Being*. (New York: Van Nostrand Reinhold, 1968); *Religions, Values, and Peak-Experiences*. (New York: Penguin Books, 1970).

Fathers of the English Dominican Province. *The Summa Theologica of St. Thomas Aquinas*. (New York: Benziger Brother Inc., 1947): *Treatise on Man*, Part I, Questions 75-102 (vol. 1, pp. 363-505), and *Treatise on Habits*, the first part of Part II, Questions 49-89 (vol. 1, pp. 703-985); Vernon J. Bourke. *Summa Contra Gentiles*, by St. Thomas Aquinas (Garden City, NY: Image, 1956), Book III, Chapters 1-48 (vol. 3, pp. 34-162); and St. Thomas Aquinas. *Treatise on Happiness*. Trans. by John A. Oesterle. (Notre Dame, IN: University of Notre Dame Press, 1964).

Erik Erikson. *Identity and the Life Cycle*. (New York: W.W. Norton, 1980); *The Life Cycle Completed*. (New York: W.W. Norton, 1997); and *Dimensions of a New Identity*. (New York: W.W. Norton, 1974).

Martin Heidegger. *Being and Time*. Trans. by Joan Stambaugh. (Albany, NY: State University of New York Press, 1996); *What is Philosophy?* Trans. by William Kluback and Jean T. Wilde. (New York: Twayne Publishers, 1958); and *Existence and Being*. (Washington D.C.: Regnery Gateway, 1988).

Gabriel Marcel. *Creative Fidelity*. Trans. by Robert Rosthal. (New York: The Crossroad Publishing Company, 1982); *The Mystery of Being*. (London, Harvill Press, 19__); *Man Against Mass Society*. Trans. by G.S. Fraser. (Chicago, IL: Henry Regnery Company, 1952); *The Philosophy of Existentialism*. Trans. by Manya Harari. (New York: Philosophical Library, 1956).

Karl Jung. *On the Nature of the Psyche*. Trans. by R.F.C. Hull. (Princeton, NJ: Princeton University Press, 1969); *Modern Man in Search of a Soul*. Trans. by W.S. Dell and Cary F. Baynes. (New York: Harcourt, 1933).

Martin Buber. *I and Thou*. Trans. by Ronald Gregor Smith. (New York: Charles Scribner's Sons, 1958); *Paths in Utopia*. Trans. by R.F.C. Hull. (Boston: Beacon Press, 1958).

Edith Stein. *Selected Writings*. Trans. by Hilda Graef. (Westminster, MD: Newman Press, 1956).

Carol Gilligan. *In a Different Voice: Psychological Theory and Women's Development*. (Cambridge, MA: Harvard University Press, 1982).

Bernard Lonergan. *Collected Works of Bernard Lonergan*, vol. 3: *Insight: A Study of Human Understanding*. Ed. by Frederick E. Crowe and Robert M. Doran. (Toronto, Canada: University of Toronto Press, 1992), see especially Chapters 6,18, and 20; *A Second Collection by Bernard J.F. Lonergan*. Ed. By William F.J. Ryan and Bernard J. Tyrrell. (Philadelphia: Westminster Press, 1974).

Lawrence Kohlberg. *The Psychology of Moral Development: The Nature and Validity of Moral Stages*. (San Francisco: Harper Row, 1984); *Moral Stages: A Current Formulation and a Response to Critics*. (New York: Karger, 1983); *The Meaning and Measurement of Moral Development*. (Worcester, MA: Clark University Press, 1981).

Simone Weil. *Lectures on Philosophy*. Trans. by Hugh Price. (New York: Cambridge University Press, 1978); *Oppression and Liberty*. (London: Routledge and Paul, 1958); *On Science, Necessity, and the Love of God*. Trans. by Richard Rees. (New York: Oxford University Press, 1968).

Max Scheler. *Ressentiment*. Trans. by Lewis B. Coser and William W. Holdheim. (Milwaukee, WI: Marquette University Press, 1994); *Person and Self-Value: Three Essays*. Ed. and trans. by M.S. Frings. (Boston, MA: M. Nijhoff, 1987); *On the Eternal in Man*. Trans. by Bernard Noble. (New York: Harper, 1960).

[2]In the Judeo-Christian view, human beings can only be "really happy" when they are at home with God, for then, at long last, they are at home with themselves. All other forms of happiness will pale by comparison to this *ultimate* happiness. Sometimes we can seek to fulfill this yearning for ultimate happiness by turning to finite, imperfect, and transitory things. But they will fail to satisfy this yearning with its divine origins, impelling us at last to find ultimate happiness in God alone. Augustine phrases it well when he says, "for Thou hast made us for Thyself and restless is our heart until it comes to rest in Thee" (*Confessions*, Book One, Chapter I).

[3]Soren Kierkegaard. *Concluding Unscientific Postscript*. Trans. by David F. Swenson and Walter Lowrie. (Princeton, N.J.: Princeton University Press, 1941), pp. 224 and 262-66; and *Fear and Trembling*. Trans. by Walter Lowrie. (Princeton, N.J.: Princeton University Press, 1954), pp. 90-93.

[4]Martin Buber. *I and Thou*, 2nd ed. (New York: Charles Scribner's Sons, 1958).

CHAPTER 7

[1]I am extraordinarily indebted to Gabriel Marcel, Martin Buber, Max Scheler, Bernard Lonergan, and Karl Jaspers for ideas that led me to the six viewpoints.

CHAPTER 8

[1]The techniques suggested here are derived from Louis E. Tice. *Smart Talk for Achieving Your Potential*. (Seattle, WA: Pacific Institute Publishing, 1995).

[2]This suggestion is amplified in great detail by Louis E. Tice in *Smart Talk for Achieving Your Potential: Five Steps to Get You from Here to There*. (Seattle, WA: Pacific Institute Pub., 1995).

CHAPTER 9

[1]Emerich Coreth. *Metaphysics*. Trans. by Joseph Donceel. (New York: Herder and Herder, 1968), pp. 103-197.

[2]Bernard Lonergan. *Collected Works of Bernard Longergan: Insight*. Ed. by Frederick E. Crowe and Robert M. Doran. (Toronto, Canada: University of Toronto Press, 1992), pp. 657-708

[3]Karl Rahner. *Spirit in the World*. Trans. by William Dych, S.J. (New York: Herder and Herder, 1968), pp. 163-230, and 387-406.

[4]Sir Arthur Eddington. *The Nature of the Physical World*. (Cambridge: Cambridge University Press, 1928), pp. 327-328.

[5]"For Thou hast made us for Thyself and restless is our heart until it comes to rest in Thee" (Augustine. *Confessions*, Book One, Chapter I).

[6]See Edith Hamilton. *The Collected Dialogues of Plato*. (Princeton, N.J.: Princeton University Press, 1963): *The Republic*, Chapter Two, Book 7.

[7]See, for example, David Hilbert. "On the Infinite," in *Philosophy of Mathematics*, ed. by Paul Benacerraf and Hilary Putnam. (Englewood Cliffs, NJ: Prentice-Hall, 1964), pp.141-151. William Lane Craig has written a more popular version of the proof in *The Existence of God and the Beginning of the Universe*. (San Bernadino, CA: Here's Life Publishers, Inc., 1979).

[8]*The Republic*, Books 6 and 7

[9]Richard McKeon. *The Basic Works of Aristotle*. (New York: Random House, 1941): *Physics*, Book q (pp. 354-394), and *Metaphysics*, Book l (pp.872-888)

[10]Augustine. *The Trinity*. Trans. by Stephen McKenna. (Washington: Catholic University of America Press, 1963), XIV 15, 21; XV 21, 40; XIV 7,9; and *Confessions*, translated by R.S. Pine-Coffin, (Penguin Books: London, England, 1961), Books X 20, 29; X 24, 35; X 25, 36-26, 37; and X 6,10. See also, Etienne Gilson. *The Christian Philosophy of Saint Augustine*. Trans. by L.E. M. Lynch. (New York: Random House, 1960).

[11]St. Thomas Aquinas. *Summa Theologica*. Trans. by Fathers of the English Domincan Province. (New York: Benzinger Bros., 1947-1948), I,Q.2. Art. 3, pp. 13-14; and *On Being and Essence.* Trans. by Armand Maurer, C.S.B. (Toronto, Canada: The Pontifical Institute of Mediaeval Studies, 1968), pp. 53-57.

[12]Etienne Gilson. The Elements of Christian Philosophy. (New York: The New American Library, 1960), pp. 46-94.

[13]Jacques Maritain. *An Introduction to Philosophy. Trans*. by E.I. Watkin. (Kansas City, MO: Sheed and Ward, Inc., 1944), pp. 190-193.

[14]Ibid.

[15]Mortimer J. Adler. *How to Think About God*. (New York: Macmillan Publishing Co., Inc., 1980), pp. 69-111.

[16]James F. Ross. *Philosophical Theology*. (New York: The Bobbs-Merrill Company, Inc., 1969), pp. 182-195.

[17]Alvin Plantinga. *Faith and Philosophy*. (Grand Rapids: Eerdmans Publishing Company, 1964), pp. ix, x, and 100-102.

[18]G.J. Whitrow. "The Age of the Universe," *British Journal for the Philosophy of Science*, 5 (1954-55), pp. 215-225, and *The Natural Philosophy of Time*. (London: Thomas Nelson and Sons, 1961). Also, "On the Impossibility of Infinite Past Time," *British Journal for the Philosophy of Science*, 29 (1978), pp. 39-45.

[19]See P.C.W. Davies. *Space and Time in the Modern Universe*. (Cambridge: Cambridge University Press, 1977), pp. 158-160, 217-219; and *God and the*

New Physics. (New York: Simon & Schuster, Inc., 1983), pp. 187-189. See also, Werner Heisenberg. *Physics and Beyond: Encounters and Conversations*. (New York: Harper & Row, 1971), pp. 82-93; and Sir Arthur Eddington. *The Nature of the Physical World*. (Ann Arbor, MI: The University of Michigan Press, 1968), pp. 327-328. There are several other works completely devoted to this subject, such as Timothy E. Toohig. *Physics Research: A Search for God*. (St. Louis, MO: Seminar on Jesuit Spirituality, 1999); *Mathematical Undecidability, Quantum Nonlocality, and the Question of the Existence of God*. Ed. by Alfred Driessen and Antoine Suarez. (Boston: Kluwer Academic Publishers, 1997); Mark William Worthing. *God, Creation, and Contemporary Physics*. (Minneapolis: Fortress Press, 1996); Lothar Schafer. In Search of Divine Reality: Science as a Source of Inspiration. (Fayetteville: University of Arkansas Press, 1997); Daniel Liderbach. *The Numinous Universe*. (New York: Paulist Press, 1989); William Lane Craig. *The Existence of God and the Beginning of the Universe*. (San Bernadino, CA: Here's Life Publishers, Inc., 1979); and Ken Wilber. *Quantum Questions: Mystical Writings of the World's Great Physicists*. (New York: Random House, 1984).

[20]In addition to the experience that many of us may recognize in our own lives, one of the key expositors in the 20th century of this natural, intrinsic awareness of God is Evelyn Underhill. See, for example, *Mysticism: A Study in the Nature and Development of Man's Spiritual Consciousness*. (London: Methuen, 1930); *Practical Mysticism*, (London: J.M. Dent & Sons ltd.; New York: E.P. Dutton & Co., 1914); *Life as Prayer and Other Papers*, ed. Lucy Menzies. (Harrisburg, PA: Morehouse Pub., 1991); and *Man and the Supernatural*. (New York: E.P. Dutton & Company, 1928).

Benedict J. Groeschel has integrated psychology and spiritual development beginning with the call of God, and proceeding through the three steps of the mystical life in *Spiritual Passages: The Psychology of Spiritual Development*. (New York: Crossroad, 1989).

C.S. Lewis describes this initial experience of God as "stabs of joy" in the autobiography of his early life entitled, *Surprised by Joy: The Shape of My Early Life*. (New York: Harcourt, Brace & World, Inc., 1955).

Rudolf Otto, "An Inquiry into the Non-Rational Factor in the Idea of the Divine and its Relation to the Rational" in his classical work, *The Idea of the Holy*. (New York: Oxford University Press, 1955).

Of course, descriptions of this fundamental spiritual experience go back to the earliest moments of the Old Testament (perhaps, 1800 B.C.), and have been given sublime articulation by many spiritual writers throughout the centuries. For a brief explanation of 26 descriptions of this experience, see Elmer O'Brien, *Varieties of Mystic Experience*. (New York: Mentor-Omega, 1964). Four of the best known expositors include Bernard of Clairvaux (Selected Works, trans. and ed. by G.R. Evans, in *The Classics of Western Spirituality*. New York: Mahwah, 1987), Julian of Norwich (*A Book of Showings to the Anchoress*. Toronto: Pontifical Institute of Mediaeval Studies, 1978), St. Teresa of Avila (*The Collected Works of St. Teresa of Avila*, Volume One. Washington, D.C.: ICS Publications, 1976), and St. John of the Cross (*The Collected Works of St. John of the Cross*, trans. by Kieran Kavanaugh and Otilio Rodriguez. Washington, D.C.: ICS Publications 1979).

There are thousands of books devoted to fundamental religious experience arising out of every religious tradition.

NOTES

CHAPTER 11

[1]The last page in this book provides information on how to obtain assimilative materials (e.g., videotapes, audiotapes, and workbooks) on the content of this book.

[2]See Chapter One (Section II.A.) on the necessity of the "win-win" in stakeholder relationships. See also, Coase's Theorem on the reduction of transactional costs in stakeholder relationships: "The Problem of Social Cost," 1960, reprinted in *Great American Law Reviews,* ed. by Robert C. Berring and Sally Gunderson. (Legal Classics Library, 1984.)

CHAPTER 12

[1]The increasing importance of this kind of thinking style within the complex and highly changing work environment is reflected in the proliferation of literature about it. See, for example: Robert K. Cooper and Ayman Sawaf. *Executive EQ: Emotional Intelligence in Leadership and Organizations*. (New York: Grosset/Putnam, 1997); David Ryback. *Putting Emotional Intelligence to Work: Successful Leadership is More than IQ*. (Boston: Butterworth-Heinemann, 1998); Hendrie Weisinger. *Emotional Intelligence at Work: The Untapped Edge for Success*. (San Francisco: Jossey-Bass Publishers, 1998).

CHAPTER 13

[1]Joseph Fletcher. *Situation Ethics: The New Morality*. (Philadelphia: Westminster Press, 1966). See also Harvey Cox, ed. *The Situation Ethics Debate*. (Philadelphia: Westminster Press, 1968).

[2]See, for example, C.S. Lewis. *The Four Loves*. (New York: Harcourt Brace Jovanovich, 1960).

[3]Note, the legal system cannot force the press to reveal its source, unless there is a law that requires it. The case mentioned here is an ethical one that attempts to show the importance of assessing and ranking principles prior to debating the severity and quantity of harm.

[4]An excellent case study, "The Analyst's Dilemma" (by J.L. Badaracco, published by Harvard Business School, October 8, 1993), can by ordered for $5.50 by calling (617) 783-7500 and asking for product #394056. See also, the Harvard case studies in ethics, which may be found in: *New Harvard Business School Cases and Related Course Materials* (Boston, MA: Harvard Business School, 1987-); and *Directory of Harvard Business School Cases and Related Course Materials* (Boston, MA: Harvard Business School, 1985-1986).

[5]I would suggest the following: *Richard T. De George. Business Ethics*. (Englewood Cliffs, N.J.: Prentice Hall, 1995); Manuel G. Velasquez. *Business Ethics: Concepts and Cases*. (Englewood Cliffs, N.J.: Prentice Hall, 1998); John R. Boatright. *Ethics and the Conduct of Business*. (Englewood Cliffs, N.J.: Prentice Hall, 1997); David M. Adams and Edward W. Maine. *Business for the 21st Century*. (Mountain View, CA: Mayfield Publishing Company, 1998).

CHAPER 14

[1]*Negotiation: Strategies for Mutual Gain*: the basic seminar of the Harvard Program on Negotiation. Ed. by Lavinia Hall. (Newbury Park: Sage, 1993).

[2]See, for example, *Ultimate Rewards: What Really Motivates People to Achieve*. Ed. with an introduction by Steven Kerr. (Boston, MA: Harvard Business School Press, 1997); Rewards that Drive High Performance: *Success Stories from Leading Organizations*. Thomas B. Wilson. (New York: AMACOM, 1999); *Quality:*

Change Through Teamwork. Rani Chaudry-Lawton, et. al. (London: Century Business, 1993).

[3]Ibid. n.1.

CHAPTER 16

[1]See Bernard Lonergan. *Insight: A Study of Human Understanding*. (Toronto: University of Toronto Press, 1992), Chapter One.

CHAPTER 17

[1]See, for example, Thomas L. Barton. *Open-Book Management: Creating an Ownership Culture.* (Morristown, NJ: Financial Executives Research Foundation, Inc., 1998); John P. Schuster. *The Open-Book Management Field Book*. (New York: Wiley, 1998); John James Jehning. *A Comprehensive Bibliography on Total Group Productivity Motivation in Business* covering such subjects as profit sharing, productivity sharing, employee stockholdership, and employer employee cooperation. (Madison, WI: Center for Productivity Motivation, University of Wisconsin School of Commerce, 1961); John Gilbert. *How to Eat an Elephant: A Slice by Slice Guide to Total Quality Management*. (Merseyside, England: Tudor Business Publishing, 1992); Darien A. Mc Whirter. *Managing People: Creating the Team-Based Organization: Total Group Participation, Employee Empowerment, and Organization Development*. (Holbrook, MA: Adams Publishing Co., 1995).

[2]See, for example, three journals: *Business Process Management Journal.* (Bradford, West Yorkshire: MCB University Press, 1997–); *Business Process Re-engineering and Management Journal*. (Bradford, West Yorkshire: MCB University Press, 1995–); and *Knowledge and Process Management*. (Chichester, W. Sussex, England: Wiley Publishing, 1998–). See also, the following books: Gary Born. *Process Management to Quality Improvement: The Way to Design, Document, and Re-engineer Business Systems*. (New York: J. Wiley, 1994); Dan Dimancescu. *The Lean Enterprise: Designing and Managing Strategic Processes for Customer-Winning Performance*. (New York: American Management Association, 1997).

How to Integrate this Curriculum

How can you expedite the integration of this material? I recommend the system currently used by The Pacific Institute in Seattle, Washington. They have made an audio-visual curriculum of this book, entitled *Purpose in Life: Ethics and Organizational Success*. This material can be tailored to the size and needs of specific organizations. It includes video-tapes, audio follow-up, workbooks, and facilitation training. The material is best facilitated by selected people from within particular organizations. The Pacific Institute trains facilitators, supports managers in facilitation, evaluates results, and shows how to integrate this material into strategic vision building. More details can be obtained by phoning them at (206) 628-4800.

The Pacific Institute
1709 Harbor Avenue SW
Seattle, WA 98126-2049
800-426-3660

Books of Related Interest from Executive Excellence Publishing

KEVIN CASHMAN
Leadership From the Inside Out
Promotes a non-hierarchical view of leadership that originates in the character of the person and radiates outward to enrich others, This vision goes beyond competencies and skill-building, focusing on character and personal development by confronting the essence of leadership, instead of focusing on its external manifestations. $24.95

WARREN BENNIS
Old Dogs, New Tricks
In today's dog-eat-dog world of competition and ongoing change, people in every position—especially the "old dogs"—must learn to work in teams rather than as "lone wolves." They must learn the "new tricks" of collaboration and innovation. $24.95

DAVID NEIDERT
Four Seasons of Leadership
Blending contemporary thought and ageless wisdom for guiding us in our life's journey, this book invites every person, young and old, to experience true personal leadership and life transformation. $18.95

WARREN BENNIS
Managing People Is Like Hearding Cats
This book spells out the dilemmas facing a leaderless society, details the qualities that successful leaders must have, and explores the challenges that today's leaders must face as they move toward change. Along the way, Bennis challenges our complacency by asking serious questions. $24.95

KEN SHELTON
Beyond Counterfeit Leadership
This book explores the causes, cures, and outcomes of both counterfeit and authentic leadership. Also included are tests to detect counterfeit in the conception and implementation of several models of leadership. $24.95

Executive Excellence on CD-ROM
The *Instant Consultant* CD-ROM will give you access to 15 years of insights from the best and brightest business minds—archived in a user-friendly format. $179.95